Systems Management

Andrew Parkin

Principal lecturer in systems analysis and data processing
Leicester Polytechnic

Edward Arnold

© A. Parkin 1980
First published 1980
by Edward Arnold (Publishers) Ltd,
41 Bedford Square, London WC1B 3DQ

British Library Cataloguing in Publication Data

Parkin, Andrew
    Systems management.
    1. Electronic data processing departments – Management
    I. Title
    658'.05   HF5548.2

ISBN 0-7131-2815-1

Printed in Great Britain by
Butler and Tanner Ltd, Frome, Somerset

Preface

SCOPE AND READERSHIP

A very large part of the practice of management lies in the domain of the everyday, where every thinking person is his own philosopher and mentor. In this domain, the guiding principle is common sense or intuition. Common sense can conform to the idea of 'scientific knowledge' if the sense comes from unbiased observation followed by deduction or inference and common means that the conclusion is shared by all who are considered rational. Intuition may be perfectly well founded, even though the reasons are unconscious. But common sense, when the sense is an intuitive feeling that arises within a person, **may** be mistaken superstition, prejudice or folklore. This could be true even when the feeling is shared by all persons in a group or culture. I suppose it could even be true of a permanent feeling shared by all persons in the world, but then only a man from Mars could educate us about our folly.

Much of management entails flying by the seat of one's pants. If I may preserve this metaphor, every aviator knows that a novice flying over strange territory, even with a map, is likely to lose his way because of mistaken recognition, or non-recognition, of ground features. There is an apocryphal story of a budding airman who set out to fly at a low height by dead reckoning and map reading from London to the Isle of Wight. He read his protractor wrongly when planning his course, and unknowingly set out in a direction diametrically opposed to the proper heading. In spite of this he managed to 'recognise' the ground features - every town, every railway, every river and lake, every aerodrome - and relate them to his map. As he approached the North Sea, he recognised The Solent. His only shock came when he set down on the Isle of Wight and found that everybody was Dutch.

Although I cannot vouch for the truth of this tale, it is only the size of the error that stretches belief, not the nature of it. One moral is that features are at least partly what we make of them. Other morals are that possession of a map alone is not sufficient for recognising features, and successfully recognising a feature does not prove the map correct.

A manager is asked to make progress in such a pit of vipers. At once both the strength and weakness of common sense can be seen. Common sense - intuition - is crucial to making anything at all out of the welter of stimuli bombarding the manager. Yet this same common sense, upon which so much action is so confidently based, is potentially full of mistakes. A manager who wishes to be rational must train himself, or be trained, to be a scientist; a lifetime exercise which is never complete. It may be a vain hope of a scientist to discover truth, but at least he is concerned to discover mistake. A manager who loses this concern would carry mankind back to the Dark Ages.

Having put management and science in the same context, I had better deal with the spectre of Scientific Management, associated with F. E. Taylor (1). This is the idea, widely criticised for lack of humanity, of the organisation as an economic engine whose component men and materials are programmed for maximum efficiency. The criticism is not that the organisation is **described** as a machine; at least, if that were the criticism, that it is an offence even to use mechanistic analogy to describe the activities of men, a very large part (if not all) of our understanding of ourselves would have to be thrown out. It is the prospect that the organisation will be **planned** as a machine, in which man's part is given only the attention due to a cog, that gives rise to the objection.

But organising with a neglect of human values, ignoring aesthetic or ethical influences, is no part of science that I can see. Just the opposite, in fact, if so to organise is a mistake and scientists are concerned about mistakes. It is a shame that scientific management has come to be equated with inhumane management. The fact is that most people in the Western world are scientific; science and rationality have pervaded our culture for centuries and we are as much creatures of them as they are of us.

Systems analysts and programmers are rational people. Anyone who has programmed computers is obliged to accept (at least temporarily) the rational philosophy of programming in which a given combination of instructions and data is always expected to produce the same result. So it is to be expected that computer people will want, and accept, a rational approach to management, and that they will be good exponents of it.

Here lies the difficult question. Will analysts, programmers, operators make managers who have the humane rationality of the scientist that I have defended? Or will they have the chilling rationality of the other Scientific Manager who thoughtlessly leaves out human values and programs his subordinates?

A worrying thought here is G. M. Weinberg's (2) statement, in a different context, that programmers have personalities which are shifted towards 'detachment'. They want to be left alone to be creative with the machine, more than working with people or striking out for wealth and prestige. Programmers, compared with the average person, are more interested in mechanical and logical things and less interested in human affairs. A person who wants to work with others, and help them, is likely to put human values at the forefront of his attention. An agressive person, concerned with being successful, may ride roughshod over other people. A detached person may simply overlook them.

A further worry is the mechanistic nature of computing. Systems design and programming requires laying down precise rules which are to be followed by computers, precise rules covering every eventuality. It is a bewitching idea, the rule-following machine which unswervingly fulfills its purpose. It would be a natural and understandable thing for a computer man to model the wider organisation as such an automaton.

These two worries conspire, at face value, to describe a person who may unwittingly program the work of others to the exclusion of human values. But, fortunately, even if this were a legitimate description, such a person is not beyond salvation. Programmers are not 100% detached; they can have their interest in people, or in success, awakened. The same is true of most people; we are all somewhat unbalanced, but rather few of us take this to pathological proportions by being totally immersed in one corner of personality. Moreover, the use of an automaton analogy for defining business procedures is not intrinsically bad. It is impossible to make plans or to organise without some appeal to mechanism, for mechanism is at the heart of our understanding and language. The mistake is not in defining man's role in terms of a cog; it is in not taking the potential cog's feelings into account when using it or when designing the running gear with which it enmeshes. Even for the designer who recognises this mistake, such is the snare of mechanism that he may yet fall into the trap of using a crude model of the cog's feelings to influence the design, when the cog is there and willing and able to declare its opinions.

I would like this book to be read by analysts and programmers who are preparing for the responsibility of supervising others, as well as by students on higher education courses. I hope they will find a concise, structured and rational explanation of some ideas for managing. But I have not pretended to touch much of that large part of management which concerns interpersonal skills, ethical and aesthetic values. The reason is simply that what I could offer there would be as nothing compared with the common sense and intuition which the reader brings with him. Indeed, it is possible that my offerings could distort otherwise balanced common sense values – a distortion which another writer has described as an excess of Maslow. Some readers may notice that theories of motivation and leadership style are given a sort of footnote status; this is no accident. For a balanced, comprehensive and uncontroversial introductory survey of organisations and the behaviour of people in them, see Hicks (3).

This is not to say that interpersonal skills and values of managers are beyond improvement: on the contrary, it is more that I cannot do much about it through the medium of the written word. In any case if a manager is thoughtful enough to be reading a book on management, such as this, the chances are I would be preaching to the converted. I hope that the case studies in chapter 16 will help teachers to explore some of these matters in classroom discussion.

Another omission is operations management and the management of operations personnel. The reason is simply that I do not feel qualified to write on that subject. Some readers may notice that there is little coverage of technical matters, although some managers in data processing are preoccupied with these questions; this is no accident either.

There is a lot of appeal to objectivity in the methods advocated in the following pages. I hope it is plain from the foregoing that I do not believe that a manager can conduct his affairs on the basis only of objective fact and rationalised choice. But the science provides **anchorage** points within which intuition and personality can operate.

A reader who has not read the companion book **Systems Analysis** (4) is particularly recommended to browse a while in the glossary on page 145. This summarises most of the terms which are used with a special meaning. Any reader might find it helpful to appreciate what terms are the subject of definitions in the glossary, especially if he chooses to dip in the chapters out of sequence.

ACKNOWLEDGEMENTS

Ideas of many people have been pressed into use. Although citations are given where remembered, this is an error-prone process and I apologise to all those who have not been given their due credit.

I am particularly grateful for the support and criticism of R. B. Coats, D. R. Howe and F. F. Land. I have yet to repay the debt of attention owed to my family, Valerie, Emma and Vicki.

Leicester   A.P.
1980

REFERENCES

(1)   Taylor, F. E., Principles of scientific management, reprinted in Vroom, V. H., and Deci, E. L. (Eds), **Management and motivation**, Penguin, 1970.

(2)   Weinberg, G. M., **The psychology of computer programming**, Van Nostrand, 1971.

(3)   Hicks, H. G., **The management of organisations: a systems and human resources approach**, McGraw-Hill, 1972.

(4)   Parkin, A., **Systems analysis**, Edward Arnold, 1980.

Contents

1 Long-range planning

1.1 MEANING AND OBJECTIVES OF LONG-RANGE PLANNING

Formulating and implementing long-range plans requires drawing resources away from shorter-term operations. If this results in the collapse of the short-term operation, the long-range plans will have been pointless. This supports the view that before attention can be given to serious long-range planning, the 'decks must be clear' in the shorter term.

What is longer or shorter in this context is purely relative. If there is a do-or-die crisis this week, then next month is long range. If this quarter's achievements are in the balance, next year is long range. Typically, in an organisation that does not have a raging fire to fight, 'long-range' will be taken to mean a time five or more years in the future.

This chapter is concerned with the long-range plans for the computer-based data processing (DP) systems of the organisation. Assuming the decks are reasonably clear as far as present DP system operation and development are concerned, long-range planning for DP can be seen as a beneficial activity which gives support to the wider long-range plans of the organisation.

Broadly, long-range DP plans focus on a point somewhere beyond any particular computer application or project. As an illustration, take the first-time computer user who asks, 'Should I have a computer, or not?' If the expense of the computer can be justified by the benefits of a specific application or set of applications, the computer purchase can be seen as fulfilling a medium-range objective. If no such justification can be supplied, then a long-range objective is in question. The issue now becomes not, 'Should I have a computer' but, 'Beyond my present range of medium-term plans, do I see the DP systems of my organisation continuing to be essentially clerical, or do I see them widely supplemented/supplanted by computers?' Naturally, an affirmative answer to this question may have far reaching consequences for medium-term, and thence short-term, plans, but it is probably a meaningless exercise to try analytically to justify the long-term view. At some point the analyst has to bow to the insight, intuition, initiative, enthusiasm or faith of the entrepreneur.

This may seem a surprising statement, considering that managers are often urged to justify all projects analytically. I am not against analytical justification, as will be seen from chapter 2 onwards. The point is that if this type of justification in terms of quantified costs and benefits is feasible or necessary, then we are talking about medium-range plans. This type of justification may be considered to be essential for selecting and endorsing the next application, but it is not the only basis for choosing computer-isation. Against a backcloth of rising labour costs, and in the knowledge that computers can make feasible a speed or volume of data processing which may be out of the question manually, thereby creating new opportunities, computers may be desired simply at face value, for the sake of learning how to use them and being ready to grasp the opportunities when they come. Computers may also be desired for their own sake, because they are fun.

Questions

(These questions illustrate and extend the points made in the text. Answers are given at the end of the chapter; they are called 'Answer pointers' because most of the questions do not have a definite answer and quite possibly your answers will be better than mine. The times are meant to indicate the maximum depth of answer expected. Each section is written on the assumption that the questions and answer pointers of the preceding sections have been read.)

1   The director in charge of a hospital employing about 200 people comes up to you and asks, 'Do you think we should consider installing a computer in the hospital? All our systems are manual at present.' What reply would you make, assuming you had only a few minutes?   (5 min)

2   The manager of a manufacturing company employing about 300 people at each of three locations approaches you and asks, 'We have small computers at each of our locations at the moment. Should we aim to centralise the computing facility more, decentralise it more or leave it about the same?' What reply would you make?   (5 min)

1.2 DERIVING ORGANISATION POLICIES THROUGH DEFINITION OF OBJECTIVES

The term 'policy' here is shorthand for a long–range plan element. The DP policies should be aligned to the policies of the organisation.

An approach to rationalising policies in top–down fashion is known as Management by Objectives (MBO). MBO descends from worthy origins, but it is difficult to demonstrate objectively that it is any more, or less, effective than any other method of managing. I like MBO because it does not supply cut-and-dried answers but instead gives an intuitively acceptable framework within which individual managers can plan, communicate, exercise their imagination and initiative and take responsibility. MBO can be tailored to suit different organisations or to adapt to organisational change. Perhaps MBO is more of a culture than anything else – a way of managing which many managers find fitting. Chapter 4 provides a detailed discussion which underpins the particular adaptation of MBO which I shall use in the development of these first three chapters. For the time being, perhaps the reader will accept that top–down rationalisation is quite an enjoyable method of planning which may also be effective.

A first step is to define the organisation's key result areas (KRAs). These may be facets of the organisation's operations in which excellent performance is likely to increase significantly the benefits won, or they may be areas in which poor performance significantly threatens those benefits. Drucker (1) has suggested a general list for businesses, which could be the starting-point for top management discussion:

   profitability;
   innovation;
   productivity;
   physical and financial resources;
   worker performance and development;
   manager performance and development;
   market position.

However, the KRAs chosen by a particular organisation will be different, to reflect the management's particular view of the world. Naturally, non-business organisations such as public administration may be the most substantially different.

I speak here of 'the management's view' as a sort of shorthand. I do not want to preclude, by this phrase, the possibility that others can or should have a say in defining the goals of the organisation. In practice the managers hold the day-to-day power to choose goals and further them. The owners may have the power to dismiss the managers, the non-manager employees may have the power to thwart the chosen goals, the public may exercise choice which defeats the managers' plans, or government may legislate to curb those plans. These are constraints or influences on a manager's powers, but he remains the principal force for positive action in choosing and furthering goals. 'The management's view' therefore means 'the management's view as constrained or influenced by the other parties who have a stake in the organisation'.

An analogy can be drawn with a linear programming problem. In Figure 1.1 managers may choose how much of each of two goals should be targets of the organisation. The shaded portion shows the constraints, i.e. those combinations which are unacceptable to the other parties who hold a stake in the organisation. This leaves a bounded, feasible region within which the managers can operate. In a linear programming problem, there is a function which must be maximised in order to identify the most desirable extremity of the feasible region, i.e. the optimum targets. In an organisation, there is usually no such function determinable, so the targets set in the feasible region are a matter of discretion or negotiation.

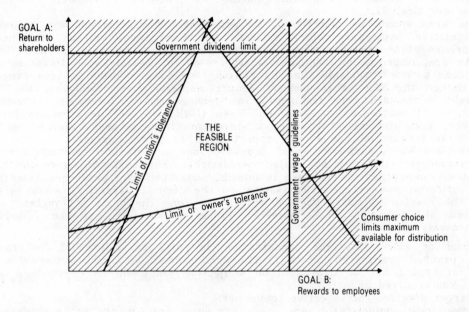

Fig. 1.1: Analogy of organisation goals with a linear programming problem. Managers can choose or negotiate targets within the feasible region. For this illustration, only two dimensions (goals) are shown: the realistic problem has many dimensions

Participation in the formulation of KRAs will be achieved if the general manager forms a team to discuss KRAs and to agree a joint definition. This team will include subordinate managers and perhaps representatives of other stakeholder groups, depending on the degree of democracy aspired to. In the discussion that follows, all the participants are called 'managers'.

If a target of listing about half-a-dozen KRAs is established, the areas which have the greatest influence on organisation performance will be selected without being diluted by lesser areas. The team should generate candidate KRAs and consider whether each candidate deserves a place in the final short list. The candidates may be generated by reviewing special features of:

the industry (e.g. a nuclear power station, candidate KRA Safety; a
university, candidate KRA Student Development);

the organisation (e.g. an employing organisation, candidate KRA Labour
Relations; a manufacturing organisation, candidate KRA Plant Replacement);

the environment (e.g. Energy Conservation, Compliance with Government
Regulations);

the time (to meet temporary opportunities or threats, e.g. Recapture Lost
Market, Provide for Succession on Chief Executive's Retirement).

What may happen in practice is not that the KRAs are much disputed, but
that the team debate centres around the precise words that should be used
to define or delineate the KRAs. Since it is intended that all the units and
sub-units of the organisation, through their managers, will align their
policies to fit in with the declared KRAs, and since their managers'
understanding of highest-level objectives will, at least in part, depend on
the words used in the 'official' definition, this concern with semantics is
important and not mere pedantry. There is ample evidence of misunderstanding between managers and subordinates in the absence of explicit objectives
(Dew and Gee, 2).

The KRAs should be prioritised, i.e. they should be assigned some measure
of relative importance which reflects top management opinion of general
priorities at the present time. Priorities should be taken into account if two
KRAs are competing for the same scarce resource. Usually, prioritisation can
be done no more precisely than by ranking the KRAs in order of importance.

Although the KRAs often concern longer-than-five-year objectives, the list
should be revised more frequently, at perhaps yearly intervals, to reflect
changed circumstances and opinion. Even if the list of KRAs remains fairly
stable, priorities may change as achievements in some areas increase or in
other areas diminish, or as new opportunities or threats arise.

Associated with each KRA there should be one or more objective **measures of
effectiveness** (MOEs; also called yardsticks, metrics). 'Objective' in this
context means that the measure is unambiguous. Different observers assessing
the effectiveness of the organisation on the defined yardsticks would agree
on the result. Objective MOEs can therefore form the basis of **targets** (also
called objectives, success criteria) expressed in terms of the following
appraisals:

true or false (Did the organisation do this, or didn't it? Did the
planned event occur or not?) The event should be clearly observable:
it should not be dependent on subjective judgement as to whether it
has occurred or not;

target date for the objective to be met;

time, cost, quantity: where these variables are, or are to be, objectively measured;

quality: if a quality standard exists or if quality can be objectively
measured in true/false fashion.

Most KRAs are multi-dimensional in the sense that there is more than one
way in which achievement on the KRA can be measured. The two or three
most important MOEs for each KRA should be identified.

Since defining MOE targets within a KRA effectively defines precise sub-
objectives, the MOEs should also be prioritised. It is hardly practical to do
this other than by ranking the MOEs within their KRA. Examples:

Profitability: yield on capital employed;
                  before-tax profits;
                  sales less cost of goods sold.
Productivity: added value per capita;
                  machine time percent utilisation.
Market position: proportion of total market by value;

turnover by value.

Industrial relations: man-days of stoppages.

Now **actions** can be formulated which, it is hoped, will influence the MOEs in the desired directions. The actions which are not expected to have an attributable payoff in the short/medium term are the strategic plans or policies.

Questions

1 Organisations may quantify the desired improvement in a MOE by specifying some target together with a date for achieving it, e.g.

'yield on capital employed to reach 22% this year'
'turnover to exceed £1 million per month by April next'.

Is such quantification desirable?   (10 min)

2 Suggest some candidate KRAs for a public lending library.   (10 min)

3 Are the example MOEs in the text (for profitability, productivity, market position, industrial relations) really objective?   (5 min)

4 It might be argued that every KRA affects 'profitability' in a profit-making concern. Why isn't it enough just to have one KRA, Profitability, and one measure of effectiveness, e.g. dividend yield on equity capital? Or is it enough?   (10 min)

1.3 DATA PROCESSING POLICIES

Using as a starting-point the KRAs, MOEs and policies defined for the organisation as a whole, a definition may be attempted of the KRAs, MOEs and policies for the data processing department; see Figure 1.2 overleaf. The DP KRAs (i.e. areas of system operation or development where excellence or failure could significantly affect a higher-level KRA) are likely to be more specialised to the particular organisation. An example list is therefore even less representative. Grindley and Humble (3) have suggested the following:

effectiveness of present applications;
return on investment of present applications;
opportunities for computerisation;
cost of operations;
hardware evaluation;
staff recruitment, development, training.

Any plan in an organisation requires actioning and monitoring by a responsible person. KRAs of the above type are therefore to be included in the plans of the responsible person, e.g. the manager of the data processing department or management services department. Naturally, if that person's responsibilities are wider than managing DP system change, there will be other KRAs which are not relevant to our present discussion.

Participation in the definition and prioritisation of the management services KRAs and MOEs can be achieved by having the objectives formulated by a team which includes the immediate subordinates of the management services manager. If these subordinates themselves manage sub-units, they will repeat the process with their subordinates, using as inputs the KRAs defined at the higher level.

Questions

1 Suppose the example DP KRAs listed in the text have been chosen by an electricity utility. Suggest one possible MOE for each KRA.   (10 min)

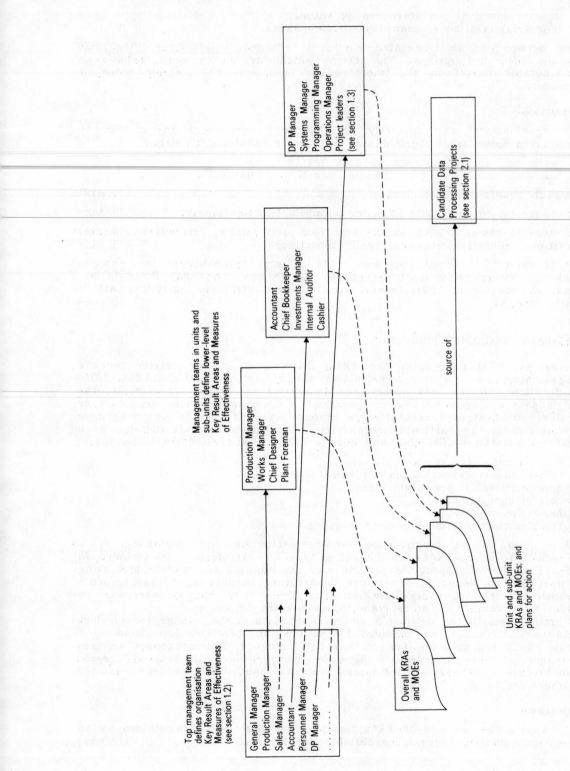

Fig. 1.2: How high–level plans can be propagated throughout the organisation

2 What is the difference between a KRA and an MOE? (5 min)

3 How much effort would be required to introduce a system for defining KRAs and MOEs into an organisation which has no MBO programme at present? (10 min)

4 Can a sub-unit have a KRA identical to the KRA of its superior unit? (5 min)

1.4 DATA PROCESSING POLICY ALTERNATIVES

The selection of DP policies will be rather particular to the organisation, both in terms of what are though fit subjects of policy and in terms of what the policy is on a particular subject. The following list shows some decisions which may be seen as matters of policy.

1 Centralisation or decentralisation of development staff.
2 Centralisation or decentralisation of computer processing operations.
3 Centralisation or decentralisation of corporate database.
4 Organisation structure and responsibilities for developing and running DP systems – who the DP manager should report to, what committees there are to be, what should be the reporting structure within the DP department.
5 Extent of participation in developing new DP systems – consultation, representation, etc.
6 Centralisation or decentralisation of project selection.
7 Use of Data Base Management System or not.
8 Charge-back of the DP development resources used – whether done, if so whether by apportionment, average cost, etc.
9 Charge-back of operating resources used.
10 Computer vendor selection, e.g. established mainfames vs microcomputers from small suppliers; new vs used equipment.
11 Single or mixed vendors.
12 Use of outside system development resources.
13 Use of outside system operation resources.
14 Selling surplus resources to outside.
15 Develop internal knowhow.
16 Develop internal standards for DP system development work.

Often there is a compromise policy available between extremes; for example, regionalisation is a compromise between centralisation and decentralisation. Each choice between major alternatives such as those listed above is potentially substantial in effect. These major, one-off decisions merit substantial thought and the manager's best tactic is probably to bone up on the subject at the time of the decision. In this book, I am dealing mainly with matters of continuing concern, so a discussion of these policy alternatives is beyond our scope.

Question

1 Which person(s) in an organisation should be deciding these policies? (5 min)

ANSWER POINTERS

Section 1.1

1 In the long run, do you see the messages, information and data of the hospital being processed by machines or by people? If the former is more likely, is now the time to start preparing? Are you happy to accept the risk

of lost opportunity if the hospital does not learn how to use computers?

2   I don't think centralisation or decentralisation of computing facilities should be considered independently of corporate aims and objectives. Do you have a long-term plan for your organisation? If so, we could consider how the computer facility alternatives would contribute to, or detract from, this plan.

Section 1.2

1   One aspect of this question could be, 'Will quantifying the improvement increase the chance of its being reached or increase the amount of benefit won?' If having quantified targets increases the motivation and effort of managers, and the managers' motivation and effort can influence the payoff, then the quantification is desirable.

Another argument concerns control. Without the quantified target, management will not know, or will not know so early, that things are going wrong. This may mean less opportunity to take corrective action or to mitigate the effects of failure. However, it is not easy to produce objective evidence to support either of these arguments.

Another tack could be, 'Is quantification desirable for its own sake?' This is a matter of opinion. Many people prefer to work to agreed targets; quantification makes their work more purposeful and meaningful.

A further aspect is that of evaluation of the responsible manager. I prefer to be evaluated by my superiors using, at least partly, some agreed, quantitative measures rather than entirely by their subjective judgement.

From here on I shall use the word 'Target' in this specific sense of a desired improvement which has been quantified on an MOE scale. The capital letter will serve as a reminder of this special meaning. By an MOE scale I am specifically including discrete 'scales' such as yes/no, true/false, as well as continuous scales.

2   Costs; Book stock; Non-book media stock; Periodicals stock; Counter service; Inter-library loans and reservations; Premises and use of space; Community activities; Staff development.

3   As a philosophical matter, I do not think it is possible to define perfectly objective MOEs. The point about the examples is that the procedure by which the measure is to be taken should be understood. If, for example, 'before-tax profits' is understood to mean 'before-tax profits as measured by the present accounting system of the organisation', then it is an unambiguous measure. However, the accounting system will not be perfectly objective in its reporting – there will be distortion caused by inflation, for instance (see Systems Analysis, section 4.4, for further discussion). For the present purpose, a measure may be taken to be sufficiently objective if the procedure by which the measurement is to be made is spelled out. If the measure is not reported in the existing information system, then a procedure should be defined along with the measure unless the procedure is self-evident. For example, if 'before-tax profits' measured by the existing accounts is **not** the measure intended, then the required adjustments to the accounts should be specified.

4   The fact that profitability may be measured in ways other than return on owner's investment is somewhat beside the point here, although it does serve to emphasise the point that profitability is not a simple notion and that the idea of profitability may find its expression in a variety of KRAs.

The argument in the question takes an owner-oriented view of the business. Although the owners have ultimate control or sanction over the managers, their powers in a large corporation are quite limited in the day-to-day sense. The KRAs form the basis of a prescription for **manager** action. Serving the owners through maximising profitability is only one of the possible goals for a manager. Other goals merit further KRAs.

Incidentally, I have repeated a rather stereotyped view of a 'profit-maximising' owner. There is no reason why some or all owners should not also have non-profit goals, such as preservation of business ethics, avoidance of pollution, furtherance of political or religious aims, etc.

Section 1.3

1 Effectiveness: mean time to send bill after reading meter; return on investment: number of times savings during five years exceed development cost (the method of identifying the savings should be specified); computerisation opportunities: number of new project ideas accepted (this assumes the existence of a norm among the managers about what constitutes a project idea); cost of operations: hardware rental cost per annum; hardware evaluation: number of complaints from users about hardware; staff: whether or not a training review and plan is made.

These are obviously speculative answers, since only the managers concerned could give answers which are realistic in context and meaningful to them.

Perhaps the main value of the MOEs is that they induce consideration of the real problem. Suppose Staff Recruitment is chosen as a KRA. Why? Is there something unsatisfactory about staff at present? Is it that staff do not stay? (Possible MOE: annual turnover rate.) Is it that staff selection is done badly? (Possible MOE: selection done by staff who have attended a selection training course.) Is it that there is insufficient choice when selecting? (Possible MOE: average number of candidates per vacancy.)

Two of the MOEs in this answer may have struck you as rather unsatisfactory. These are 'whether or not a staff training review and plan is made' and 'whether or not selection is done by staff who have completed a selection training course'. These are reasonably objective, but they are distinguished from the other MOEs by being less of an end in themselves. They imply that there is another MOE which is desired in itself and which it is hoped to influence through these MOEs.

To a certain extent this is true of all MOEs; but with the two just cited it is more so. In practice, it may be necessary to resort to MOEs phrased in this manner when the truly desired end is not measurable with a reasonable amount of effort. When defining these MOEs, attention should be given to the reliability of the connection between the MOEs and the desired end.

2 An MOE is an objective which has a known procedure to determine whether or not the objective was fulfilled, or by how much it was fulfilled. A KRA is not so quantified. An MOE specifies a goal in more detail than the KRA of which it is part. However, they are both goals of managers. What is a KRA or an MOE exists in the minds of the managers. Leaving aside the quantification aspect, one manager's MOE could be another manager's KRA.

3 The scheme certainly cannot be implemented just by declaring, 'As from tomorrow, we will deal in KRAs and MOEs.'

If the managers are not already attuned to spelling out and quantifying objectives, they will need training in doing this. One or two days instruction is needed to permit practice in setting and quantifying objectives, and a further day or so for practice in monitoring and reviewing them. The periodic round of defining, monitoring and revising objectives will make further demands on each manager's time. The crucial question is 'What **should** the manager spend his time doing?'; I would sooner defend than deny the proposition that effort spent in defining, monitoring and revising objectives is effort well spent.

4 Yes, although it would be unusual if many sub-unit KRAs were the same as the superior unit's KRAs. Functional division of the sub-units means that

some sub-units can influence some higher-level KRAs more than others. The DP manager may have 'cost of computer operations' as a KRA for his department; the operations manager is likely to see this expanded into, say, 'cost of data preparation and control', 'cost of hardware rentals', 'cost of consumables', etc. Both might have 'staff development' as a KRA, even with the same MOEs; the operations manager's KRA would apply to a subset of the staff of the DP manager.

Section 1.4

1   It is difficult to believe that any one person should decide such important questions. Certainly, because of their implications for the whole organisation, they should not be the province of only DP personnel. The people most concerned are the general management of the organisation, the existing and potential users of the system, and DP management.

REFERENCES

(1) Drucker, P. F., **The practice of management**, Harper and Row, New York, 1954.
(2) Dew, R. B., and Gee, K. P., **Management control and information**, Macmillan, London, 1973.
(3) Grindley, K., and Humble, J., **The effective computer: an MBO approach**, McGraw-Hill, 1973.

2 Medium-range planning

2.1 IDENTIFYING DP OPPORTUNITIES

Given the long-range plans, the medium-term plans for DP system development
(when a centralised project selection policy is adopted) will include selecting
and prioritising a collection of projects to be started during the planning
period (typically 3-5 years). Naturally, this project selection and prioritisation will also be subject to review in the light of the revised long-range
plans. The aim, simple to state but not so easy to do, is to:

generate ideas for new projects;
choose from these the most beneficial collection which can feasibly be
started;
sequence the chosen projects in time of start-date.

Usually, the forecast effect on funds (measurable money costs and benefits,
or, often, only money costs) are incorporated into the budget plans of the
organisation for future years.
Ideas for DP projects can be classified as follows:

1 systems to provide defined operational messages, such as accounts,
   paycheques;
2 process control systems;
3 management information systems;
4 systems which aid the communication, storage, retrieval of undefined
   messages;
5 time-sharing systems.

Ideas in the first two classes may come from review of the existing
operational messages and processes.
Management information may be classified into the following:

1 monitoring information - how well are we doing? Do we need to take
   action?
2 decision support information - what is the best action to take?

If KRAs and MOEs throughout the organisation have been rationalised as
outlined in chapter 1, the 'monitoring information' needs of managers are
defined, at least partly and possibly completely, by the MOEs. Each MOE
merits some sort of information system. Probably most of them can use
informal channels and many others may be unsuited to computerisation; the
balance can give rise to ideas for DP projects which will supply 'monitoring
information'.
Review of the decisions that are or could be taken by managers in each
KRA will also identify pieces of information which can help. Again, many
pieces may be unsuitable for computerisation; the balance can give rise to
ideas for DP projects supplying 'decision support information'.
The fourth category includes word processing, communication networks and
the 'electronic office'. The fifth aims to provide a general-purpose service
to specialist users who may be able to use prescribed calculator facilities
or to write their own programs.

Question

1   Identifying project ideas requires an act of intelligence. As with most instances where invention is called for, it is wise to consider more than one way of generating ideas. Apart from reviewing KRA decisions and MOEs, existing messages and processes, what other ways of getting project ideas can you think of?   (5 min)

2.2 PROJECT SELECTION

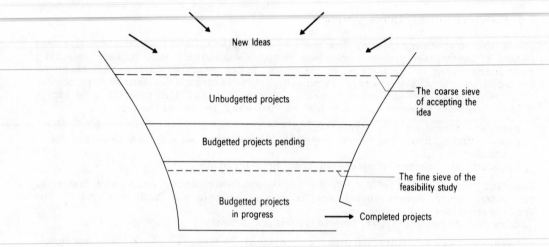

Fig. 2.1: Project selection hopper

Figure 2.1 illustrates how a given project, once the idea is identified, may be added to the list of unbudgetted projects. It may be decided to budget the project forthwith (so it joins the budgetted projects pending) or possibly to initiate it straight away (in which case it joins the budgetted projects in progress). These decisions are not irreversible and it may be decided to move projects up in the hopper as well as down.

A management team, such as a long-range DP steering committee, may be put in charge of the project selection hopper. This team should include representatives of general management, present or prospective users, and the DP manager. Their job includes vetting new ideas, budgeting them, authorising and cancelling projects.

Some new ideas considered by the steering committee may be rejected out of hand. Figure 2.1 illustrates this by means of the 'coarse sieve' at the top of the hopper. Patently flawed or unfruitful ideas will fail to get through this sieve. The steering committee must use their insight, experience and judgement to decide whether or not an idea should join the list of plausible possibilities in the hopper.

A more detailed evaluation of the idea will be necessary when priorities dictate that the project should go forward to completion. This is the feasibility study, which is considered in chapter 3 onwards. Figure 2.1 illustrates the feasibility study as a fine sieve encountered after some resource has been allocated to the project, i.e. when it is in progress.

When prioritising projects, the following factors may influence ranking. These factors probably cannot be quantified with any precision, but it may be possible for each project to be rated on a five-point scale.

1   Forecast effect on funds. Possible five-point scale: very significant

increase, significant increase, average increase, small increase, non-improving or deleterious.

2 Manageability. This term covers the ability of the management to achieve the ends they have perceived. Factors influencing judgement of this criterion will include management knowhow about the type of project, departmental morale, labour relations, involvement of sponsor, the organisation structure for DP system development, technical expertise.

3 Risk. Again, risk of failure of a project may be assessable on a five-point scale from very risky to low risk. See next chapter for some risk-influencing factors.

4 Timespan for development.

5 Forecast return on investment. Forecast effect on funds was absolute; return on investment is concerned with the ratio of the eventual benefits to the costs initially advanced.

6 Congruence with DP policies.

7 Congruence with present DP system architecture.

It is not suggested that this list is necessarily complete, nor that the items are orthogonal. A tabulation of project ideas with their marks on each chosen criterion may aid steering committee judgement of relative worth (McLean and Soden, 1).

Questions

1 How can project money expenditures be budgetted 3-5 years ahead without substantial investment in fact-finding, such as is normally done in a feasibility study?   (20 min)

2 What can be done if the steering committee lacks the insight or experience to make good advance judgements about project ideas?   (3 min)

2.3 PROJECT INITIATION

Project initiation is what happens when a project idea is changed in status from 'budgetted project pending' to 'budgetted project in progress'. The first progress to be made on the project is to carry out the feasibility study.

The steering committee's problems at this time include:

what should be the objectives of the feasibility study?
who should lead the study team and who should be in it?
what should be the study team's terms of reference?
what preparation does the study team need?
how long should the study team be given and what target for the output
     of the team should be stipulated?

Figure 2.2 summarises, by means of an example, the background to project initiation as described in this and the last chapter. The main activities of a feasibility study are taken to be simply those of 'systems analysis and design', the difference, if any, being one of the level of detail to which the analysis and design is taken and the emphasis given to finding out facts which will help in evaluation. Techniques of systems analysis and design are discussed in Systems Analysis.

Question

1 Define a possible set of responsibilities for a long-range DP steering committee.   (20 min)

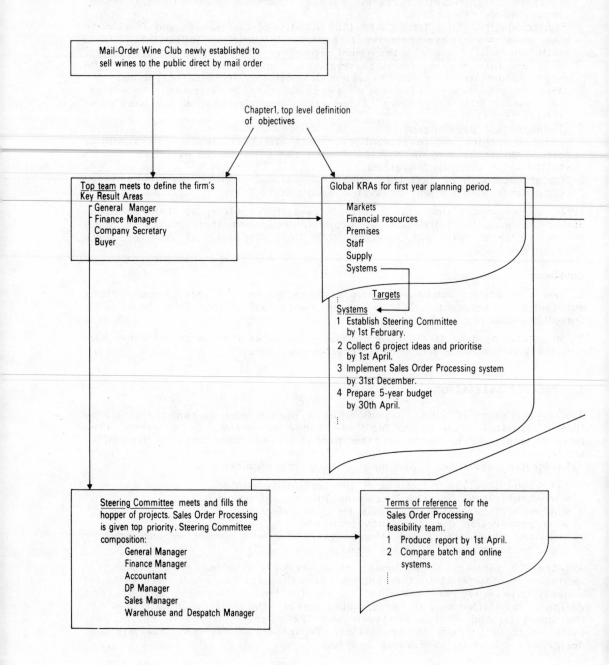

Fig. 2.2: Example of MBO adapted to a case. Note that the steering

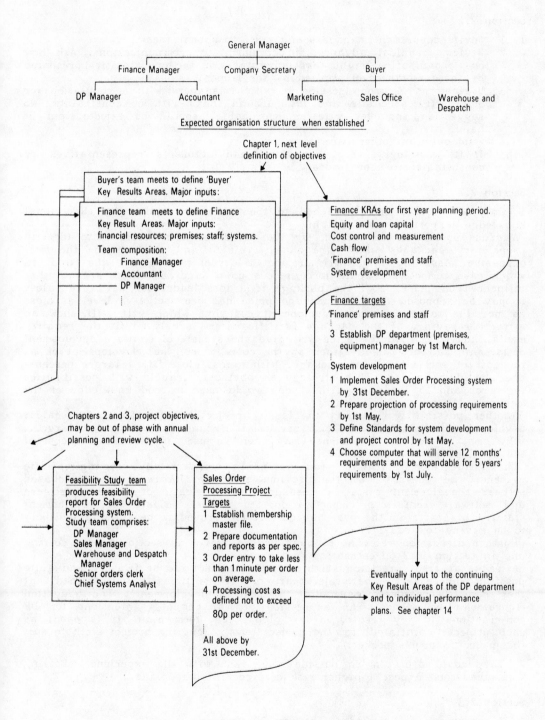

General Manager

Finance Manager — Company Secretary — Buyer

DP Manager — Accountant — Marketing — Sales Office — Warehouse and Despatch

Expected organisation structure when established

Chapter 1, next level
definition of objectives

Buyer's team meets to define 'Buyer'
Key Results Areas. Major inputs:

Finance team meets to define Finance
Key Result Areas. Major inputs:
financial resources; premises; staff; systems.

Team composition:
 Finance Manager
 Accountant
 DP Manager

Finance KRAs for first year planning period.
Equity and loan capital
Cost control and measurement
Cash flow
'Finance' premises and staff
System development

Finance targets
'Finance' premises and staff

3 Establish DP department (premises,
 equipment) manager by 1st March.

System development

1 Implement Sales Order Processing system
 by 31st December.
2 Prepare projection of processing requirements
 by 1st May.
3 Define Standards for system development
 and project control by 1st May.
4 Choose computer that will serve 12 months'
 requirements and be expandable for 5 years'
 requirements by 1st July.

Chapters 2 and 3, project objectives,
may be out of phase with annual
planning and review cycle.

Feasibility Study team
produces feasibility
report for Sales Order
Processing system.
Study team comprises:
 DP Manager
 Sales Manager
 Warehouse and Despatch
 Manager
 Senior orders clerk
 Chief Systems Analyst

Sales Order
Processing Project
Targets
1 Establish membership
 master file.
2 Prepare documentation
 and reports as per spec.
3 Order entry to take less
 than 1 minute per order
 on average.
4 Processing cost as
 defined not to exceed
 80p per order.

All above by
31st December.

Eventually input to the continuing
Key Result Areas of the DP department
and to individual performance
plans. See chapter 14

committee is monitoring plans that transcend department boundaries

ANSWER POINTERS

Section 2.1

1   1   Invite department managers and staff to submit ideas.
    2   Review technical advances in computing or communications. Ask how our organisation might take advantage of the opportunities presented by these advances or implied by the trends.
    3   Brainstorm. A group session in which managers with a reputation for originality speculate and toss around ideas with no constraints. No suggestion, however wild or improbable, should be rejected out of hand.
    4   Find out what others are doing.
    5   Invite outsiders, e.g. computer manufacturer's representatives or consultants, to submit ideas.

Section 2.2

1   Only with great error attached to the estimates, and/or by exceptional knowledge, experience and insight.
A crude possibility for getting an idea of development costs is to identify proprietary packages which are closely related and to determine the most expensive. Assuming that there are not a lot of packages in the field, in which case competition would force prices down, and that there are no other influences on price, e.g. the package is a loss leader for hardware sales, it may be supposed that the package price has been set at a level as close as possible to an in-house development cost but which will still show an attractive saving. If the package facilities seem largely to fit the requirements, adding 50% to the price will give an estimate of software development costs: this can be viewed either as the costs of original development or as the cost of specialising the package. With a less close fit, a larger percentage should be added. This strategy is obviously fraught with possibilities for error and to get away with it one would need a good knowledge of the market.
Another possibility is to try to classify projects on two five-point scales: development costs (very large...very small); running costs (very large... very small). Previous experience may then be used to estimate the cost of the development and operation.
The influence on hardware and purchased software may, failing specific evidence, be guessed from the previous ratios of hardware and purchased software development costs (as measured by the ratio of annual hardware and software rentals or amortisations to annual salaries of development staff). This ratio in the past has quite often proved to be 1:1 and is likely to be moving towards 1:2.
Further discussion relevant to budgetting is given in section 6.1 on costing and in section 10.2 on estimating.
Attempts at great precision at this stage are likely to be illusory and quite possibly unnecessary. The projects are not yet sufficiently well-defined that they can be considered as having a 'cost of development'. The budgetted figure can be seen as an expression of management's intentions for DP contributions to key results in the global long-term plan. It is open, as each project is initiated, for the project team to cut the project cloth to suit the project budget's pocket.

2   They could draft in an outside consultant with the experience. Failing this, they must expect a higher risk of error in their plans.

Section 2.3

1   To encourage and vet ideas for new DP projects.
    To define DP policies.

To decide between competing projects, including projects in progress, in the light of priorities.

To budget projects in the medium term.

To initiate projects and thereby authorise feasibility studies.

To decide the objectives, composition, terms of reference and preparation of the feasibility study team.

To cancel projects or authorise continuation.

To establish, or satisfy themselves about, arrangements for detailed planning and control of authorised projects.

REFERENCE

(1) McLean, E. R., and Soden, J. V., Strategic planning for MIS – a conceptual framework, **Proceedings of the National Computer Conference,** 1976.

3   Conduct of feasibility studies

3.1 OBJECTIVES OF THE FEASIBILITY STUDY

A feasibility study means here the activities in the first phase of a new project after it has been initiated (see also chapter 9).

The project idea has been through the coarse sieve to become an accepted unbudgetted idea. It has then been budgetted, or at least the feasibility study has, and is presently viewed as the most urgent project to start. Now it faces the fine sieve. Bearing in mind that, at least in the context of this discussion, the project at face value gives expression to a long-term plan of top management, the question at this stage is not so much 'Does the project go through the fine sieve?' as 'Can we force the project through the fine sieve?'

What is the fine sieve? The holes of the sieve can be seen as a more precise definition of the evaluation criteria used for prioritising the project (see section 2.2). The edges of the project are made more rigid as a result of more precise definition of requirements (see Systems Analysis, chapters 4 and 5). A more precise definition of the evaluation criteria can take the form of **project Targets**, i.e. objective measures of the DP system performance by which the success (or failure) of the project can eventually be judged. What measures are chosen in a particular instance will obviously vary with the prioritising factors, but examples of common measures are as follows:

- money cost of system development (measured by project accounting system);
- money cost of system operation (measured by cost accounting system);
- ease of use (e.g. number of times ad hoc enquiry service used, number of official complaints from users);
- speed per transaction, or response time (measured by a specially-kept log; both the average and the distribution are of interest);
- accuracy (error correction entries per 1000 transactions);
- timespan to develop system (project event log);
- money return on investment (e.g. measured money return on measured money investment – but see chapter 5);
- congruence with DP policies (lack of revision to this system to permit the development of subsequent systems).

'Number of complaints' is a good example of a **lumpy** measure, since some complaints may be serious and others not. These limitations are discussed further in chapter 4.

Measures of the sort listed above might be dubbed **close** MOEs, since they are relatively independent of disturbance from the environment of the system. MOEs such as

- customer satisfaction (proportion of customers closing accounts),
- job satisfaction (labour turnover ratio), and
- productivity (added value per capita),

are **distant** MOEs in this context, in the sense that although it is postulated that the DP system may affect them, environmental disturbance is large and likely to swamp out the system influence on these measures. The project sponsor may want to see a thread connecting close MOEs to distant MOEs, but the magnitude of the DP system effect on distant MOEs may never be known with much confidence.

1 To propose the (close) MOEs of the project.
2 To consider major alternative system designs and reject unacceptable ones on any reliable ground – economic, technical, social, timescale, manageability, risk (chance of failure, cost of failure), etc.
3 To choose the most promising remaining alternative and to develop the design of this to the point where, with acceptable reliability,

i) a forecast can be made of the effect on the close MOEs, thereby defining Targets, and
ii) an assurance can be given that the project is free from unacceptable side-effects.

   More than one attempt at this may be necessary if the development reveals that the chosen alternative is not the most promising one.
4 To lay the foundations for subsequent planning and control of the project, should continuation be authorised, by preparing an outline plan for the whole project and a more detailed plan of the activities to the end of the analysis phase.
5 To document the Targets, design and plan in a way that allows subsequent analysis, design and post-implementation evaluation teams to benefit from the work of the feasibility study team.
6 To present the findings in a way that will allow the sponsors to decide whether or not to authorise continuation.

Fig. 3.1: Feasibility study objectives. Note that continuing with the existing system, or improving a manual system, should always be considered as major alternatives

Figure 3.1 summarises the general objectives of a feasibility study. What is meant by 'acceptable reliability' in this figure is difficult to quantify. The feasibility study can be seen as reducing the chance of the worst failures occurring or as reducing the cost if failure does occur; the higher the prior chance or cost of failure, the more reliability is required. The reliability can be increased by demanding a finer attention to detail from the study team, or by increasing the representation on the team. In very high risk cases – say, where the cost of failure could be several times the system development cost – the study team could be asked to develop a pilot or prototype system to operational status in order finally to assess system performance. A pilot system is generally taken to mean a version of the system implemented in one place; this system will, when all the bugs are out, be replicated in other places. A prototype is a quick and dirty version of a system, or some aspect of it, or a mock-up, which will aid assessment of effectiveness.

Questions

1 Is there any point in proposing a project MOE which is not presently measured?   (5 min)

2 An MOE proposed for a system which it is hoped will produce bills more speedily is average delay between customer ordering goods and customer paying for goods. Is this a close or distant MOE? Is it lumpy or smooth?
                                                                                 (5 min)

3.2 COMPOSITION OF THE STUDY TEAM

The study team should be of such a number, and mix, of people that they can achieve the feasibility study objectives within the desired time scale. Consideration of the objectives suggests that the study team should include a person or persons who can:

    make up MOEs;
    design and document systems;
    predict main and side effects;
    plan DP projects;
    make reports to management.

In addition, it is virtually prerequisite that study team members should be intelligent and able to use their initiative. All these abilities together are usually found only in top calibre personnel.

In view of a substantial proportion of projects which fail to realise the benefits originally anticipated (estimates have been as high as 70%), there should be a strong presumption that there are risks in the project which are not yet fully understood. To help combat these, the factors in the project which increase the chance of failure or which give rise to serious consequences if failure occurs should be identified; see Figure 3.2. Team participants should then be selected from those available persons who can apply special knowledge, skill or experience to the risky factors. The available personnel can be seen as a pool of data processing personnel, user personnel and outside consultants; outside consultants can be selected to combat a high-risk factor, or to fulfil other roles if they cannot be covered from within.

1   System needs to fit the requirements of human operators or users, e.g. order entry system, management information system.
2   System directly affects organisation's dealings with customers (in a buyer's market) or other sensitive outside influences, e.g. airline seat reservation, point-of-sale system, production control.
3   System demands unusually high reliability, e.g. air traffic control, railway signalling.
4   System may use unfamiliar technology, e.g. distributed database, new or untried software, unusual file organisation, first-time user.
5   System may require algorithms not well understood, e.g. production control, pattern recognition.
6   System has diverse functions, e.g. integrated system crossing department boundaries.
7   System has diverse locations, e.g. international network where local requirements may differ.
8   System has changing or ill-defined requirements, e.g. ad hoc management reports.
9   Any other factors which can be identified in the particular case, e.g. change of location or organisation structure concurrent with change of system.

Fig. 3.2: Factors increasing the chance or cost of failure. Factors 4 and 5 must be judged relative to the experience or knowledge of the intended implementors

It may be, in a given case, that one factor is thought to be so high-risk as to warrant several persons being involved with different aspects of it; for example, a system which changes the established patterns of work of a large workforce could call for representatives from each affected section. Some people may be able to bring skills to bear on more than one factor. Some projects may be sufficiently low risk to bear study by a solo all-rounder.

Questions

1 This section concentrates on feasibility study team composition from the point of view of reducing risks and of achieving the objectives of management. What other influence on team composition might there be? (2 min)

2 What can be done if it is decided not to use consultants and if the available personnel do not have the desired feasibility study skills? (3 min)

3.3 TERMS OF REFERENCE

The terms of reference are the official brief to the study team given by the project initiators. Often, in practice, the team leader is asked to propose terms of reference for approval by management.

Spelling out terms of reference with well-chosen words contributes to genuine understanding between initiators and team. It also gives a chance to make clear the balance required in the study effort and the particular responsibility of team members picked for their special skills or knowledge. The terms may be more generally or specifically couched, according to how much licence the initiators are prepared to give the team, or how much initiative is expected. The terms are more helpful if they refer to desired outputs or achievements of the team, as shown in Figure 3.3 overleaf, avoiding phrases such as 'to study' or 'to investigate', which only describe activity.

Other points to consider when drawing up terms of reference are as follows.

Bounds of the study may be included to reduce the risk of misapplied effort or to ensure referral for management decision should the study need enlargement.

Constraints caused by company policy, future plans, etc. should be mentioned.

Any specific authorities which are needed should be granted, and limitations of authority should be specified. The resources available to the team should be spelled out if these are not clear.

Method guidance may be needed, e.g. the team may be required to inspect known similar systems, search literature, etc.

Especially when high risk factors are present, consideration should be given to requiring the team to furnish fallback or standby emergency plans which could be called upon should the recommended system prove infeasible when it is brought into operation.

Even short written reports may remain unread by busy managers. A verbal presentation of the findings might be good insurance against misunderstanding.

The terms of reference should not be considered as cast in concrete. The team should expect to apply for revision as they encounter new possibilities or facts.

Question

1 Suppose some terms of reference read: 'John – Go to the Boston works and do a feasibility study on their production planning. Report to me in four weeks.' Could this be an adequate definition? If so, what circumstances do you envisage? (20 min)

3.4 PREPARATION OF THE STUDY TEAM

Of course, the study team should be informed about any previous similar

From: Computer Steering Committee   To: Order Entry Study Team
(A. Brown, Systems
J. Roberts, Orders
B. Johnson, Warehouse)

TERMS OF REFERENCE

1 Propose objective measures of effectiveness of the sales order entry system. Of particular concern are the speed of getting orders to the warehouse, the speed of raising invoices and the proportion of invoices which need retyping or which are sent out containing errors.

2 List the advantages and disadvantages of two alternative possibilities (or more at the team's discretion), including:

(a) on-line order entry using minicomputer with terminals in sales department and warehouse;

(b) off-line order entry, input from sales department by optical mark read documents.

3 For the system recommended by the team, provide firm forecasts of the effect on each of the proposed measures of effectiveness and of the cost of development and operation. Define in detail the inputs and outputs of the system, with draft order forms/displays, picking lists and invoices. Document the manual processes foreseen in the sales department and warehouse.

4 J. Roberts is particularly to appraise the effect of the proposed system on customer service, order staff job satisfaction and other side effects.

B. Johnson is particularly to appraise the effect of the proposed system on picking speed, and the productivity and job satisfaction of picking staff.

Messrs Roberts and Johnson are also to ensure that each person in their departments is kept fully informed of plans and possibilities and that interested staff and shop stewards are invited to participate in the team's activities. It is company policy that no redundancies take place as a result of computerisation and that established work-groups will not be broken up if this can be avoided.

The authority of the study team does not extend to negotiating wage rates nor to other matters connected with sharing any productivity benefits which might result.

5 Make the proposed system extensible so that stock control and sales ledger systems can be added at a later date. Investigation of these systems is authorised only to the extent necessary to establish extensibility.

6 Furnish plans for standby operation in the event of prolonged cessation of computer facilities or electricity supply.

7 The expected duration of the study is five weeks. The team is to submit forthwith a detailed plan of their activities, stating their planned achievements at approximately weekly intervals.

8 The feasibility report is to be drawn up as outlined in the company standards manual. The report is to be copied to Steering Committee members, order/warehouse personnel at supervisor level and above, and warehouse shop stewards. A management presentation should be made approximately three days after submitting the report.

Fig. 3.3: An example of fairly specific terms of reference

projects and supplied with background information and available documentation.

There is no means of appraising a project proposal completely independently of context. The evaluation facts relevant to a project cannot be completely listed without a full knowledge of the purpose. Although, perhaps, many evaluation facts are predictably required by every project - e.g. cost of development, change in costs of operation under new system, development time needed – the analyst is guided to seek out and record other facts only by his understanding of the purpose of the project and the mood of the initiators. This means that the study team should be made fully aware of the long-term plans and management reasoning relevant to the project.

Study team members may require training prior to undertaking the study. All members of the team should have a good understanding of

long and medium-term planning for DP
conduct of feasibility studies

ans some understanding of

principles and practice of systems analysis and design.

Collectively, the team should have a complete set of systems analysis and design skills. User department members should have skills in factfinding and design of business procedures.

The team leader should have a comprehensive understanding of feasibility studies and project management. Other participants who might be involved in managing the implementation of the system in their departments should also have a knowledge of project management.

The required skills are reviewed in Systems Analysis. The present state of team skills should be weighed up against the target skills. The gap shows what training is needed.

Question

1 A feasibility study was authorised for a small work-in-progress system. The analyst discovered that two other feasibility studies had been done in earlier years, both of which recommended substantially the same system as the one he now had in mind. How should the analyst apply his effort now?

(5 min)

3.5 TEAM TARGETS

The activities of the team will be a subset of those undertaken in a complete systems analysis and design exercise. These activities should be planned, estimated, scheduled and controlled as with any other project, and the target date for completion will be established in the usual way from the estimated work and resources available (see chapter 9 onwards).

Often, team leaders feel less sure about planning feasibility study activities than later stages of a project. In such cases, they should look back to the terms of reference: are they not sufficiently well-defined that the team activities can be spelled out? Being more specific in the terms of reference will make planning the study easier.

Sometimes the terms of reference cannot be more specific because no one feels confident enough about what has to be done. This is a danger sign. In this case it should be recognised that the project has 'research' (not development) status and the first task of the analyst should be to undertake sufficient research to enable more specific terms of reference to be drawn up. In the absence of other clues, an arbitrary time – say, one week – may be authorised for this, with ad hoc extensions.

The deliverable product of the team at the target date is the feasibility report. A possible content of the feasibility report is outlined in Figure 3.4 overleaf, but initiative should be used to adapt this example to the emphases or facts of a particular case. All other documentation collected or created by the team should be filed for use in the next phase of the project.

The feasibility report is not only for a yes/no decision. It is also to allow management an opportunity to modify specific weaknesses or to take

Terms of reference	As modified.
Justifications	Statement of system objectives and scope. (This should specify what messages will be supplied by the system, what processes will be controlled, what decisions are to be supported. Operational messages, monitoring information and decision support information should be listed.)
	Major alternatives considered and preferred solution (premises, assumptions and unknowns influencing choice should be emphasised).
	Fit with long- and medium-term plans.
	Cost and benefit summary, project Targets.
	Limitations of preferred solution.
	Other implications or side effects of interest to management.
Present system	Background information if necessary.
	Summary of procedures, staffing, equipment.
	List of inputs, outputs and files.
	Control and security features.
Proposed system	Summary of procedures, staffing, equipment.
	Outline design of the inputs, outputs and business procedures.
	Data dictionary or summary of the database content, listing the entities and relationships and their attributes which are to be recorded by the system.
	Control, integrity and security features.
	Other implications.
Conversion	Conversion requirements and conversion plan.
Future plan	Overall project plan.
	Detailed plan for the analysis phase.
	Recommendations for participation in the next phase.
Appendices	References to documents read or mentioned in report.
	Supporting detail of present system, proposed system, conversion plans, volumes, estimates, costs, benefits, hardware, software, data transmission, terminal network, etc., being mainly copies of or extracts from the standard system documentation files.

Fig. 3.4: Example feasibility study report content

advantage of strengths not previously recognised, to check out for side-effects which only the management are in a good position to predict, and to weigh up their confidence in the feasibility effort.

Question

1 Figure 3.5 summarises this chapter. If there is no steering committee, who should undertake their functions? Does this person need any more training than the steering committee members?   (5 min)

ANSWER POINTERS

Section 3.1

1 Only if it will be measured in the future. It should be an additional Target of any DP system to supply information about project MOEs if these are not presently measured.

2 Distant. Length of credit taken is affected by liquidity in the trade, the

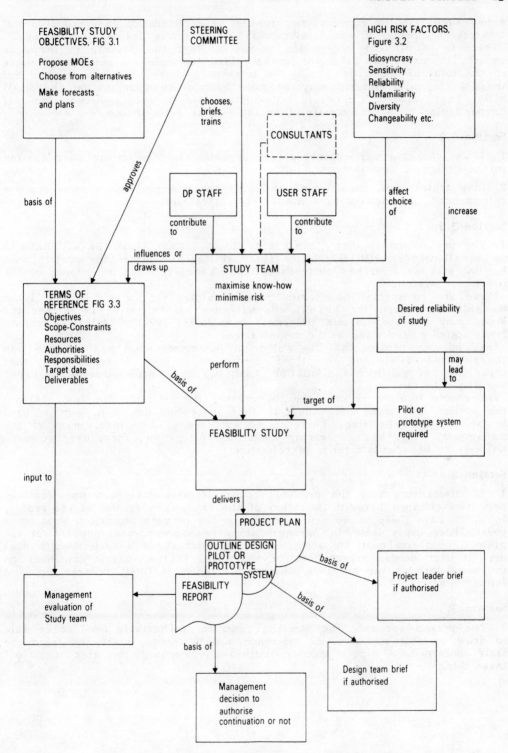

Fig. 3.5: Overview of feasibility study conduct

money supply in the economy, improvement or deterioration in speed of postal services. A closer MOE would refer to the delay before despatching the bill.

There is insufficient information to say whether the measure is lumpy or smooth. If one or two bills are for very large amounts – a substantial share of the total of the bills – then the measure is lumpy. Failure to send out those large bills quickly may be more harmful than delays on the small bills. The proposed MOE would not differentiate between the two cases. If no particular bills predominate, then the MOE is quite smooth.

Section 3.2

1   I was thinking particularly of the organisation's policy on participation in the design of new systems.

2   Give training in the missing skills. Otherwise, postpone project or, not recommended, go ahead with a higher risk of failure.

Section 3.3

1   The implication is that 'John' is to do the study alone. He will have to be an all-rounder with feasibility study skills, and either the project must be low risk or John has quite exceptional knowledge and experience of the particular system.

There are no special boundaries or constraints, etc. which John will not be able to discern for himself. He will use his initiative to further the study and can use his own judgement over MOEs, level of detail, alternatives, standby, reporting and communication.

This in turn implies that the author of the memorandum has insights into the proposed system and exceptional confidence in John. It seems likely that this level of confidence could be built up only after several years of working with him.

The remote location reduces the chance that the initiator has insights into the system. The memo tone suggests that there has not been, nor is there to be, an oral briefing. There is no evidence of any involvement of the management, e.g. via a steering committee. Altogether, these are extremely unlikely to be adequate terms of reference.

Section 3.4

1   In discovering why the previous proposals were not taken up. Possibly priorities changed between initiation of the study and receipt of the report, in which case there is no evidence against the proposed solution. Most other possibilities imply something wrong: lack of management/user support for the project; no clear benefit to users; lack of participation; a system which does not fit user needs, expectations or tolerance. If the analyst continues on the same path as the previous studies, his report is likely to meet the same fate.

Section 3.5

1   The project sponsor. The steering committee **collectively** need to be able to draw up suitable terms of reference and to choose, brief and train the staff concerned. A single sponsor individually needs to be able to do all these things.

4 Utility analysis

4.1 TWO–GOAL INDIFFERENCE CURVE

The aim of this chapter is to lend theoretical support to the methodology of the previous chapters. It serves to emphasise that a feasibility study can hardly hope to come up with simple yes/no answers, and to clarify some of the problems of making rational choices when the possibilities are complex. It is not the intention that the reader should aquire any particular skill from this chapter, but that he should understand rather than take on trust the philosophical principles upon which rest the KRAs and MOEs already introduced. Some readers may prefer to continue directly to the next chapter.

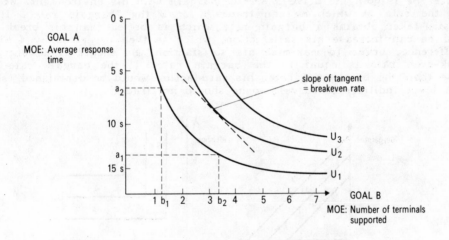

Fig. 4.1: Two–goal indifference curves

Figure 4.1 shows, on the horizontal and vertical axes, the extent to which any two goals in a system are met (increasing as one moves away from the origin). The two goals might be, for example, A, Minimising Average Response Time and B, Maximising Number of Terminals Giving Access to the System. These two goals happen to be quantified and are usually systematic-ally related, i.e. response time might deteriorate because an extra terminal is added. However, for the purpose of the present discussion any two goals, even trivial, unquantified or independently achievable ones, will suffice as examples; say, A, Maximising the Niceness of the Computer Room Colour Scheme and B, Maximising the Travelling Salesman's Job Satisfaction.

The indifference curve U_1 joins all points which give a decision–taker equal satisfaction. The curves U_2, U_3 etc. show higher levels of satisfaction, increasing as the curves are more distant from the origin. The decision–taker for the purpose of the discussion is the sponsor and 'satisfaction' is synonymous with 'utility'. Economists in the past used the word 'value' instead of 'utility', but 'value' has become so associated with money value that this term is generally avoided when talking about personal, internal values. The normal association of the word 'utility' with 'usefulness' is misleading in this context. For example, a particular colour scheme of the computer room might be useless, but it might have utility if it is valued for its own sake.

So, it is supposed that a decision-taker is indifferent between any two points on the curve U_1, i.e. he will be equally satisfied whether he has a_1 of A and b_2 of B or a_2 of A and b_1 of B. The slope of the indifference curve at a particular point shows the rate of trade-off, of one goal for another, that the decision-taker considers as 'breaking even'. This slope will be referred to as the 'break-even rate'. It will be seen from the figure on the preceding page that the curve may become vertical as B is diminished, i.e. there is no increase in A which will compensate for further loss of B. For example, no further improvement in Average Response Time will compensate for having fewer than the minimum acceptable Number of Terminals. A similar position may arise as goal A is diminished and the indifference curve becomes horizontal. It will also be seen that, unless the indifference curve is a straight line, the break-even rate will change as one goal becomes more or less fulfilled.

It may be imagined that the decision-taker is contemplating taking some action which will change the proportions at which he presently enjoys A and B, i.e. he is going to drive a sort of bargain with his environment. We will call the rate at which he can trade A for B the 'bargain rate'. If the decision-taker obtains a bargain rate which is better than his break-even rate, he can increase his satisfaction, which is then described by a higher indifference curve. To maximise his satisfaction, he should trade until the break-even rate is equal to the bargain rate. If the bargain rate were worse than the break-even rate, his satisfaction would be diminished (shown by a lower indifference curve), so he should not trade.

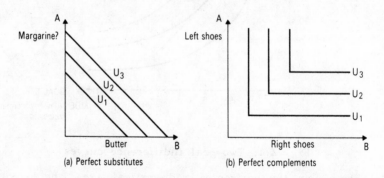

(a) Perfect substitutes   (b) Perfect complements

Fig. 4.2: Special cases of indifference curves

Figures 4.2 (a) and (b) illustrate special cases of indifference curves – perfect substitutes and perfect complements. It is difficult to defend practical examples of these. It is more realistic to speak of goals as being relatively substitutable or relatively complementary.

To summarise, if a decision-taker sees a bargain rate of trade between two of his goals which is better than his break-even rate of trade, then he can improve his position. After the bargain is concluded, though, his break-even rate of trade may have changed so that a repeat bargain is less attractive. Furthermore, when the goals are systematically related, both the break-even rate of trade and the bargain rate offered by the environment may have changed as a result of the bargain.

Questions

1   Using either example in the text, explain what is meant by the horizontal portion of U_1 in Figure 4.1 (p. 27).   (5 min)

2   In Figure 4.2 (b), does it matter whether or not the shoes are of the same size and colour?   (5 min)

3   If the sense of the curves of Figure 4.1 are taken as concave, what would a convex curve mean? Could such a curve be descriptive of behaviour?   (5 min)

Exercise

Draw specimen indifference curves to describe your own, or a hypothetical decision-taker's, preferences for A, Number of Chinese Dinners had in a Year and B, Number of Visits to the Pictures in a Year.

4.2 MOE NORMALISATION: SCORES AND WEIGHTS

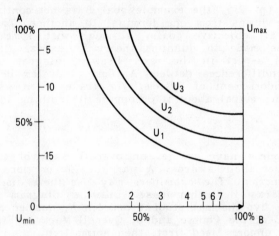

Fig. 4.3: The 'scored' degree of fulfilment of the goals gives a linear scale (the original MOEs of Figure 4.1 are shown inside the axes of this figure)

Figure 4.3 revises the axes of Figure 4.1 to a standard unit. The origin of these axes represents the least possible utility that comes from lack of fulfilment of the goal. This is fairly easy to conceive as, for example, the utility of 'less than one terminal' in the case of the example previously offered for goal B, but is more hazy in the case of A, response time. I can only define it as the point beyond which any further deterioration of the MOE does not significantly cause further diminution of utility. For example, the Average Response Time above which all higher average response times are for practical purposes equally inutile.
  The extremes of the axes, marked 100%, represent the pinnacles of the decision-taker's satisfaction from more of the goal (as he sees things at a particular instant). This may be conceived, in the case of A in the example, as an instantaneous Average Response Time. (Perhaps that should be qualified, since there is an argument for having a 'natural delay' in responses from a computer system, to avoid pressuring the user. The most utile time in this case may be greater than zero. The MOE scale marked has to be imagined so that the best time, say $\frac{1}{2}$ second, appears at the 100% mark and the balance of the scale descends away from 100%.) In the case of B, we have to imagine a Number of Terminals above which an additional

terminal does not significantly increase utility. (Both examples given show diminishing returns of utility with unit improvements in the MOE. This is usually, but not necessarily, the case.)

This normalised scale now permits a measure of the utility of an MOE, expressed as a fraction, percentage, mark–out–of–ten etc. on a linear scale between zero and unit utility. This measure is called the **score** of the MOE.

Considering a decision–taker whose present state of fulfilment is described by a point on one of the indifference curves, the normalised rate of trade is given by the tangent to that curve. This rate can be used to measure the relative 'weight' of the two goals. For example, if 5 percentage points of A would be traded away for a gain of 4 percentage points in B, a percentage point of B therefore being valued 25% more than a percentage point of A, then B would be assigned relative weight 5 while A would be assigned relative weight 4. It is hoped that expressing weights in this way corresponds to the intuitive idea of a higher weight for the goal which is more prized at the present moment.

Question

1   In Figure 4.1 (p. 27), the example goal B is not continuous but instead moves in discrete jumps from one terminal to another. To a certain extent this is true of all objective goals, although with some goals an appeal would have to be made to quantum theory to expose the discreteness. I glossed over this aspect in the text. Draw a diagram of a hypothetical decision–taker's indifferences between A, Cost of System Development and B, Trade Union's Endorsement of System. The trade union will either endorse the system, remain neutral about it or oppose it; nothing in between.

(10 min)

Exercise

Students on a course have to get an overall mark of 40% in their final examinations to get their awards. A mark of 70% or more will warrant the award of a distinction. The examiners may use their discretion to condone slightly lower marks in either case. Draw a diagram to illustrate the indifferences of a hypothetical student between A, Number of Chinese Dinners in the Final Year of the Course and B, Overall Mark in Final Examinations. Draw the diagram unnormalised first, then normalised.

4.3 MULTIPLE GOALS

A proposal for evaluating the utility of alternative bargains is known variously as weights and scores, multi–criteria utility analysis, or multi–attribute utility analysis (Gilb, 1; Land, 2: for a comprehensive biblio-graphy, see Dujmovic, 3). The suggested method is to add up the weighted score improvements of all the goals concerned in the bargain to produce an overall measure of the utility won, as in Figure 4.4. The bargain with the highest utility improvement (the greatest weighted score gains) is to be preferred.

It is assumed that the decision–taker, maybe after some training, can reveal his preferences by voicing his weights and scores or that an analyst, maybe after some training, can deduce the weights and scores by questioning or observing the decision–taker.

It is also assumed that the utility of the individual goals is additive, i.e. the overall utility is equal to the sum of the indepently–considered utilities of the goals. This is not true in the case of complements, i.e. a left shoe on its own may have zero utility, as may a right shoe on its own, but a left shoe and a right shoe together have some utility. The assumption of additivity can only be completely defended when dealing with perfect

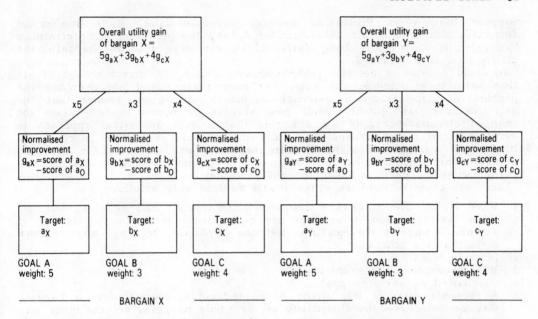

Fig. 4.4: Comparison of alternatives by weights and scores. In this example, there are three goals affected by the projects; the first alternative leads to the set of Targets called Bargain X, the second leads to the set of Targets called Bargain Y. In this example the present state of the MOEs in the existing system is a_0, b_0, c_0, so the 'overall' utility of the existing system can be taken as 5 x score of a_0 + 3 x score of b_0 + 4 x score of c_0

substitutes.

The assumption of substitutability is also embodied in the weights adopted. Recall that the weights reflect the instantaneous break-even rates of trade as seen from the present position (marginal rates, in the economist's jargon). These rates are assumed to persist even when a bargain drives the decision-taker to a new position. Such consistent rates of trade reliably exist only with perfect substitutes.

A further implication of the assumption of additivity is that of a square utility space, as in Figure 4.3 (p. 29). It is assumed to be meaningful to speak of increasingly utile A/B combinations right up to 100% A and 100% B. This is contradictory to the assumption of substitutability if the existence of a limit on the utility of further fulfilment of any one goal is accepted. In Figure 4.2 (a) (p. 28), for example, if the axes of the perfect substitutes are taken to be normalised and if the line U_3 is the hypotenuse joining 100% A to 100% B, then U_3 is the highest attainable utility.

If we wish to preserve the weights and scores method, then, we must declare that we are dealing only with alternatives that are closely grouped together, with goals that are fulfilled far from completely (well away from the hypotenuse of the utility space), and which do not contain complements. (We could hope that the assumptions of linearity and additivity, which usually tend to overstate the utility of a bargain, are compensated for by the lack of treatment of complements, which tends to understate the utility of a bargain. I cannot conceive of any reason, though, why these might be supposed to be at all balanced in their effects.) Such close alternatives, distant from the perfect goal, are relatively linear and addable.

We must now face up to another corollary, namely that of independence. The linear additivity assumption means that if we strike a bargain of A against B, the utility of C remains unchanged. This is difficult to accept.

Suppose that A is Minimising Average Response Time, B is Number of Terminals and C is a fair substitute for A, say the provision of Entertaining Messages to While Away Long Waits. If we win more A in our bargain, the utility of C is diminished.

We could provide a decision-taker who was willing to invest enough of his time with some defences for this, but even these would not overcome the problem of dependence on **external** variables unless we assume that the decision-taker can quickly voice new weights or scores to compensate for changed circumstances. (I am assuming that a more analytical approach to weighting and scoring takes time, and during this time it is increasingly likely that variables not included in the model will change.) For example, overnight announcement by the government of a surprise credit squeeze may change what the decision-taker thought yesterday.

There are other difficulties which I will mention only briefly.

1   Weak MOEs. The MOEs are assumed to be smooth and regular, but the MOEs fastened upon in practice are quite likely to be lumpy. Number of Terminals may be the measure, but one particular terminal may be more utile than the others.
2   Discrete MOEs.
3   MOEs incompletely measure goal.
4   Overlooked or unvoiced goals.
5   A person's view of the utility of an individual component of a bargain may be determined by the utility of the whole bargain, not the other way around.

Cures might be advanced for each of these ills, except perhaps the last, but with each fresh assumption and each fresh cure, my personal confidence in the weights and scores method, as a tool for use by the general run of decision-takers in the present context, diminishes.

Questions

1   Weights and scores methods are often advocated for choosing computer hardware. Weights are allocated to computer characteristics such as memory size, cycle time, online backing storage, price, vendor support, etc. Competing tenders are scored on the characteristics and a choice made according to the summed weighted scores. Would you say weights and scores are more suitable for choosing hardware than for choosing between alternative DP systems proposals? (10 min)

4.4 GROUP GOALS AND THE MBO METHODOLOGY

A group goal is one agreed (or 'thrashed out') by individuals in a group. It is not necessarily a conjunction of the goals of the separate individuals, were they to be quizzed separately on their aims. The break-even rates between group goals are not necessarily the average of the break-even rates of the individuals. People may even change their goals momentarily, according to whether or not they are in a group. Psychologists have noted, for example, that individuals are more willing to entertain risk in a group decision than when considering the same possibilities alone. Whether this is because the individuals value freedom from risk less when they are part of a group or because they find comfort in shared responsibility, or for some other reason, it is difficult to say. Whether the 'group' utility, or some sort of sum of the individually-ascertained utilities, is to be preferred as a basis for choosing between alternatives does not appear to be a question of objective fact.

In the MBO (Management by Objectives) scheme I am proposing, there are three components concerned with goals: Key Result Areas; Measures of

Effectiveness; Side-effects. I have not mentioned side-effects so far, except incidentally in Figures 3.1 and 3.4, but they are an important addition to the methodology of earlier chapters. It should be recognised that human beings are not perfect; given the complexity of management problems, it is highly likely that there is a fault in the KRAs or MOEs identified. The KRAs may fail to cover all the goals or the MOEs may be an incomplete measure.

'Side-effects' is a catchnet for the balance of the goals and the desired measures. A feasibility report should inform about side-effects as well as giving Targets or forecasts of the MOEs.

The philosophy of the MBO method described in chapters 1 and 2 is that the most important thing for the analyst to do is to marshal the facts of interest to the decision-takers in a way that brings out the features of their decision problem. What they do with the facts is up to them.

The team approach to defining KRAs, in addition to allowing the rationalis-ation of high-level goals into goals which can be taken on board by subordinate units, also allows agreement of group goals. The limited number of goals allowed at each stage tends to ensure that complementary goals and strong substitute goals are lumped together as a larger goal. The KRAs will therefore tend to be weak substitutes. The prioritisation of the KRAs is intended to reveal, or to ensure reflection on, the present break-even trading rates of these larger, longer-term, faintly substitutable goals. Numbers can be put on these weights if it helps. The review of priorities is vital since break-even trading rates will change both with goal achieve-ment over time and with external variables (one of which will be the composition of the group). I have to leave it to the decision-taker to decide how frequently to review priorities, since organisations vary so much in the stability of the work they do; there is no general rule.

The MOEs which are to measure facets of the goals are set out in their raw state, helping the decision-takers to make their own subjective adjustments for complementariness, lumpiness and discreteness. Prioritisation is again intended to force consideration of break-even trading rates. The MOEs can be ANDed or ORed when they are complements or substitutes, for the purpose of prioritisation. For example:

number of branches served online by system AND
amount of online backing storage.

It is assumed here that one without the other is no use.

It is possible that a single MOE may crop up in more than one KRA. Since this MOE is measuring a facet of the fulfilment of different goals, or goals of different people, I think it should be left to appear in both places.

The collected KRAs and Targets allow the decision-takers to compare the **whole** proposed position with the present position, making their subjective adjustments for non-linearity and inter-goal dependence.

The need to report and consider side-effects allows overlooked or unvoiced goals to be brought into the marshalled facts, even at the last moment.

Questions

1 Where do money values come into the decisions?   (2 min)

2 In Public Administration applications, who should identify the KRAs and MOEs and who should discern the break-even trading rates, etc.?   (2 min)

3 Why bother to have KRAs? Why not just deal in MOEs?   (5 min)

ANSWER POINTERS

Section 4.1

1 At about a 15 second Average Response Time, there is no increase in the

Number of Terminals which will compensate for a further deterioration in the Average Response Time.

Below a certain level of Niceness of the Computer Room Colour Scheme, there is no increase in The Travelling Salesman's Job Satisfaction which will compensate for further reduction in niceness.

2   Assuming the decision-taker has equal-sized feet and is not an eccentric, yes; only matching shoes are complements.

3   After a bargain is concluded, the break-even rate of trade changes so that a repeat bargain is more attractive. This could occur if the sample trade revised the decision-taker's opinion about the utility of the goals. In this chapter I have assumed that the decision-taker has a perfect understanding of the goals.

Section 4.2

1

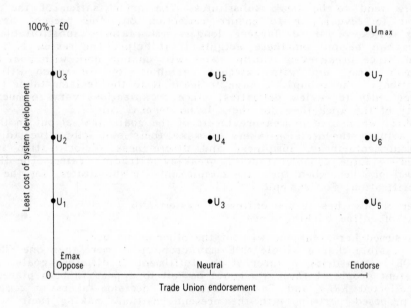

Fig. 4.5: Answer pointer to question 1, section 4.2

Section 4.3

1   I would, but I am not sure that I can justify this opinion objectively. It can be considered that the problem of alternative computers is better understood than the problem of alternative DP systems. There is less likelihood of unvoiced or overlooked goals. Usually, the most highly weighted goals - cost, power or throughput, reliability - have smooth, continuous MOEs and, within the confines of a range of alternative systems actually presented in response to a call for tenders, are relatively substitutable. In other words one computer tendered tends naturally to be a close alternative to another. Weights and scores methods are most applicable to close alternatives. It is hard to see alternative DP systems in the same light.

Section 4.4

1 Money is a candidate MOE, no doubt an important one. Money is a lumpy measure if it accrues at different points of time. More about this in chapter 5.

2 In a democracy, the public (through their representatives).

3 Not a very clear-cut answer. KRAs lend structure to the definition of objectives. MOEs may be too fine a level of detail for easy consideration. KRAs allow discussion to start by centering around fuzzy ideas, then to progress to a more detailed level. This makes the method easier to use.

REFERENCES

(1) Gilb, T., **Controlling the computer**, Studentlitteratur, 1974.
(2) Land, F. F., Evaluation of systems goals in determining a design strategy for a computer-based information system, **The Computer Journal, 19**, 4, 290-4, 1976.
(3) Dujmovic, J. J., The preference scoring method for decision making – survey, classification and annotated bibliography, University of Belgrade, Department of Electrical Engineering, 1977.

5 Net Present Value

5.1 FINANCIAL COST-BENEFIT ANALYSIS

The purpose of this chapter is to explain the philosophy behind using Net Present Value (NPV) as a smooth, close MOE, and to explain some practical considerations. A cost-benefit analysis is taken here to mean an evaluation of a project by converting all the costs and benefits into monetary equivalents. In some quarters a cost-benefit analysis is defined in just the opposite sense; in those quarters, what I am talking about is often called 'return on investment'.

A cost-benefit analysis is distinguished here from a cost-effectiveness analysis. In the former, all costs and benefits are valued in money terms and the criterion for judging alternatives is return on investment (payback period, yield, net present value, internal rate of return). With a cost-effectiveness analysis, not all the costs and benefits are valued in money terms (those not so valued being the 'effectiveness'). The criterion for choosing between alternatives is either the least cost for a given effectiveness or the most effectiveness for a given cost. If effectiveness is a single continuous variable, it may be meaningful to make judgements on 'effectiveness for cost'. The method of the previous chapters is similar to cost-effectiveness analysis in that not all costs and benefits are valued in money terms, but similar to cost-benefit analysis in that neither a level of effectiveness nor of cost is given. The criterion is 'maximise utility', but unlike the weights and scores approach there is no attempt to add goals measured in different units.

In practice, a cost-benefit analysis often ends up with goals left over which cannot be translated within acceptable limits of time and effort into money values. These are termed **intangibles**. These intangibles are almost equivalent to the non-money MOEs of previous chapters. If the intangible is not quantified, there may be a difference since the non-money MOE chosen may fail to measure completely the intangible goal. The influence of the project on the residue of the goal, if any, is a side-effect. Figure 5.1 illustrates these concepts.

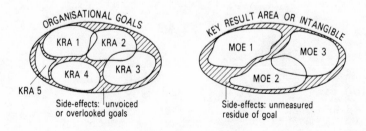

Fig. 5.1: Illustrating the sources of side-effects

Where intangibles are present, the cost-benefit criteria are inappropriate to the extent that failure to account for the intangibles distorts the calculated return on investment. For example, payback period (time taken for a money benefit to accrue to equal an initial money cost) is a senseless measure if a significant benefit or cost is omitted. With data processing projects, intangibles frequently play a large, even dominating, part.

There would be some hope for continuing with 'return on investment' criteria if it could be assumed that the intangibles were the same between alternatives, with only the tangibles differing. This view is hardly tenable when the alternatives are 'going ahead' and 'not going ahead'. Also, between alternative data processing projects which do have the same intangibles, the dominant proposal can usually be quickly identified, and the dominated solution rejected at an early stage. Thus the question of a detailed analysis and comparison by management of two projects which have the same intangibles rarely arises.

For these reasons, return on investment as a judgement criterion must be rejected unless all significant costs and benefits are money-valued. The discounted cash flow technique known as Net Present Value, on the other hand, is endorsed as a **measure of effectiveness**.

Question

1   The text speaks of 'converting' costs and benefits to money. This implies that project costs and benefits are real costs and benefits, not money. Is this always the case?   (10 min)

5.2 MONEY AS A MOE

Which goals are measured in money and which in non-money is a choice for the decision-taker; this choice is offered explicitly and early in the MBO method (section 3.1). It is more the analyst's concern to ensure that double counting is avoided. Either the money value of an improved goal achievement should be recorded, or the improvement should be measured in a non-money MOE, but not both.

In practice, direct costs of developing a new system are measured in money (analysts' and programmers' salaries and salary overheads, materials and computer time used on program development and testing, plus other direct expenses in developing a new system).

The increased, new or reduced costs of recording and communicating the formal messages concerned (change in user department salary costs and overheads, operating materials used, cost of computer and other machinery operating time, other data processing operations, e.g. keying) are also usually given a money Target. Beyond this, the viewpoints of organisation managements vary widely from little further attempt to place money values on costs and benefits (e.g. public administrations such as police, welfare, community medecine) to as much quantification of costs and benefits as can be achieved within reasonable limits of time and effort (e.g. profit-oriented management).

The money Targets are linearly additive (this does not mean that their **utilities** are linearly additive), except that the present value of monies accruing at different points of time will vary. As a first step, the cash flows (i.e. the effect on the chosen money MOEs) over time need to be analysed. A quarterly analysis is probably amply precise in practice; see Figure 5.2 overleaf. How these estimates are derived is covered in other chapters.

Note that the entries in the table should reflect the time associated with the **cash** movement. For example, if a computer is to be purchased for cash, the whole of the cash purchase price should be entered in the quarter in

Year	Quarter	Development and Maintenance Costs	Operating Cost Old System	Operating Cost New System	Other Money Targets	Total
1	1	(10)				(10)
	2	(10)				(10)
	3	(15)				(15)
	4	(15)				(15)
2	1	(4)	24	(23)	2	(1)
	2	(4)	24	(23)	2	(1)
	3	(4)	24	(23)	2	(1)
	4	(4)	24	(23)	2	(1)
3	1	(4)	30	(25)	2	3
	2	(4)	30	(25)	2	3
	3	(4)	30	(25)	2	3
	4	(4)	30	(25)	2	3
4	1	(4)	37	(27)	2	8
	2	(4)	37	(27)	2	8
	3	(4)	37	(27)	2	8
	4	(4)	37	(27)	2	8
5	1	(4)	47	(32)	2	13
	2	(4)	47	(32)	2	13
	3	(4)	47	(32)	2	13
	4	(4)	47	(32)	2	13

Fig. 5.2: Example quarterly analysis of money Targets (cash flow). An example of an 'other money Target' here is the value of better information

which the cash will be paid. If a computer is to be rented or leased, the rental/lease payments should be entered in the quarters in which they will be paid. If a nominal cost-per-hour of computer time is included in the analysis, the nearest practical approximation will probably be to accumulate the costs-per-hour in the quarters in which the time will be used. It is the cash flowing to and from the organisation which should be counted, not the expected profit or loss as measured by the books of account of the organis- ation. The MOE is money as measured by an actual flow of funds; the accounts may seek to show a fair view of profit or loss over a limited timescale, neglecting whether funds have flowed or not.

It **may** be necessary to forecast the effect of the project on the books of account ('make a budget') in order to exercise budgetary control over the project as it progresses, but that is another matter. Also, some Targets may depend upon the state of the books of account (e.g. corporation tax is calculated on a book profit, not on cash flow). If it is desired to money- value these accurately, it will be necessary to forecast the project's effect on book account balances. This takes us somewhat off the present point, but it might be observed in passing that the complete effect of taxation cannot be assessed unless the effect of non-money MOEs on account balances is forecast; this is tantamount to requiring that all costs and benefits must be measured in money terms. This may be an added reason for profit-oriented management to require quantification in money values. Against this, the differences of taxation effects between projects is less significant than the differences in the pre-tax cash flows. It is often decided to take tax effects into account only broadly, or to omit them from the analysis, leaving the decision-taker to make his own, possibly subjective, adjustments.

Questions

1 The entries in the cash flow analysis are not necessarily equal to the expected changes in 'profit' of the company as measured by the books of account at year end, but the total cash flow over several years will be similar to total profit change over the same period. Why is this?   (15 min)

2 There is nothing to stop a project sponsor from choosing book profit as a MOE if he desires. Would this be a money MOE or a non-money MOE?

(2 min)

5.3 NET PRESENT VALUE

The money realised in each quarter (Figure 5.2) is not addable, since the unit of measure has a time bias. If a cash benefit is postponed in time, the present value of the benefit may be taken as equal to the sum which, if invested now in the best available investment, would grow during the period of postponement to equal the future sum. The return to be gained on the investment depends on specific investment opportunities. In the absence of information about specific investment opportunities, the best assumption would be **either** that the cash would be invested in the equity of the business, in which case it could be assumed to earn the rate of interest to be earned generally on equity capital employed in the business, **or** that the cash would be invested in reducing the indebtedness of the business, in which case it can be taken to earn the rate of interest to be paid generally on loans borrowed by the business. Which of these views is preferred depends broadly on whether the growth of the business is limited by its ability to raise loan capital. If it is, the equity view is preferred. (Another way of looking at this is that if a project is to be financed out of equity capital, the equity interest rate is the opportunity cost; if out of loan capital, the loan interest rate is the actual cost.) In organisations that do not seek to make profit, only the loan view makes sense.

If the loan view is taken, then the interest rate earnable may be considered fairly secure. If the equity view is taken, then it is the custom of investment analysts to mark down the interest rate earnable by an amount which compensates for the riskiness of the return. This action may make the interest rate on either view rather similar.

The chosen interest rate is therefore that expected to prevail during the project lifetime and will probably be equal to a past prevailing rate adjusted for risk and trends. Prevailing interest rates include an element which is ascribable to 'inflation'. To preserve comparability, the forecast cash flows in each quarter should be those expected assuming that inflation occurs at the rate embodied in the interest rate. Alternatively, if cash flows are not to be forecast in this way but are to be left uninflated, the interest rate assumed should be diminished by its inflation content; this may make it zero or even negative. Of course, **real** trends of costs and benefits, i.e. those independent of inflation, should still be taken into account when forecasting cash flows.

We therefore have, for any quarter's cash flow,

$$F_q = P(1 + i)^q$$

where F_q is the future cash flow in quarter q, P is the present value equivalent, i is the assumed interest rate and q is the postponement in quarters (this assumes interest is to be compounded quarterly). Thus,

$$NPV = \sum F_q/(1 + i)^q \ , \quad q = 1, 2, \ldots, n$$

where n is the number of quarters to be included in the analysis. In a cost-benefit analysis the criterion would be that if the NPV were positive, the project is justified. In our context, NPV represents the positive or negative value of money Targets in present equivalent. The criterion is, 'Does the decision-taker wish to take up the bargain offered by the NPV and the non-money Targets?'

There are a couple of other aspects to NPV which should be mentioned briefly.

1   Rate of compounding. This should be equal to the rate at which earnings are compounded, or at which loan interest is payable. This will vary with the business.
2   Period of analysis. This should correspond to the expected life of the system, i.e. the period involved in the 'bargain'. Likely periods chosen will be 5–10 years. A shorter period should be chosen if a 'quick and dirty' approach to system development is adopted and only routine maintenance revisions are allowed for in running costs. Of course, the decision-taker should understand that the non-money Targets in the bargain also survive for this period of time.

Questions

1   The investments manager of your company tells you that he currently uses a rate of 20% in his NPV calculations. Should you adopt the same rate?
(2 min)

2   A company has forecast cash flows for an investment:

	Year 1	Year 2	Year 3	Year 4
	(70)	15	30	50
Corporation tax @50%				
12 months in arrears		35	(8)	(15)
	(70)	50	22	35

Assuming this is a cost-benefit analysis as defined in the text, and that the cash flows occur at the beginning of each year, is this a worthwhile investment if the proper interest rate to use in a NPV calculation is 20% per annum compounded annually?
(20 min)

3   A public authority has raised loans on which it pays 10% p.a. interest. Finding itself with a surplus of cash, it invests in gilt-edged stocks which yield 12% p.a. interest. Which rate should be taken for NPV purposes?
(5 min)

4   The idea of the life of a system is a difficult one. If an important component of a system is a machine, which will wear out, one can fix the life of the system at the lifetime of the machine. If, however, the system consists of 'software' and 'human behaviour', and ample provision has been made for continued maintenance of the system, then a tenable view is that the benefits of the system continue in perpetuity. What mathematical series expresses the present value of a quarterly benefit lasting for ever?   (2 min)

DISCUSSION CASE

The accountant had proposed a new computerised system which involved the purchase of a large mainframe. With the aid of the systems analyst, he was preparing a budget for submission to top management. The accountant originally told the analyst to write off the purchase price of the computer over five years in the budget. However, when the analyst had completed his estimates, and his figures were added to the budget, the proposition did not look favourable. 'We were pretty cautious with the original five-year write-down, weren't we?' said the accountant. 'Look, let's make that a seven-year period instead; after all, I think we could rely upon the machine being usable for that period.' The revised budget, looking more favourable to the proposed system, was submitted to top management.

ANSWER POINTERS

Section 5.1

1 The costs and benefits are real if they consume or release a tangible resource. Taking money in the sense of one of man's images of tangible things, a case could be made that money always reflects a real resource, although the money value placed on the resource will vary according to the supply of money and the supply of and demand for the resource.

But from the viewpoint of the organisation, it may not be possible to trace all project costs and benefits to a specific resource within the organisation. Take, for example, a cash development grant from the government – this may represent a real sacrifice somewhere, but from the standpoint of the organisation it is a monetary benefit without a real basis. A money benefit in coin, note or bank balance etc. might also be desired for its own sake.

This is not important, except to make the point that there may be some costs or benefits that are meaningfully valued **only** in money. With most costs and benefits, there is a choice of expressing them in money or real values.

Section 5.2

1 One possible explanation could be as follows.

The book profit is the difference between debts incurred **by** the company (whether or not they have yet been paid) and debts incurred **to** the company (whether or not they have yet been paid). In deriving a book profit, a debt incurred in one year may be nominally apportioned over several years to give what is thought to be a fairer view of trading in a year.

The money MOE is the cash flow that pursues these debts. Only if debts are settled immediately and no apportionments to different years are made will cash flow equal profit within a year.

In the long run, though, debts will be settled by a transfer of funds. Looking at the total of several years it will make little difference whether apportionment was done or not. Cash flow and profit over a long period therefore tend to be equal.

2 I could not blame you for hesitating over this one, since no definition of a money MOE has been offered in the text so far. The two–minute time limit was to prevent a serious attack of cognitive dissonance reducing your brain to jelly.

If money MOEs are to be discounted and added to find a net present value, as described in section 5.3 which follows, then only cash flows are admissible as money MOEs. Book profit must be taken as a non–money MOE.

There is a certain similarity between book profit and the idea of overall utility in a weights and scores evaluation. Book profit is a reflection of the value of real costs and benefits as seen through the eyes of accountants and expressed in terms of currency. Overall utility is a reflection of the value of real costs and benefits as seen through the eyes of the decision taker and expressed in terms of utiles. A difference is that the choice available to the accountant, e.g. how to apportion, is rationalised by referring to the objective facts such as how long a machine will last before it needs replacement, although it is open to a particular accountant to bias his interpretation of the facts by letting his subjective feelings of utility play a part. The weights assigned in utility analysis are entirely internal to the decision–taker, although it is open to a particular decision–taker to rationalise his weights if he desires by appeal, for example, to profit-ability.

My insistence on a money MOE being a cash flow serves to direct attention to the objective question of how much funds will change hands, and when.

Section 5.3

1 Only after you have established that he has made the same assumption about inflation as you have.

2

Year	Postponement year (n)	Cash flow (F)	$(1 + i)^n$	Present value (P)
1	0	−70	1	−70
2	1	50	1.2	41.7
3	2	22	1.44	15.3
4	3	35	1.728	20.3
			Total NPV	7.3

The NPV is positive, so the investment is worthwhile.

3 12%. This does not contradict the text if it is accepted that this particular public authority is a profit-seeking organisation.

4 Where i is the quarterly interest rate, P the present value and F the quarterly benefit, and assuming that the benefit accrues at the end of each quarter:

$$P = F(1/(1 + i)^1 + 1/(1 + i)^2 + 1/(1 + i)^3 + \ldots)$$

This can be shown to be equivalent to $P = F(1/i)$. So if the quarterly interest rate is 5%, 20 times the perpetual quarterly benefit can be taken as its present value; if the quarterly interest rate is $\frac{1}{2}$%, 200 times.

6 Evaluation facts

6.1 COSTING

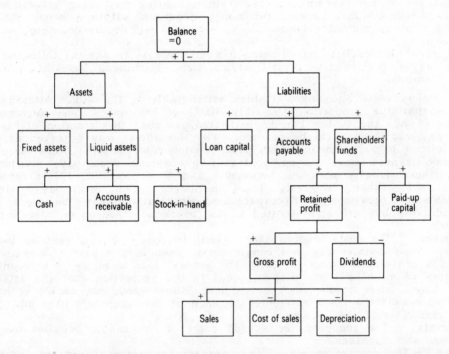

Fig. 6.1: A much-simplified Chart of Accounts showing the aggregation of
accounting categories. In the familiar double-entry bookkeeping system, any
transaction will be recorded such that the balance is zero. For example: sell
fixed asset for cash: decrease fixed assets, increase cash; write off stock
for scrap: decrease stock-in-hand, increase cost of sales; purchase stock
on credit: increase stock-in-hand, increase accounts payable; settle the
purchase: reduce cash, reduce accounts payable. The accounting convention
is that an increase of an Asset item is called a Debit and an increase of
a Liability item is called a Credit

Organisations take different views of how money costs should be counted and
aggregated. The view is broadly dictated by the organisation's Chart of
Accounts, that is to say, the classifications, designated by the organisation
management, under which transactions may be recorded; see Figure 6.1. This
in turn has been influenced by the nature of the business and, no doubt,
its history and traditions. In order to communicate effectively the money
costs and benefits, the analyst may find he has to adapt the guidelines of
this section to the conventions of the organisation.

The aim is to estimate the changed cash flows, associated with a money

MOE, that are wrought by a proposed system. The money MOEs will usually be Cost of Development and Changed Cost of Operation, but others may be included at the sponsor's discretion. For the present purpose, I shall assume that if a source of cash flow can be identified (for example, a need to write a program, hire an analyst or buy a computer, or an opportunity to release an employee) then the amount of the cash flow can be estimated. This is obviously a large assumption and a later chapter will consider the problems of estimation. Meanwhile, this leaves us 'only' with the problems of identifying the sources of cash flow which are to be costed, i.e. all the constituents of a money MOE.

The main tactic is to partition the money MOE orthogonally so that all significant money items (costs or revenues) are included and so that no significant double counting occurs. Double counting may occur between money and non-money MOEs, between two money MOEs and **within** a money MOE. In practice, it is virtually impossible to eliminate all double counting, as will be seen.

A general approach to partitioning a money MOE is to use the following five 'M's as a preliminary classification: Men, Machines, Materials, Money, Miscellaneous.

Men   Pay costs and pay variables attributable to the MOE. 'Attributable' means that the proportion (possibly 100%) of the man's time consumed in (released by) the system can be estimated, so that this fraction of his pay and pay variables is to be counted. 'Pay variables' may be taken as costs which tend to vary linearly with pay: pension contributions; social security; holiday/sickness pay; maternity leave; guaranteed week pay; redundancy pay. These usually work out between $\frac{1}{3}$ and $\frac{2}{3}$ of pay (UK, 1977); typically about 40%. Other relatively fixed manpower costs, such as training, supervision, provision of floorspace and workstations may be even more considerable but are often treated as an 'overhead' (see under Miscellaneous below).

Machines   The costs incurred (or saved) in the purchase, rent or leasing of machines; maintenance and repair costs. When only a part of a machine's hours are attributable to the MOE, the general rule to follow is to count the fraction of machine costs that is equal to the proportion that the attributable hours bears to the total hours used. (Note **used**, not **usable** – this is to ensure that the costs attributed to each of the machine's uses add up to the total costs of the machine.)

Materials   The incurred (or saved) costs of consumable supplies used by the men and machines.

Money   The cost of increased indebtedness (or value of reduced indebtedness) attributable to the system. This does not include the effect (on interest paid or earned) of costs or revenues recorded under the other four Ms. This would amount to double counting, since the effect of the other costs on interest payable is to be accounted for in the NPV calculation. However, a system may change the cash flow of the organisation in a way which has not been counted under one of the other headings. For example, a new system may provide for monthly bills where quarterly ones were previously sent and, as a consequence, it is forecast that customers will reduce the average amount of credit they take. Interest earnable (or reduced interest payable), as a result of this improved cash flow, can be counted. A similar position may arise if the working capital tied up in stock is released as a result of a reduction in stocks.

Miscellaneous   This is a catchnet for anything not recorded elsewhere and as far as the present explanation goes includes 'overhead'. Broadly, this covers the more fixed costs which must be shared out among the variable costs counted for Men, Machines, Materials, Money. In figures presented to management, this overhead is usually taken to increase the figures reported under the other headings. There may be nothing left to report under

'Miscellaneous'. Thus, the pay and pay variables costs may be increased by an amount to allow for their share of other manpower costs of training, recruitment, relocation, supervision and management, secretarial and support services, personnel and payroll administration, workstations, leaving, subsidised meals, staff discounts and loans, furniture, rent, heat, light, telephones. Manpower overhead is even more dependent on the particular case (type of men, type of organisation) than pay variables; 100% overhead is possible. Overhead may similarly be attributed to machines and materials, to represent the costs of storing, husbanding and replenishing them. Overhead should be added to costs in either sense, i.e. whether cost incurred or saved.

To be strictly accurate, it is the opportunity cost of the five Ms that should be counted, although the costs measured by the conventions of accounting are usually taken as being a sufficient approximation; this assumption is especially tenable in a market economy. However, should the analyst encounter a significant case where the opportunity cost exceeds the accounting cost, for example where there is an earmarked alternative use for the resource which would derive a benefit much greater than the cost of the resource, then the opportunity cost should be counted. Fanciful opportunities should be neglected.

It is between the Miscellaneous 'overhead' and the others that double counting is most difficult to avoid. For example, suppose a user is to go on a training course as part of the system development plan, and the user's salary, salary variables, salary overhead, training course fees and expenses are to be counted. There may be subtle double counting if 'average' costs of training are embodied in the salary overhead. Whether this is significant or not depends upon the particular case; probably not significant in this example. Another instance: suppose the cost of materials, materials overhead (re-ordering and storage of supplies) as a percentage of materials cost, and interest on working capital tied up, are counted under Materials. If the average cost of working capital was included in the cost of storage used for assessing the materials overhead percentage rate, again there is double counting; quite likely significant in this case.

Given the limit to the amount of effort which it is usually thought worth-while to invest in costing, the best advice for combatting this problem would seem to be:

a)   understand how any supplied costing rules, e.g. overhead rates, rate-per-hour of machine time, were calculated;

b)   keep a clear head.

A systematic method is to partition one's original idea of expected costs until no one cost item dominates the others. In this way, proper attention will be given to the most significant items. One could start off picturing a matrix of money MOEs against the five Ms, as in Figure 6.2, and then perform a step-by-step analysis as follows.

Step 1   Probably there is an entry which could be made in each box even though in some boxes it may be a very small amount. Reject any boxes which are clearly insignificant. Speculate on the likely magnitude of the cash flows which are to be recorded in each remaining box, and identify the dominant items; say those which are likely to contribute 10% or more to the total cash flow for the MOE. By way of example, I have put £ signs in the dominant boxes for a hypothetical case (Figure 6.2, overleaf). These are the items which must be examined in more detail.

Step 2   Consider partitioning the dominant items according to type of factor (e.g. Box 1, Men: analysts, programmers, user personnel, other; Box 5, Money: reduced inventory, improved debtors' balances) and according to subdivisions of the MOE (e.g. Box 1, Cost of Development: cost of analysis, cost of design, cost of construction, cost of trials). It may be that no

Factors / Example MOEs	Men and men overheads	Machines and machine overheads	Materials and materials overheads	Money	Miscellaneous
Cost of development	1 £	2 £			
Change in data processing costs		3 £	4 £		
Change in object system costs				5 £	

Fig. 6.2: Starting point for analysing money MOEs

natural division is seen for a particular item; in that case, one can leave it as it is since it will probably be treated as a single entity when it comes to estimating.

The result can be translated into a working schedule for the MOE, as illustrated in Figure 6.3.

This schedule now forms a guide for the detailed evaluation facts sought and, when completed, is in a form suitable for calculation of the NPV and for submission as a summary of the money MOE estimates. It can also form the basis of a project budget. For this purpose, some adjustments may be needed to bring the forecasts into line with the project cost reporting system. These adjustments may include replacing opportunity costs by outgoings, or removing some fixed costs which will not feature in reported costs.

Questions

1   The project sponsors claim that the fixed costs will be incurred anyway so you are only to report on the variable costs. Are they right?   (15 min)

2   The cost accountant tells you he uses a figure of 150% to increment pay costs so they reflect pay variables and overhead. Should you use his figure?
(2 min)

3   Your system calls for an extra clerk, who is presently surplus to requirements in another department. There may be no actual costs incurred in training, recruitment and no increase in supervision or support services, etc. Does this mean that the 'overhead' for this clerk can be omitted from your analysis?   (2 min)

4   Some organisations have a standard form for analysing system costs, along the lines of Figure 6.3, for all projects. Is this a good idea?   (5 min)

6.2 ATTRIBUTES OF FORMAL MESSAGES AND DP SYSTEMS

The money MOE evaluation facts sought as above usually concern the resources used to supply the new DP system and run it thereafter – the cost of developing the system, the increased or reduced cost of providing the desired messages when it is in operation.

The non-money MOE evaluation facts sought generally relate to attributes of the messages and message system other than the resources used in providing them. These attributes may affect the expenses or revenues of the object system, so they are **potentially** money MOEs. The main difference is that the expenses and revenues of the object system are usually relatively

BCD system
MOE: Cost of Development

Men	Analysts	Progs	Users	Other	Totals
Analysis					£
Design					£
Construction					£
Trial					£

Total Men: £U

Machines	Computer	Other	
Construction			£
Other			£

Total Machines	£V
Total Materials	£W
Miscellaneous (ex. overheads included in above)	£X
Total Cost of Development	£Y

Time analysis by quarter

quarter	Year 1				Year 2				Totals
	1	2	3	4	5	6	7	8	
Men									£U
Machines									£V
Materials									£W
Miscellaneous									£X
Total cash flow									£Y

Fig. 6.3: Working schedule for analysis of a money MOE. Note that arithmetic sign must be accounted for when adding NPV of different MOEs; this example, being all outflow, will be negative

'distant' (as previously defined) whereas the message, or message system, attributes are relatively 'close'. The fact that the financial costs of developing and running new DP systems are close MOEs may explain why money is a natural choice for measuring the resources committed to development and operation. Measuring the money value of other attributes of messages, by reference to the monetary effect of those messages on the object system, often introduces a wider distance between cause and effect. When the object system turns in an improved or deteriorated performance, it may be difficult to say how much of this is due to the changed message attribute and how much is due to changed environmental factors. Chapter 7 deals with some possibilities for money-valuing some message attributes, should the investment of time and questionable reliability of the results be acceptable. In the meantime, this section considers the non-money aspects.

This discussion is complicated in published works by imprecision in the notion of an attribute; imprecision about whether it is the qualities of the 'system' or of the 'message' which are being classified; confinement of the discussion to 'information' (which may be taken in a narrower sense than 'message', i.e. all informations are messages but maybe not all messages are informations); mixed 'distance'; mixed formal and informal messages. Some examples of attributes, broadly at the 'system' level, catalogued by authors are given in Figure 6.4. (I have edited out of the lists those attributes that correspond to close money MOEs. Some of the authors' original phrasing is also abbreviated.) Examples of attributes which are ascribed to 'information' are given in Figure 6.5. My attempt at a unified list of close attributes of formal messages is given as Figure 6.6, but other classifications are defensible. The list does not claim to be complete and the attributes shown are not necessarily independent.

King and Schrems (1)	Sanders (2)	Schwartz (3)
Accuracy (error rate)	Processing time	Decision-making
Response time	Processing capacity	Operations speed
Security (secrecy)	Accuracy	Operations accuracy
Reliability	Comprehensiveness	Operations quality
(lack of interruption)	Control	Competition opportunities
Flexibility	Customer service	Firm's image
(ease of adaptation to	New information	Institutional
change)	Planning	(corporate plans,
	Prestige	management aspirations)
	Combat labour shortage	
	Prepare required	
	government reports	

Fig. 6.4: 'System' attributes (excluding close money MOEs)

It should not be thought that there are general, regular relationships between the sense of a change in a particular attribute (e.g. more or less of it) and the value of the message. This is plain in the case of, say, secrecy – some messages have privacy as a goal, some have publicity as a goal. Aggregation may reduce a manager's search, but fineness may reveal a need for action that would be concealed in the aggregate. Smaller time interval between regular reports improves currency, but if this interval is smaller than the time needed for the resulting action to take effect, future control actions may overcorrect (see Systems Analysis, section 4.5, q. 5). Reduced report period may improve currency, but increased period may reduce sampling error (see Systems Analysis, section 4.5). Even accuracy is double-edged when one considers a pair of messages which jointly are meant to support a decision; there may be compensating inaccuracies, or compensating arithmetic sense to the inaccuracies, with the result that

Lasfargue (4)	Gorry and Scott Morton (5)	Smith and Weschler (6)
Objectivity	Source	Relevance
Precision	Scope	(appropriateness of
Verifiability	Aggregation	content)
Age	Time horizon	Accuracy
Frequency	Currency	Timeliness
	Accuracy	Sufficiency
	Frequency	(ability to satisfy all
		user needs)
		Conciseness
		Reliability
		Discovery

Swanson (7)	Verhelst (8)
Degradation from perfect information by:	Accuracy (exactness and precision)
error	Information interval
distortion	Information period
delay	Information delay
sampling distortion	Level of detail
threshold	Exception degree
saturation	
bias	

Fig. 6.5: 'Information' attributes

A solidus, /, divides an attribute and its synonyms from its antonyms or converse

Likelihood, surprise value, discovery
Scope (subject-matter entities and relationships and the attributes of them that are reported)
Credibility, verifiability (the source, and whether or not the source can be traced)
Secrecy/publication
Accuracy, objectivity/degradation through error, distortion and bias
Precision, exactness
Period, referent time (period or instant alluded to by the message - there may be several)
Delay (time between close of period and receipt of message)
Interval (time between successive close-of-period or referent times, as with a regular report)/frequency
Persistence, reconstructability/ephemerality
Reliability/lack of interruption
Response time (time between requesting and receiving message)
Fineness, level of detail/aggregation, summarisation
Filtration, exception degree
Wording
Formattedness/clutter
Conciseness/length
Noticeability
General purposeness (ability of a message to meet more than one purpose)
Age/currency of information
Timestamp (of message)

Fig. 6.6: Some close attributes of formal messages

improving the accuracy of one of the pair degrades the joint effectiveness of the messages (see section 7.2 for an example). More mundanely, a lie may achieve a desired goal, while the truth may obstruct it . (This sentence should not be construed to mean that I am advocating lying!)

Questions

1   Suggest example target MOEs for ten attributes in Figure 6.6.   (20 min)

2   A process control computer is passing 'messages' to machines to control a process in a chemical plant. Is money a more or less suitable MOE in this case than in a business management case?   (5 min)

6.3 SIDE-EFFECTS

'Side-effect' is a catchnet for any positive or negative consequence which has not been made the subject of a MOE. These are not necessarily less important than the MOEs so if a substantial side-effect is discovered, consideration should be given to making up a MOE to cover it. The point of having side-effects in the method is to encourage the analyst to think beyond the initial bounds of his problem and to allow the decision-taker to bring in inexplicit goals, at the last moment if necessary.

Although this is obviously an indefinite classification, in practice the analyst may be advised to give special attention to (a) unrepresented stakeholders, and (b) organisation social effects.

Stakeholders   Land (9) reminds us that different interest groups have a 'stake' in a system and that a proposed change may be beneficial to some stakeholders but adverse to others. The analyst may be advised to identify the stakeholders and their regular representatives, for example:

Internal	The owners	Shareholders/taxpayers/ratepayers Owners' representatives: directors, ministers, auditors
	The managers	Manager interest groups Manager representatives (rare): managers' union, professional societies, consultative committees
	The employees	Non-manager employee interest groups Employee representatives: trade unions, professional societies, consultative committees
External	Customers or clients	Customer interest groups Customer representatives: consumer councils, internal salesmen acting as surrogates
	Suppliers	Supplier interest groups Supplier representatives: suppliers' trade associations, internal buyers acting as surrogates
	Other	Government departments, the community at large Representatives: government inspectors, public pressure groups

Some of these stakeholders or their regular representatives will already have a voice in the system design. They may have been selected by:

being the sponsor;
being members of a sponsoring committee (high-level steering committee) or a project monitoring committee (see later);
being members of the feasibility study team (see section 2.3).

The sponsor should now consider (a) do the represented stakeholders have the voices, votes or power desired? and (b) should the unrepresented stakeholders have a voice, vote or power? If so, how should it be given them?

While the point of this explanation is to provide a model which will meet many different circumstances, the following participation philosophy is one which I believe suits a number of organisations (see glossary for definition of terms used).

Owners   Consulted through designated outsider representatives such as directors on a high-level steering committee. The auditors should be consulted and asked to approve the system.

Managers   A sponsoring manager, or the manager of the unit most concerned with operating the new system, should be designated project manager, giving him insider participation in, and authority over, the project development team. (This philosophy may entail training for the designated user manager.)

Other designated managers (including the DP manager) directly concerned with the project should be consulted through membership of a project monitoring committee. (The project manager should also be on this committee.)

Other managers not directly concerned with the project, but who may have an interest through the relative priorities of projects, should be consulted through being designated members of the high-level steering committee.

Employees   Groups with a predominant interest in the whole project (e.g. because their jobs are 100% related to the particular DP system) should be represented by designated or elected insider participants in the project team, working as equal partners with other members of the team. (This representation may be additional to the next type. Training may be needed for this role.)

Groups with a predominant interest in only a part of the project should have consensus outsider involvement as partners in the design of the part of the system which concerns them. (Again, consider training for this role.)

Groups with a minority interest (their jobs have only a small content related to the particular DP system) should be consulted through outsider elected representatives (e.g. shop stewards) or consulted in consensus.

Customers, suppliers, other   Consulted by designated outsider representatives, possibly internal surrogates, if they have an interest in the DP system.

Most business organisations are loth to create new committees or needs for consultation, on the grounds that they generate words but inhibit action. Much depends on the particular organisation and the particular personalities involved. My opinion is that there is no substitute, in this sort of political arena, for the insights and initiatives of thoughtful managers for choosing the most suitable organisation: horses for courses.

Unrepresented stakeholders   Following the sponsor's decision on stakeholder representation (or lack of any such decision) the analyst may be advised to analyse for himself the effect of the proposed system on the unrepresented stakeholders, and their possible reactions. Relevant forecasts should be presented to the sponsor, either orally or in the feasibility report.

Organisation social effects   Even when stakeholders are represented, the representatives may overlook possible effects on their own interests. The analyst may be advised to consider the following common effects of a proposed change (these effects may be beneficial or adverse) and draw them to the attention of the sponsor (after Mumford and Ward, 10).

The organisation structure.
The relationships between organisational units, the system of checks and balances, the supervision or coordination of organisation activities, the ability of the organisation to adapt to new needs.

Power relationships: if 'information is power', a message system change may shift power to a new point accidentally or on purpose.

Jobs: the new system may impoverish or enrich jobs (see Systems Analysis, sections 8.2, 8.3).

Social relationships: new procedures may inhibit established social contact or permit new contacts; a high-morale work group may be dissipated or a new high-morale group created.

Pay: a pay-related DP system may directly affect pay, possibly in subtle ways, e.g. when bonus or commission payments are calculated by the system or the calculations use data collected by the system. The intrusion of new workers or the redeployment of existing staff, or job redesign, may affect pay differentials.

Management style; the expectations of employees for negotiation and consultation. The DP system may permit, or preclude, new ways of managing or working. The example or precedent established by participation in DP system development may have repercussions on expectations for participation in other matters.

Discussion question

1 You are an analyst in a large engineering works where there are entrenched attitudes both in management and on the shop floor. The management in the past has ruled out participation by the shop floor workers, even at consultation level, mainly because they believe that an invitation to participate would be taken as an invitation to negotiate. In other words, they fear that shop floor representatives would demand compensation for changed methods of working if management were to make a special issue of a planned change. If a small change is presented as a fait accompli, this is likely to be accepted unquestioningly by the shop floor. Equally, the trades union shop stewards' main contact with the management is in reconciling disputes or making bargains. They have historically seen their role as representing their members only on pay, working conditions and related matters.

You have been assigned to design a new system for collecting job progress information from the shop floor operatives. This system will affect only a small portion of their duties, but you believe that the operatives should be at least consulted and preferably encouraged to design for themselves their own part of the system. What should you do?

6.4 RISK

The forecasts of money and non-money MOEs which are to be included in the feasibility report may not be accurate. The estimators should somehow communicate their uncertainty about the estimates so that the sponsor can take this into account when trying to assess the sensitivity of the overall project goals to error in the forecasts.

One way of doing this may be for the estimators to record their personal uncertainties by displaying their estimates of the discounted cash flow associated with each project item as a personal probability density function (PPDF). The error attached to the total NPV could then be illustrated by adding the PPDFs of the money MOEs; the easiest way to do this is probably by stochastic simulation, drawing samples from the recorded PPDFs. However, apart from philosophical objections to adding the PPDFs of different people, or, if all the estimates are made by one person, the possibly self-fulfilling nature of the result, this process would be something of an overkill on a typical project. Also, the project sponsors may be in no position to interpret meaningfully the resulting distribution of NPV, or they may be deluded by the precision.

The following is a practical proposal which will be found workable and which will allow the sponsor to assess subjectively the sensitivity of project success to error in the estimates.

Step 1   Classify each constituent element of a money MOE. The 'constituent elements' can be chosen at any convenient level of detail: for example, the level of the boxes in the working schedule (Figure 6.3). A simple classification could be as follows (after Davis, 11).

Class A   Reliable estimates, accurate to plus or minus 10%. You will be surprised if the actual cost or benefit turns out to be more or less than 10% either way of the estimate. On the whole, these will be 'measured' items, for example:

> hardware and software costs where you have a firm quotation;
> costs of supplies, where you have directly relevant past experience to go on;
> value of saved clerical time, where this has been determined by reliable experiment or prototype system.

Class B   Fairly reliable estimates, accurate to plus or minus 50%. You will be surprised if the actual cost or benefit turns out more than 50% away from the estimate. On the whole these will be items where a forecast has been constructed indirectly from past measured experience, for example:

> systems analysis and design costs where you have recorded experience of substantially similar systems;
> value of reduced inventory when inventory holding costs are recorded by the cost accounting system and a high-confidence model has been used to forecast this quantity reduction.

Class C   Guesses. You will not be surprised if the actual cost or benefit turns out more than 50% away from the estimate. Probably you have little past experience to go on or the past experience you have was not quantified. For example:

> loss of revenue due to errors;
> value of improved customer service;
> value of improved management information;
> systems analysis and design costs when you have no records of a substantially similar system.

Step 2   Add up the constituent estimates to get a total for each class (A, B and C) within the MOE. (Purists should add up the NPV for each estimate, but the improved accuracy is probably not worth the effort.) Work out the proportion that each class contributes to the whole, e.g.

MOE: Cost of Development.	Class A reliable estimates:	20%
	Class B fairly reliable estimates:	70%
	Class C guesses:	10%
		100%

Report these ratios for each money MOE.

Step 3   Classify the non-money MOEs as belonging to class A, B or C. For some non-money MOEs you may need to adjust the definition of the classes in your own mind (e.g. when the target is a discrete state of affairs, class A: the state of affairs is more than 95% probable; class B: more than 80% probable; class C: less than 80% probable). The important thing is to choose the class which most meaningfully communicates your uncertainty to the sponsor.

Report the class of each non-money MOE or group non-money MOEs according to their class.

Question

1   Under what circumstances, would you suggest, is it unnecessary to report your uncertainty about the MOE forecasts?   (2 min)

ANSWER POINTERS

Section 6.1

1   A tongue-in-cheek answer could be that project sponsors, like customers, are always right. Another is that by definition a fixed cost is not taken into account.

Economists have a maxim that in the long run all costs are variable. To neglect fixed costs (or to believe they exist) is to take a short-term view. If the organisation is to be sold or wound up next year, the sponsors may be right to worry only about variable costs.

Suppose the computer and computer room are considered to be a fixed cost. Charging only for the variable costs of computing, mainly supplies, may lead to increased use of the computer. Eventually, a new computer and computer room will be needed to accommodate the increased workload. Allocating fixed overheads reflects this long-run consequence and leads to better long-term decisions, other things being equal.

The sponsors could still be right even if they are worried about the long term. Maybe they have spotted that the fixed costs for the particular system are associated with a substantially under-utilised resource. It will be a long time before the maximum capacity of the resource is reached and the spare capacity cannot be sold. Maybe they want to increase utilisation of the resource in the short term and plan to revise their policy, or abandon the system, when the time of full capacity approaches.

Technological advance may also run counter to the long-run forecast of the economist. For example, computers are not only getting cheaper but also smaller; a replacement computer of higher power will probably manage in a smaller computer room than that of its predecessor.

2   Not before you understand how the figure was calculated.

3   The same arguments apply as in question 1. It is difficult to accept that this clerk is a long-term under-utilised resource, so the most likely answer is that this overhead should not be omitted from the analysis.

4   If projects are all very similar, there is a clear case for a standard form. If projects are dissimilar, a simple standard form might invite lack of attention to the important features of the particular project. One could argue that a standard form is a good idea if analysts are sufficiently trained or experienced to ignore it or adapt it to meet the case. Standard forms found in the opposite circumstances may tend to be followed blindly without proper regard to meaning and purpose. On the other hand, perhaps costing is not being done or is being done so badly that even costing on a standard form is deemed better than none.

Section 6.2

1   (a) Likelihood   There is no MOE for likelihood in the present context because likelihood is not an attribute of a message which can be changed by a DP system. That is, given that a nominated message is to be passed under specified circumstances, its likelihood is out of the control of the designer. The most relevant MOE would be 'whether or not the nominated message is passed', e.g. 'the new system will report every work accident to the personnel manager'.

   (b) Scope, relevance   'The accident report will state employee details, accident details, details of previous accidents as per specimen attached.'

(c) Verifiability   'The original notification in writing is to be signed by the originator. Given any report reaching the personnel manager, it must be possible to trace the corresponding original notification.'

(d) Secrecy   'The accident report is not to be inspected by personnel other than ...'

(e) Accuracy   'Fewer than one accident report in every ten will bear a detected error in date of accident, time of accident, injury code or severity code.'

(f) Precision   'Time of accident will be reported to the nearest minute.'

(g) Period   'The accident report will cover accidents occurring in a working week.'

(h) Delay   'The report will be delivered by 12 noon on the Monday following the end of the working week.'

(i) Frequency   'Weekly.'

(j) Reconstructability   'A further copy of a report for any week within the last two years will be supplied on request.'

(k) Response time   'Further copies will be supplied within three working days of requests.'

(l) Aggregation   'The end-of-year report will show frequency of accidents by week, by hour of day, by injury code and by severity code.'

(m) Exception degree   'Only accidents with severity code 3 or greater will be reported.'

(n) Wording, formattedness, conciseness   'The report will appear as per specimen attached.'

(o) Reliability   'The deadline for report delivery will be met nine times out of ten.'

(p) Noticeability   'Reports of accidents with a severity code 5 or more are to be highlighted as per specimen.'

(q) General-purposeness   'A copy of the report is also to satisfy the reporting requirements of the Ministry.'

(r) Age   See Period, Delay, Frequency.

(s) Timestamp   'The report is to be dated.'

I do not mean to suggest that MOEs such as these must always be spelled out at such length. In practice it may be possible to summarise many of them in one, e.g. 'produce a report as per example attached'; and in a given instance, some of the attributes may be 'don't cares'.

2 Probably more. The chemical process is a relatively closed system, undisturbed by the environment, because the designer of the process will have sought to reduce such disturbances by insulation or by environmental control. Following a message system change, changes in the resources used by the object system can be attributed to the change, provided that no other changes are made at the same time. Thus if a forecast is made in terms of money benefits, it can later be established whether or not the forecast was correct. Money is therefore a close MOE in this case.

The business results are more affected by influences outside the control of the managers – the market, the government, the supply of raw materials and labour, etc. Also, the managers are likely to make adjustments to the business process in addition to adjustments to the message system. The effect of the former influences and adjustments are more likely to swamp out any effect of message system change. If a forecast is made in terms of money benefits, it probably cannot later be established whether or not the forecast was correct. Money is a distant MOE in this case. The cash flow resulting from a changed attribute of a message is often a matter of an a priori argument, or of a subjective opinion, and not a matter of experiment. It has been my argument that in such cases a non-money MOE should be chosen to reflect closely the changed attribute. Such a MOE can be decisively tested. The relationship between the MOE and cash flow remains a matter of debate or opinion and is beyond decisive practical test.

Section 6.4

1 When they are all class A. This is rather unlikely to be the case with money MOEs since few money forecasts connected with DP systems can be made up totally from reliable estimates. Non-money MOEs, especially when they are discrete ones, as in the case of most of the examples in the answer pointer to question 1, section 6.2 above, are more likely to be considered reliable. In this case, a feasibility study could reasonably report the non-money MOEs without comment on risk. Only the money MOEs would have their uncertainty illustrated.

REFERENCES

(1) King, J. L., and Schrems, E. L., Cost-benefit analysis in information system development and operation, **Computing Surveys, 10,** 1, 19–34, March, 1978.

(2) Sanders, D. H., **Computers and management/text and readings,** McGraw-Hill, 1970.

(3) Schwartz, M. H., Computer project selection in the business enterprise, **Journal of Accountancy,** April 1969, reprinted in Li, D. H., **Design and management of information systems,** Science Research Associates, 1972.

(4) Lasfargue, Y., Les facteurs de la rentabilite d'un systeme d'informations, **Direction et Gestion,** Nos 3 and 4, 1969.

(5) Gorry, G. A., and Scott Morton, M. S., A framework for management information systems, **Sloan Management Review, 12,** pp. 55–70, Fall, 1971.

(6) Smith, W. A., and Weschler, B. L., **Planning guide for information system evaluation studies,** Computer and Information Systems Division, AIEE Inc, Norcross, Georgia, 1973.

(7) Swanson, C. V., **Evaluating the quality of management information,** Working paper no. 538.71, MIT, Cambridge, Mass., June, 1971, reported in Verhelst (8).

(8) Verhelst, M., **Contribution to the analysis of organisational information systems and their financial benefits,** Ph. D. Thesis, Katholieke Universiteit Leuven, 1974.

(9) Land, F. F., Evaluation of systems goals in determining a design strategy for a computer-based information system, **The Computer Journal, 19,** 4, 290–4, 1976.

(10) Mumford, E., and Ward, T. B., **Computers: planning for people,** Batsford, 1968.

(11) Davis, G. B., **Management information systems: conceptual foundations, structure and development,** McGraw-Hill, 1974.

7 Money value of message attributes

7.1 EXPERT'S GUESS

One way of valuing attributes of messages is by intuitive guesswork of one sort or another. Another method is to model the object system, in one way or another, using measured data as a basis for the model. A combination of the two may supply the required balance of accuracy for effort expended. This combination may take the form of analytical modelling based on guesswork data or of sensitivity analysis to give additional insight into the system when formulating an intuitive guess.

This section is concerned with a brief review of guesswork. The possibilities for modelling are endless and should be considered for each case separately. The next two sections illustrate analytical models which are paradigms for the construction of models to meet further specific cases.

The sponsor can supply his own guesses. Alternatively, the sponsor can rely upon the guesses of someone else: presumably someone who, he believes, has a better insight into the problem; an expert. So, for an assessment of the effect on sales of a change in customer service, the sponsor may turn to the Sales Manager. For effects of improved production scheduling on productivity, to the Production Manager, and so on. Perhaps the sponsor believes that the expert will have special insight into only a familiar part of the problem. For example, the Sales Manager may be relied upon to forecast increased sales in units or money turnover (the measures familiar to him), but not to come up with a figure for 'value to the organisation', which should be the NPV of the net cash flow arising from the increase. In this case the sponsor may turn to another expert, e.g. the Accountant, to translate the first expert's assessment from familiar units to NPV.

Some possibilities most relevant to DP feasibility studies are outlined below. See Moore and Thomas (1) for a more comprehensive discussion.

Direct assessment

This involves asking the expert directly for his guess. Examples of simple questions are as follows.

1 To a Sales Manager in an organisation where departments are profit centres and each manager is accustomed to consider the profitability of his department: 'Regarding the proposed monthly contribution-by-value sales analysis, broken down by product within area, what is the most you would be prepared to pay for this report?'
2 To a Sales Manager who manages out of an appropriation budget: 'What is the most you would recommend be spent to get this report?'
3 To a Sales Manager for whom sales value is the familiar unit: 'What is your considered opinion of the increased sales you will derive as a result of having this report?'

There is some argument for a more analytical approach which will force the expert to review his PPDF, especially if he is expert in his normal function but not expert in estimating. It may be that the expert fixes upon the 'mode', the most likely value of his PPDF – see Figure 7.1 – and fails to compensate for the skewness of the distribution. From a technical point

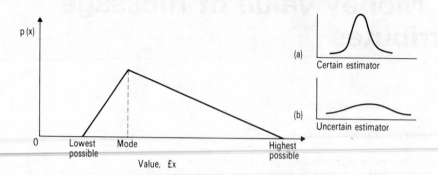

of view, the value the estimator should supply is the 'expected monetary value', i.e. the sum of (each value times the probability of that value): the integral of $x.p(x)$ for all the values x. Possibly some estimators are skilled enough to draw their PPDF and so permit the analyst directly to deduce the expected value, but I would be suspicious of this precision.

A simple adjustment, which is not defensible except on the grounds of simplicity and (probably) being better than no adjustment, could be made by taking the **mean** of the answers to the following three questions.

1 'Being reasonably optimistic, what is the **lowest** value you would place on the sales analysis report?'
2 'Being reasonably cautious, what is the **highest** value you would place on the sales analysis report?'
3 'What do you consider is the **most likely** value of the sales analysis report?'

The range of the answers could be used to risk-classify the estimate as proposed in section 6.4. In the case of an inexpert estimator, though, it would be safer to class his guess in category C, whatever his personal certainty.

Indirect assessment

The philosophy here is that even if an expert has no direct insight into his own PPDF, perhaps his PPDF can be deduced from suitable questioning about his preferences or, possibly, by observing his behaviour when he faces choices.

Suppose we wish to find the percentage sales increase, resulting from the new sales analysis report, which is considered by the Sales Manager as equally likely to be exceeded or not exceeded. We could present the Sales Manager with two wagers.

a) If sales increase by 10% or more as a result of the report, you get £1000. Otherwise, you get nothing.
b) We toss a coin. If it comes up heads, you get £1000. Otherwise you get nothing.

We ask the Sales Manager, 'Which wager do you prefer?' If he says 'a' he believes a 10% increase has more than 0.5 probability and we can offer a fresh wager with a higher percentage. If he says 'b', a fresh wager with a lower percentage is offered. If he is undecided, we have struck the right figure.

Having found the 50th percentile in this fashion, say a 10% or more increase, questioning to discover the upper quartile would continue in this fashion: 'Suppose we know that in fact sales will increase by more than 10% per annum. Which of these two wagers would you prefer?

a) £1000 if sales increase by more than 20%. Otherwise (the sales increase is in the interval 10% to 20%), you get nothing.
b) £1000 if the coin comes up heads, nothing if tails.'

Similarly for the lower quartile.

Obviously there is some overhead of effort in doing an analysis of this type and perhaps the potential value lies mainly in the way it helps train estimators to decribe their own PPDFs directly.

Delphi technique

If the sponsor has alternative experts at his disposal, he should consider the Delphi technique to harmonise their views. Possibly the result is more reliable than simply taking the mean of the estimates from a group of experts.

The experts are invited to make their estimates independently and to record their reasoning. The collected estimates and reasons are then circulated to all the experts, so that each can see all the others. The experts are invited independently to make a further estimate in the light of this sharing of ideas, and so on until a consensus emerges.

Reliability of guesses

Probably the most reliable thing about guesses is that they are not very reliable. There is evidence that an expert estimator who has statistical training gives better estimates (more accurate, more certain) than an unskilled estimator. However, there are several reasons why guesses may be suspect, as follows.

1 Reporting bias. The estimator may wittingly or unwittingly bias the report of his 'true' feelings. The sales manager may value the report more if he is eager to have the new system for other reasons.
2 Unfounded certainty. Give people only two past points in a time series and they are all likely to make the same straight line prediction of the next point. This consensus is due to ignorance. It does not reflect certainty based on knowledge. Individual inexperienced estimators are also commonly more certain than warranted by the evidence available.
3 Lack of statistical intuition. Untrained estimators misconceive chance, pay too much attention to the latest clues (forgetting the prior probabilities), are insensitive to sample size and misconceive correlation and regression.
4 Wager bias. Indirect guessing based on wager analogies may be biased by the estimator's attitudes to wagering and risk-taking.

Questions

1 If the effects of message attributes are forecast only in terms of non-money MOEs, might it be argued that the sponsor will still supply his own guess of the money values anyway?   (10 min)

2 If an estimator is aware of the sources of bias, does this make him immune to them?   (2 min)

7.2 ANALYTICAL EXAMPLE 1: STOCK CONTROL

There are many cases where an analytical model may be proposed which is much simpler than this example; e.g. value of reduced errors = expected number of errors avoided times average cost per error. The purpose of this section is to illustrate some of the possibilities by reviewing the sensitivity to error of the well-known stock control model (see Systems Analysis, Appendix A).

For the purpose of this example, it is supposed that the new system of stock control will:

1   reduce the cost of placing orders and receiving replenishment stocks;
2   improve the forecasts of demand by accounting for seasonal variation;
3   allow disaggregation of stockholding costs so that more accurate inform-ation is available about the holding costs of each type of stock;
4   provide new information about costs;
5   reduce the time taken in placing orders with suppliers.

Basic stock control model

Let

I = annual cost of holding a unit of stock of a given type;
D = annual demand in units;
R = re-order cost per order;
Q = re-order quantity in units;
S = safety stock;
L = lead time as a fraction of a year.

The safety stock may be set at some multiple, **lambda,** of the demand in the lead time, DL, to give a tolerable risk of run out in the light of variances in previous periods, i.e.

$$S = lambda.DL \tag{1}$$

The re-order level in a two-bin system (constantly monitored)

$$= S + DL \tag{2}$$

The total costs

$$= \text{cost of stockholding} + \text{costs of re-ordering}$$
$$= SI + \tfrac{1}{2}QI + (D/Q)R \tag{3}$$

This is minimised with respect to Q when $\tfrac{1}{2}I - (D/Q^2)R = 0$, i.e. when

$$Q = \sqrt{2DR/I} \tag{4}$$

Substituting this value of Q into (3), we get

$$\text{total costs} = \text{fixed costs} + \text{variable costs}$$
$$= SI + \sqrt{2DRI} \tag{5}$$

In the discussion that follows, it is assumed that this is the model being used by the organisation in question to calculate re-order quantities on both old and new systems.

1   Reduced re-order costs

Let R_0 be the old re-order cost and R_1 be the new re-order cost. From (5), neglecting errors in the data for D, R and I, the total saving will be

$$\text{total saving} = \sqrt{2DR_0 I} - \sqrt{2DR_1 I} \tag{6}$$

Note the danger of double counting. If costs saved under the old volume of orders have already been accounted for in the calculation of another money MOE, e.g. changed cost of operation, an estimate of the additional benefit would be

$$\sqrt{2DR_0 I} - \sqrt{2DR_1 I} - (D/Q)(R_0 - R_1) \tag{7}$$

If $(R_0 - R_1)$ is reliable, these expressions, (6) and (7), are rather insensitive to error in R_0, D or I.

2, 3, 4   Improved accuracy of information

Improved forecasting will bring the reported figure for demand, D', closer to the true value D.

Disaggregation will reveal for each stock line a better approximation to the true value I than the reported figure I'.

Information about re-order costs will allow a better understanding of the true value R than does the existing figure R'.

That is,

$I' = I + Ie_i$
$D' = D + De_d$ where e is the error as a proportion of the true value
$R' = R + Re_r$

From (3), the true costs being met at present are

$$SI + \tfrac{1}{2}Q'I + (D/Q')R \tag{8}$$

where

$$Q' = \sqrt{2D(1 + e_d)R(1 + e_r)/(I(1 + e_i))} \quad \dots \text{ see } (4)$$

Substituting this value of Q' into (8) and deducting (3), the costs of the system with perfectly accurate information, we have the cost savings of perfectly accurate information:

$$\sqrt{2DRI(x + 1)^2/4x} - \sqrt{2DRI} \quad \text{where } x = (1 + e_d)(1 + e_r)/(1 + e_i) \tag{9}$$

$$= \sqrt{2DRI}(\sqrt{(x + 1)^2/4x} - 1) \tag{10}$$

which as a fraction of the minimum variable-stock costs is

$$\sqrt{(x + 1)^2/4x} - 1 \quad \text{or} \quad \sqrt{(x + 2 + 1/x)/4} - 1 \tag{11}$$

A graph of this function is given in Figure 7.2.

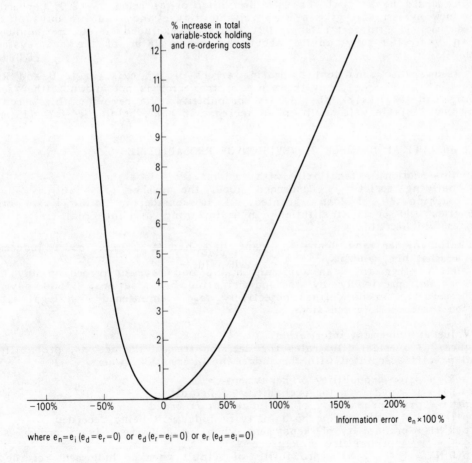

% increase in total variable-stock holding and re-ordering costs

Information error $e_n \times 100\%$

where $e_n = e_i$ $(e_d = e_r = 0)$ or e_d $(e_r = e_i = 0)$ or e_r $(e_d = e_i = 0)$

Fig. 7.2: The effect of error in either I, D or R on variable-stock holding costs

5 Reduction in order processing time

This may mean safety stock can be reduced without significantly increasing the risk of run-out (this assumes a demand in the lead time of over 10). Where L_0 is the old lead time and L_1 is the new lead time, if the present cost

$$SI = lambda.DL_0 I \qquad (12)$$

then the saving can be estimated

$$= lambda.DI(L_0 - L_1) \qquad (13)$$

Questions

1   Inert Sludge order about 500 000 tons of sludge for stock each year for their continuous-process plant. It is bought in at £4 per ton. Storage costs are estimated at 10% per annum. Company policy is to aim for safety stock equal to average demand in the lead time, i.e. 30 days' supply. Each order and delivery costs (it is thought) about £1000, which the new system will cut by £100.

The new order system will keep an exponentially-smoothed forecast of demand which is expected to be very good. Present forecasts have proved to be 20% out on average. Re-order cost estimates are guesses; the true figure could be as little as £500 per order or as much as £2000 per order. The new system will give a more reliable figure and take two days off the lead time. The interest rate for NPV (inflation excluded) is 10% per annum.

Can you offer any advice about the money value of the new system's benefits? (120 min)

2   Assume that consistent estimating errors of 10% exist in **I**, **D** and **R** in equation (10) on p.61, but the sense of the error is not known, either sense being equally likely. What is the probability that removing this error in any one variable will result in an **increase** in stock holding costs? (15 min)

7.3 ANALYTICAL EXAMPLE 2: REVISION OF PROBABILITIES

For this section, a familiarity with decision trees is assumed.

A building society is concerned about the number of defaulters — now approaching 4% of loans granted. It is considering joining with other societies and credit institutions in maintaining a joint credit information system which could

1   tell whether any loan applicant had had a county court judgement against him, and/or
2   tell whether any loan applicant had a bad payment record on any loan granted previously by the participating organisations. ('Bad payment record' is to be defined objectively, e.g. 'threatened with legal action on three or more occasions'.)

1 Value of judgement information

Figure 7.3 overleaf illustrates the decision tree of the actions, probabilities and payoffs associated with the judgement information, where

$p(R)$ = prior probability of Repayment
$p(D)$ = $1 - p(R)$ = prior probability of Default
$p(N)$ = prior probability of No Judgement recorded
$p(J)$ = $1 - p(N)$ = prior probability of Judgement being recorded
$p(R|N)$ = probability of Repayment when No Judgement is recorded (said 'probability of **R** given **N**')
$p(D|N)$ = $1 - p(R|N)$ = probability of Default when No Judgement recorded
$p(R|J)$ = probability of Repayment when Judgement is recorded
$p(D|J)$ = $1 - p(R|J)$ = probability of Default when Judgement is recorded
a = average NPV payoff from a repayment

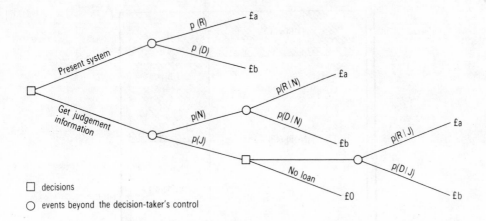

Fig. 7.3: Judgement information decision tree

b = average NPV payoff from a default.

Of course, if **b** is not less than zero, the information will have no value since it is always worthwhile giving the loan. If **b** is less than zero, then the maximum possible value of the information can be quickly determined as –p(D)b, i.e. the expected monetary value of the losses avoided. The judgement information would have to be a perfect predictor of defaulters and repayers to be worth this, though.

The expected monetary value (EMV) of the present system is given by

$$p(R)a + p(D)b \tag{14}$$

If p(R|J)a + p(D|J)b is greater than zero, the EMV of the proposed system is also equal to

$$p(R)a + p(D)b \tag{15}$$

since the action – grant loan – would be unchanged.

Otherwise, the EMV of the proposed system is given by

$$p(N)(p(R|N)a + p(D|N)b) \tag{16}$$

Figure 7.4 shows a unit square of probabilities. On the base are marked the prior probabilities of repayment or default as measured from past cases. The areas of the rectangles above the segments of the base line representing p(R) and p(D) are also equal to p(R) and p(D), since the square has unit height.

The left side is marked with p(N|R), the probability of No Judgement being recorded against a person who has Repaid, and p(J|R), the probability of Judgement being recorded against such a person. The area of the rectangle marked p(N|R)p(R) is equal to the joint probability that a payment has been made and No Judgement is recorded against the repayer. Similarly, the area of the rectangle above is equal to p(J|R)p(R).

The right side is marked with the probabilities of Judgement and No Judgement respectively against a person who has defaulted. Again, the probability of default is divided into two cases: p(J|D)p(D) and p(N|D)p(D). The question is this: given that in the past we have measured all the marked probabilities, suppose we are now presented with an application for a loan, and the information that the applicant has No Judgement recorded against him. By how much should we revise our prior estimate of repayment p(R) so that we have the new probability that repayment will be made, given that the applicant has a good record – p(R|N)?

If No Judgement is recorded against the applicant, we cannot be looking at either of the shaded cases in Figure 7.4, since they both concern applicants with Judgements. The information about No Judgments has excluded

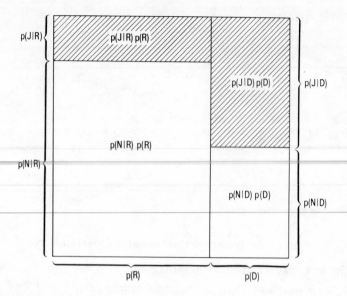

Fig 7.4: Revision of probabilities according to Bayes' theorem

those possibilities. We must therefore be dealing either with a potential Repayer with No Judgement or a potential Defaulter with No Judgement. The probability of the applicant being a Repayer is given by the ratio that the rectangle $p(N|R)p(R)$ bears to the total unshaded portion, $p(N|R)P(R)$ + $p(N|D)p(D)$. This unshaded portion exhausts the ways No Judgement may arise, so it is simply equal to $p(N)$. Thus we have arrived at Bayes' theorem:

$$p(R|N) = \frac{p(N|R)p(R)}{p(N)} \tag{17}$$

where $p(N|R)$ is the probability that No Judgement was recorded in the cases where a Repayment has occurred. Similarly,

$$p(D|N) = \frac{p(N|D)p(D)}{p(N)} \tag{18}$$

where $p(N|D)$ is the probability of No Judgement being recorded in the cases where a Default occurs.

So, substituting in equation (16),

$$EMV = p(N|R)p(R)a + p(N|D)p(D)b \tag{19}$$

from which it follows that the expected value of the information (EVI), i.e. the EMV of the proposed system (19) less the EMV of the old system (1), is given by

$$EVI = (p(N|R) - 1)p(R)a + (p(N|D) - 1)p(D)b \tag{20}$$

To continue, from (15), case (16) will apply if

$$p(R|J)a + p(D|J)b \text{ is less than } 0 \tag{21}$$

i.e. $\quad \dfrac{p(J|R)p(R)a}{p(J)} + \dfrac{p(J|D)p(D)b}{p(J)} \quad$ is less than zero $\tag{22}$

i.e. $p(J|R)p(R)a$ is less than $-p(J|D)p(D)b$ $\tag{23}$

The point of these manipulations is that equations (20) and (23) are expressed in terms which can reasonably be measured from inspection of the existing records of the society, i.e. $p(D)$ (from which $p(R)$ follows), $p(J|D)$ (from which $p(N|D)$ follows) and $p(N|R)$ (from which $p(J|R)$ follows). The values of **a** and **b** must also be measured or estimated.

Worked example

The values are as follows: $p(D) = 0.04$; $p(J|D) = 0.15$; $p(N|R) = 0.99$; **a** = £100; **b** = −£400.

From (23), 0.96 is less than 1.8, so case (16) applies.
From (20),
  EVI = ((0.99 - 1)0.96 x 100) + ((0.85 - 1)0.04 x (-400))
      = **£1.44 average per applicant.**

In practice, the usefulness of this method may lie as much in the sensitivity analyses possible as in the measurement of EVI. For example, suppose the cost of obtaining judgement information was £x per applicant. For what values of **b** (cost of default on average) will the judgement information be worthwhile?
  The information is worthwhile when
    EVI - **x** is greater than 0
i.e. $(p(N|R) - 1)p(R)a + (p(N|D) - 1)p(D)b - x$ is greater than 0   (24)
or **b** is greater than $\dfrac{x - (p(N|R) - 1)p(R)a}{(p(N|D) - 1)p(D)b}$
In the case of the numerical example already quoted, this is when
  -**b** is greater than 167**x** + 160
  Another example: for what values of $p(N|R)$ will the information be worthwhile?
  From (24), the information is worthwhile when
    $p(N|R)$ is greater than $1 + \dfrac{x - (p(N|D) - 1)p(D)b}{p(R)a}$
In the case of the numerical example, when
  $p(N|R)$ is greater than 1 + 0.0104**x** - 0.025
e.g. if **x** = 1, $p(N|R)$ must be greater than 0.9855; if **x** = 1.44, $p(N|R)$ must be greater than 0.99.

2 Value of bad payment record information
If this case is considered independently from 1 above, the analysis proceeds in the same way. To find the **additional** EVI, the revised probabilities from case 1 can be taken as the priors for case 2, or the joint probabilities can be analysed to permit procedure in similar fashion to 1.

Question

1 The City Council is thinking about a computerised traffic control system which has been given a crude development and running cost estimate of £1800 000 NPV. The project would be considered a success if average vehicle speed rose by 20% in rush hours, a failure if there were less increase than this. A computer simulation of rush-hour traffic could be built for about £40 000 NPV, but the reliability of the model in predicting the effect of the system is uncertain. Forty similar cities are known who have tried to computerise their traffic control, and at least five of them count it a failure. Have you any advice to offer to the Council?   (120 min)

ANSWER POINTERS

Section 7.1

1 Neglecting side-effects, the sponsor has to decide whether to take up the 'bargain' of NPV and non-money MOEs. If NPV is negative and the global utility of the non-money MOEs is positive, the sponsor is facing a 'value for money' problem – are the advantages of the project worth the expense? If the sponsor decides to go ahead, then (on this financial view) he has money-valued the non-money MOEs at an amount at least equal to the NPV.
If NPV is positive and the global utility of the non-money MOEs is negative, the sponsor is facing the problem – do the savings of the project justify the disadvantages? Again, the sponsor's decision may allow one to

impute a minimum or maximum financial valuation of the non-money MOEs.

Even when the sign of the global utility of the non-money MOEs is unknown, if the sponsor goes ahead it may be taken that he values them at least equal to the negated NPV. For example, NPV = £10 000, least possible value of rest of bargain = -£10 000. If the sponsor does not go ahead, he values them at most equal to the negated NPV.

All this suggests that the sponsor has made a money valuation. However, it may be argued with equal strength that he has an implied utility valuation of the NPV. On this counter-argument, the sponsor has not money-valued the non-money MOEs, but utility-valued the money. If utility is **defined** in such a way as to make it the reason for exercising choice, the proposition that the sponsor has utility-valued the money becomes superior definitionally, but somewhat tautologically.

2   Unfortunately, probably not. The most that might be expected is that he is somewhat less susceptible.

Section 7.2

1   The variable stock holding costs and re-ordering costs can be estimated as $\sqrt{2DRI} = \sqrt{2 \times 500\,000 \times 1000 \times 0.4} = £20\,000$.

If future demand forecasts are perfectly accurate, this will lead to savings (neglecting errors in holding costs or re-order costs) of

$$\sqrt{\frac{(1.2 + 1)^2}{4(1.2)}} - 1$$

= 0.416% of variable costs, or £83.

The savings from the reduction of £100 in re-order costs could be put at

$$20\,000 - \sqrt{2 \times 500\,000 \times 900 \times 0.4} = £1026$$

of which $100D/Q = 100 \times 500\,000/50\,000 = £1000$ is attributable to cost reductions in ordering calculated on the old volume of orders, and £26 is attributable to the lower stock holding which is enabled by the more frequent re-ordering that can be done when re-order costs are reduced.

If the true figure for re-order costs were £500, e_r = 100%, and the saving with perfectly accurate information would be:

$$2000 \times \left(\sqrt{\frac{(2 + 1)^2}{4(2)}} - 1 \right) = £1213$$

If the true figure were £2000, e_r = 50% and savings would be £412. If the true figure were equally likely to be anywhere in the range £500 to £2000, the expected savings could be valued at (£1213 + £412)/4 = £406. (It might be more reasonable to assume that the true costs were not uniformly distributed, but peaked around £1000. This would cut down the expected savings somewhat.)

The two days saving in lead time allows safety stock to be reduced by 2/365 x 500 000, showing a saving of £1096.

To summarise, the new system will save about £2100 each year from cost reductions due to reduced re-order costs and lead time and, less certainly, a further £400 or so each year from improved accuracy – a total of £2500 a year. If the real interest rate is 10% p.a. and these are perpetual benefits, the NPV of the attributes dealt with is about £25 000.

If the re-order cost reduction and lead time were measured improvements, they could be class A estimates. If I had confidence in the supplied figures and the validity of the stock control model, the other estimates to my mind would be class B. So, uncertainty surrounding the NPV would be classified

A – Reliable estimates (£2100/£2500)   84%
B – Fairly reliable estimates   16%

If the re-order cost reduction were measured but, say, the reduction in lead time were based only on good arguments from first principles, and I did not have much confidence in the model, I would classify as follows:

A – Reliable estimates (£1000/£2500)   40%
B – Fairly reliable estimates (£1100/£2500)   44%
C – Guesses   16%

2   Suppose e_d were negative.
If e_r were negative and e_i were negative, eliminating e_d would reduce costs.
If e_r were negative and e_i were positive, eliminating e_d would reduce costs.
If e_r were positive and e_i were negative, eliminating e_d would increase costs.
If e_r were positive and e_i were positive, eliminating e_d would reduce costs.

This exhausts the cases with e_d negative. A similar position arises with e_d positive. The same arguments apply with e_r and e_i. Each time, one case in four increases costs. So the probability of increasing costs by removing the error on one variable only is 0.25.

Section 7.3

1   A short and tempting answer is no; there is too much uncertainty. Let us see how far we can get with courageous assumptions and return to this aspect later.
In this problem we have rather a large number of unknowns, particularly the expected payoff from success or loss from failure, and the reliability of the model. Reliability here means whether or not the simulation gives an accurate prediction. We do have an estimate of the prior probability of failure, $p(F)$, at $5/40 = 0.125$, and from this the probability of success, $p(S) = 0.875$. If we knew the population of the city we could perhaps make an inspired guess at average journey time and through that deduce total savings in fuel, wear and tear, etc. But even this is denied to us in the question, so the most we can attempt is some illustration of sensitivity which will help the council decide whether or not to buy the simulation.
In the absence of other information, the EMV of going ahead without the simulation could be considered neutral, i.e.

$$0.875\mathbf{a} + 0.125\mathbf{b} = 0 \qquad (26)$$

where $\mathbf{a}$ and $\mathbf{b}$ are the net gain on success and the net loss on failure respectively. If the project is unsuccessful, the worst net loss would presumably be £1800 000 – average vehicle speed does not rise at all so the whole outgoing is lost. (I am assuming that if computerisation made average speed worse, someone would have the sense to pull the plug out. Would it be too cynical to say that this is the most courageous assumption of the bunch?) More than this is scarcely open to speculation on the data supplied.
The reliability of the simulation could be defined by the probability of success being predicted, given that success occurs, $p(Sp|S)$, and the probability of failure being predicted given that failure occurs, $p(Fp|F)$. We have no reason to distinguish these probabilities so let us make a start by assuming them to be equal.
A totally useless simulation model would have a reliability of 0.5. If technical matters of traffic flow were the only factors in success, it would not be surprising to find that the built model had a reliability of 0.9 or more. Let me stab at 0.75 reliability as being a reasonably unfavourable assumption (I return to this later). That is:

$$p(Sp|S) = p(Fp|F) = 0.75 \qquad (27)$$

The decision tree is illustrated in Figure 7.5.
Assuming we will not go ahead if the model predicts failure, the EVI is

$$(p(Sp)p(S|Sp)\mathbf{a} + p(Sp)p(F|Sp)\mathbf{b}) - (p(S)\mathbf{a} + p(F)\mathbf{b}) \qquad (28)$$

By Bayes' theorem,

$$p(S|Sp) = p(Sp|S)p(S)/p(Sp)$$

and

$$p(F|Sp) = p(Sp|F)p(F)/p(Sp)$$

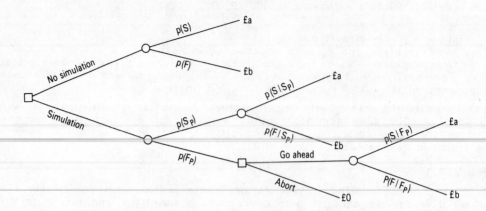

Fig. 7.5: Simulation model decision tree

Substituting in (28),
    EVI = $(p(\mathbf{Sp}|\mathbf{S}) - 1)p(S)\mathbf{a} + (p(\mathbf{Sp}|\mathbf{F}) - 1)p(F)\mathbf{b}) - (p(S)\mathbf{a} + p(F)\mathbf{b})$
        = $(p(\mathbf{Sp}|\mathbf{S}) - 1)p(S)\mathbf{a} + (p(\mathbf{Sp}|\mathbf{F}) - 1)p(F)\mathbf{b}$
From (27),
    EVI = $(0.75 - 1)0.875\mathbf{a} + (0.25 - 1)0.125\mathbf{b}$
From (26), $0.875\mathbf{a} = -0.125\mathbf{b}$, so
    EVI = $(0.75 - 1)(-0.125\mathbf{b}) + (0.25 - 1)(0.125\mathbf{b})$
        = $0.125\mathbf{b}(0.25 - 0.75) = -0.625\mathbf{b}$
Figure 7.6 illustrates this EVI together with the EVIs of other reliabilities.
We can perhaps advise the council that if expected monetary value is the
test it is fairly certain that a study with reliability less than about 0.75

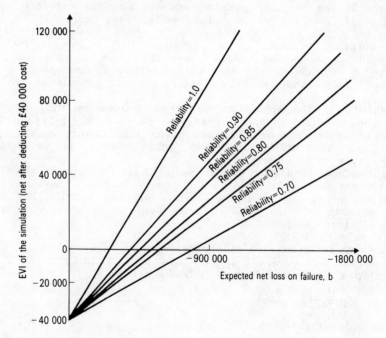

Fig. 7.6: Sensitivity analysis of the EVI of the simulation

is not worthwhile. Above this, the value of the information is sensitive to the expected net loss if the project is unsuccessful, as illustrated. If the simulation was 90% reliable, the expected net loss on failure of the project would have to exceed about £800 000 for it to be worthwhile.

The sensitivity of this advice to the opening assumptions in equation (26) can be tested if desired by making different assumptions. Also, the prior probability of failure is somewhat suspect, especially considering that the criterion for classifying the outcome as a failure may not be standard. Sensitivity to this figure may be explored if desired.

Another dimension to this answer is opened up if EMV is not an adequate criterion for the council. Unlike the granting of loans by the building society, the council intends to computerise traffic control only once. There may be no profits on roundabouts to compensate for losses on swings. Maybe the disutility of a severe net loss on the project is greater than that suggested by its EMV, and maybe the council is prepared to suffer the smaller disutility of a net loss of EMV on the simulation in order to reduce the risk of the project. In other words, the council may consider the expected cost of the simulation (development cost less EVI) as a sort of premium for an insurance which will mitigate the worst possible outcomes of the project.

REFERENCE

(1) Moore, P. G., and Thomas, H., **The anatomy of decisions**, Penguin, 1976.

8   Project failures and pitfalls

8.1 CAUSES OF FAILURE

Many computer projects, it is thought, end in failure. Not failure in the sense of not providing a system, but failure in the sense of not providing all the anticipated benefits. If the cause of failure of past projects can be systematically identified, maybe the chance of future failures can be reduced by appropriate action.

Although not without force, this hope of systematic learning from the past is a little forlorn. Asking 'Why do projects fail' is like asking 'Why do people miss buses?'. There is an indefinite number of truthful responses and an indefinite chain of causes of the causes. For example, the reasons why people miss buses can be superficially given as (a) the person arrives late or not at all, or (b) the bus arrives early or not at all. In looking for the causes of (a), we may consider the cause 'the person does not have an alarm clock and oversleeps'. Should we advance this as a cause? Maybe some people do not have alarm clocks because they are too poor, and some people oversleep because they go to parties the night before. Should we assert 'People sometimes miss buses because they are poor or go to parties'?

In practice we **select** causes to advance in answer to the question; causes which are not too superficial nor too remote. One reason for selecting cause **X** is that in the past we have ourselves found it useful to consider **X** a cause. Another reason is that by advancing **X** as the cause we believe we are offering the questioner helpful advice which may guide his actions. We mention 'Some people miss buses because they do not have alarm clocks' because we think our questioner may not have an alarm clock and might oversleep. But perhaps we omit to mention 'Some people miss buses because they do not have any clock or watch' or 'because they cannot tell the time' because we believe it unlikely that the questioner wants to hear this.

The point of this sidetrack is that any attempt to review past failed projects through questioning the participants, or even by questioning oneself if one has participated in a failed project, is of dubious objectivity. The causes one is likely to dredge up are the subjective opinions or prejudices of questioner and questionee. What one is really getting is more like advice for the future.

There is a defect in the analogy with missing buses. Missing a bus is an objective event which all rational observers, even independently, will agree has occurred. The success or failure of a project is subjective and can be a matter of dispute which is not reconciled even when observers have discussed their viewpoints. This is a reason for definition of project MOEs. It would be too glib to claim that the Targets make a complete definition of success, since side-effects may play a part in this. But if the Targets are reached, at least it can be claimed that the project is a success according to all the criteria which talented personnel of the organisation deemed it worthwhile to specify at the outset. Failure may be considered more excusable if its source is a side-effect which eluded the best brains available.

Questions

1   At a conference about project failures, a speaker meticulously described the events which occurred in a project up to the point of its implementation. He then invited conference participants to predict what would happen next. The respondents predicted a failure of the project caused by the hostility of a particular user manager who had not been much involved during the design stages. This was indeed what had happened in the real case, but none of the project team concerned had predicted such an outcome at the time. What possible reasons are there for the conference participants' success where the project team had failed?   (20 min)

2   Comment on the following assertions.

   a   The cause of the project failure was that the estimate of project duration was incorrect.

   b   The project failed because it was inadequately defined.

   c   The project failed because one of the tasks necessary for completion was overlooked during initial planning.   (20 min)

3   If you take advice about something from a lot of people, is the most commonly-given advice the best?   (2 min)

4   In a survey (McKinsey and Co. 1968), it was found that less successful users of computers tended to have projects which were not planned. 'Not planned' meant that in the consultants' opinion there was nothing deserving the name of an overall plan for a full range of computer applications and that the economic and operational feasibility of projects were seldom fully explored. Operational feasibility was defined to mean whether or not the computer system, once developed, would be successfully used by the people concerned. On this evidence, could this be another self-fulfilling case, like 2b above?   (5 min)

8.2 LACK OF PLANNING AND CONTROL

One possible heading under which causes of project failures could be classified is lack of planning and control. These causes are appealing to the 'control system' model of achieving a target.

A controlled system must have a standard (well-defined objectives), a controller (which will seek to reach the objectives) and control actions (which the controller may take). In a computer project, the objectives are the Targets, the controller is the project manager and the control actions are principally the application and organisation of the project resources, mainly people, used in furthering the objectives.

If a control system is to reach its objective within a specified time, the control action must be able to draw on sufficient resources to drive the system to its objective on time. If this system can be disturbed while the control action is being implemented, there must also be slack resources (or slack time) available to overcome the disturbance. The Targets of computer projects are usually given a deadline within which they must be reached. Disturbances can occur rather easily in computer projects while the resources are driving towards the target, since there is usually a long elapsed time between committing the resource and reaching the objective. The disturbance may be an unforeseen or newly-arising obstacle to progress, or it may be an interruption to the supply or application of resources.

A feed-forward or input-controlled control system uses the present state of the system 'inputs' to make a prediction of the 'output'. The difference between the predicted output and the standard or target output is used for **anticipatory** control actions by the controller. To exercise feed-forward control, the controller must have a prediction formula and information about

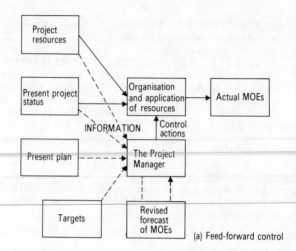

(a) Feed-forward control

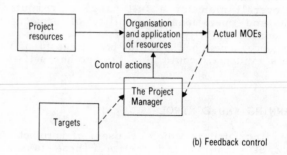

(b) Feedback control

Fig. 8.1: Feed–forward and feedback control

the inputs, and must have this information early enough for the control actions to take effect. In a computer project, the inputs are the project resources (mainly man and computer time). The information needed for prediction is the state of project achievements to date, the nature of the activities to which resources are presently applied and the expectations of future supplies of resource. The prediction formula is a model of system development which identifies all the tasks of the project, how they depend on one another, and what resources are needed to complete each task or plan.

A feedback or output–controlled control system senses the present state of the system outputs and supplies this information to the controller for after–the–event corrective action. Feedback control is rather ineffective compared with feed–forward control, especially when there is a long time between deciding to take the control action and the action having the desired effect. The desired outputs of a computer project are the Targets. The information needed is the state of the MOEs. Throughout most of the system development, the Targets are simply 'unfulfilled', so the feedback model is not very helpful. Towards the end of a project, or after implementation, there may be relevant measurements to be made of the MOEs to permit evaluation of the system status. Some Targets, such as cost of development or target date for implementation, may be beyond correction at this stage. Others, such as response time, may be tunable.

To summarise, the causes of project failure through lack of planning and control could be classified as follows, with reference to the missing constituents of a control system.

1   Lack of objectives; in other words insufficiently or inadequately stated Targets resulting in the controller not knowing what he is aiming for.
2   Lack of a controller; no one designated as, trained as, and with the personal qualities needed by, a project manager.
3   Lack of control actions; insufficient opportunity to redeploy or reorganise resources or call upon new resources, particularly manpower; insufficient resource allocated at the outset.
4   Susceptible to disturbance; insufficient slack resource or slack in deadlines to overcome unpredictable obstacles and interruptions.
5   Insufficient information for feed-forward control; lack of information about the state of the project or the deployment of resources, or information comes too late for corrective action.
6   Inaccurate prediction model; defective analysis of tasks, dependence of tasks or resources required to achieve tasks; no plan.
7   Feed-forward control not exercised; no revision of plans, no revision of MOE forecasts, no identification of forecast variances, no anticipatory control action taken.
8   Insufficient feedback information; lack of measurement of project MOEs, or information comes too late.
9   Feedback control not exercised; no post-implementation evaluation.

Questions

1   The following are some reasons why projects fail. Classify each one under one of the nine headings listed above. Have you any left over?

a   Unrealistic budget.
b   Insufficient cost control.
c   Unrealistic completion schedules.
d   Insufficient control of activities.
e   Firm commitments were made on the basis of specifications which were inadequate.
f   An adequate set of specifications was not developed.
g   Necessary tasks were overlooked.
h   Interdependence of tasks was overlooked.
i   Clearance was not obtained on delivery dates or turnaround rates on which planning was based.
j   The project leader was overburdened with detailed tasks.
k   Plans made no allowance for contingencies.
l   Checkpoints were not used to monitor progress.
m   Performance was not adequately monitored.
n   Planning was not done in sufficient detail at an early enough stage.
o   Insufficient weight was given to, and insufficient time was spent on, both long-term and short-term planning.
p   Inadequate skills or experience of DP staff in identifying and scheduling tasks.
q   Lack of appreciation of the complexity of tasks and practical problems to be encountered.
r   Control is not exhaustive enough or is intermittent.
s   Short lead times are allowed for in estimates.
t   Personnel availability for the project is unknown.
u   Project leader responsibility is undefined.
v   Definition of project is vague, misleading or totally wrong.
w   The project, between time of original estimate and its initiation,

changed without a corresponding change in in estimate.
x   Resource requirements were not scheduled for the project.
y   Reporting of project information is not performed.
z   Project reviews are exercises in trivia.
aa Change of personnel during project.
bb Resource requirements were not anticipated.
cc Lack of a project log.
dd No account taken of differing abilities of staff.
ee Success or failure of project not evaluated.   (30 min)

2   A project leader feels that the regular project cost reports he gets for
the periodic checkpoints and reviews contain information that is too old to
be useful. In what three ways can he improve this information?   (2 min)

3   What would you suggest should principally determine the frequency with
which feed-forward control is exercised, i.e. how frequently checkpoints
and reviews are held for the purpose of revising forecasts and plans?
                                                                     (5 min)

4   In Figure 8.2 unrealistic estimates are ascribed to failure to analyse
project complexity and human problems. Can you suggest other reasons for
unrealistic estimates?   (5 min)

THE SQUEEZE

1   If the complexity of the project is not fully analysed, or if the human
    problems to be encountered are omitted, there will be a tendency to
    assume that the project is easier and simpler than in reality.
2   Estimates made at the outset will tend to give unrealistic target dates
    and resource requirements.
3   Staff at all levels commit themselves to the targets.
4   As the deadlines approach, the pressure leads to skimping of:

    ▌ planning and control   ▌ quality of work
    ▌ testing   ▌ documentation

as well as abandonment of standards and unauthorised deviations from
plans and specifications.

Fig. 8.2: A not uncommon symptom

8.3 LACK OF PARTICIPATION

Causes of failure of this type generally make appeal to the resistance of
the users to accepting a changed system of work, or to the decisive
influence of the users over the effectiveness of the operation of the users'
system. Resistance is a variable which ranges from, say, tacit reluctance
to open hostility.
  The components of resistance might be classified into (a) predispositions
of the users and (b) their revised dispositions as a result of contact with
the project team.
  Predispositions which contribute to feelings of resistance may result from
the following factors.

  The climate of personnel relations in the organisation and suspicion
  of motives.
  The history of innovation in the organisation. Previous changes may
  have a bad reputation; earlier change, perhaps in another department,
  may have worked to the disadvantage of colleagues; previous attempts
  at innovation may have been abortive or ineffectual.
  The image of computers. Popular broadcasts, films, books and articles

on the whole, I think, promote a negative image of computers for those people who have never worked with them before. Fictional computers are often portrayed as all-knowing or all-powerful machines controlling the destiny of men, and they have a remarkable propensity to explode if given an insoluble problem. A person who knows his work is to be computerised may be excused for feeling apprehensive before he has sampled the reality.

The present job satisfaction of users. Users dissatisfied with their work may clutch at any change in the hope of improvement, but may just as quickly reject the change if it does not prove the panacea they hoped for.

The personality of the users. Some people are more temperamental, easily upset, anxious or plain cussed than others.

These predispositions can nearly always be counteracted by suitable conduct on the part of the project team (but one case in my experience involved the negative personality of a user who was so intractable that he was considered paranoid by those who dealt with him). In most cases, 'suitable conduct' comprises no more than a sympathetic and sensitive appreciation of the mood of the users, and the use of everyday interpersonal skills to keep people informed and alleviate fears. This still leaves a minority of cases where more than everyday skill is required.

The project team may promote resistance as a result of the following.

The team's foci of interest. The team may concentrate on technical considerations and ignore the preferences of users or the effect of change on their work and job satisfaction.

The team's personal behaviour. The team may neglect user talent, they may believe their own solutions are superior, they may patronise users; all giving rise to negative feelings or apprehension.

The team's use of persuasive method. 'Selling' a system can promote sales resistance; an offer of compensation may promote an expectation of negotiation; a command may promote an obstinate refusal.

Overcoming or avoiding resistance is a rather negative approach to participation. Lack of resistance does not make a system a success. This is governed as much by the willingness, enthusiasm or determination of the users to make the system succeed as by anything else. How much more willing, enthusiastic or determined will they be if they have actively participated in the design of the new system to the point where it is the system they have chosen, invented or built?

Questions

1 (a) Can a system in which users have not participated in the choice, invention or construction be willingly, enthusiastically and determinedly operated by them?
(b) Can a system in which users have so participated be unwillingly operated by them, without enthusiasm or determination?
(c) Why should users participate in the system design?   (5 min)

2 Human behaviour and reactions are notoriously difficult to predict and attitudes may be difficult to discern. People can be wrong in predicting their own reactions to change, let alone those of others. Participation, although necessary to reduce risk, is not **sufficient** to ensure positive reactions, not can such reactions be forecast reliably. What steps can a project manager take to plug this gap?   (5 min)

3 In this book it is proposed that users should participate through membership of the steering committee and the project monitoring committee, and by supplying the project manager and members of the feasibility study and project development teams. Is this enough?   (5 min)

4   Are the following plausible reasons for project failure?

ff   The user was not the prime mover behind the project.
gg   The chief executive was not aware of the need for user involvement.
hh   The DP department was not aware of the need for user involvement.
ii   The systems analysts believed in their own superiority.
jj   The systems analysts acted like prima donnas.
kk   The systems analysts were too glib.
ll   User approval of the specification was not required.
mm   No project monitoring committee was established.
nn   User morale was lowered.
oo   No working relationship with user department.
pp   Users were not involved early enough.
qq   Involvement was 'one-way' from the DP department to users by selling ideas or education.
rr   A brute force approach was adopted to steamroller the project through.   (5 min)

8.4 LACK OF MANAGEMENT

Lack of management in this context may be seen as the 'cause of the causes' of project failure, i.e. the cause of lack of project planning and control or the cause of lack of user involvement.

An appeal can be made to the management by objectives prescription to managers which advances the following steps for managing their employees.

Agree with the employee what is expected of him.
If it is not agreed what a person is supposed to do, by a reasonably precise definition of his individual objectives and priorities, it will not be very surprising if in practice he does something else.
Give the employee an opportunity to perform.
This means giving the employee authority to match the responsibilities he is taking, supplying him with the information he needs, and making sure the political and organisational lines are clear for him to act. Failing this, there may be obstacles to his getting on with the job; obstacles which he cannot reasonably be expected to overcome by himself.
Let the employee know how he is doing.
This means evaluating the employee so that he understands the manager's opinion of his performance, be it good or bad, and specific strengths he can capitalise on or weaknesses he can correct.
Give the employee guidance and training.
Enthusiasm and intelligence on their own can go a long way in any endeavour, but guidance and training will make it go further.
Reward the employee according to results.
The reward may be not only financial; for instance, it may be the psychological reward of praise, recognition or status.

This prescription is to help the manager get the best out of the people he has got. The other side of the coin is to get the best people in the first instance, through effective recruitment and selection.

To summarise, failure of a project through 'lack of management' means that managers have failed to provide the conditions under which a project can succeed.

Questions

1   Is there any difference between 'agreeing with an employee what is expected of him' and the definition of Targets?   (5 min)

2   Systems analysts and programmers are talented and able people. Is there then less need to spell out their individual objectives?   (5 min)

3   Re-examine the causes of failure in section 8.2, question 1, and in section 8.3, question 4. Supposing these causes were themselves caused by failures in the management of systems analysts and programmers, tentatively classify each cause under one or two of the five points of the prescription for MBO on the previous page. Place the five points in order of frequency you use them for this classification.   (10 min)

ANSWER POINTERS

Section 8.1

1   a   The project team did not consider making, nor were they asked for, any predictions; or
b   the conference participants had better insight than the project team; or
c   the speaker had related the events of the project development in the knowledge of the actual outcome. Despite his attempt to be meticulous, his selection of events was biased so as to bring out, or at least to include, the feature facts which he believed explained the outcome. Wittingly or unwittingly he prompted the conference prediction. In the real case, though, the project team had not seen those same facts as features at the time. They were dealing with a much richer set of facts in which the 'cause of failure' facts were not highlighted.
d   The 'cause of failure' facts were not objective facts, recognisable by the project team at the time, but are an interpretation particular to the speaker.

2   a   At face value, this looks objective. The original estimate can be examined. The project duration is recorded. All observers agree that the latter exceeds the former.
 However, a flaw in the assertion is the assumption that it is the estimate that was wrong. Maybe it is the project duration that was wrong. Perhaps the estimate could have been fulfilled if the project had been handled properly. This would make the disparity between estimated and actual duration a **symptom** of failure rather than a cause of it.
 This problem is like having one equation with two unknowns. We cannot find the right answer (see also section 10.2).
b   'Adequately defined' is not an objective fact. Indeed, one suspects the possibility that the same definition may be regarded as 'adequate' or 'inadequate' according to whether the project succeeds or fails. In that case, the assertion is self-fulfilling. On the other hand, perhaps a definition of project failure is that a project fails to meet its sponsor's objectives, whether or not they were clearly stated. Inadequate definition of a project could mean that not all the sponsor's objectives were clearly stated; so this assertion could mean something like 'the project failed because the project development team did not know everything expected of them'. Quite plausible.
c   Assuming that the task concerned can be nominated and its omission clearly led to the failure, this is quite objective and plausible. However, any project has a myriad of small 'tasks' which are necessary for completion but which are not explicitly considered at the outset. Perhaps the definition of a task for the purpose of this assertion is that it is something that will cause failure if overlooked during initial planning.

3   Necessarily the best, no. Usually the best, I don't know.

4   It could be (I'm not saying it is). One of the corollaries of the preamble

to the question is that 'less successful users tended not to explore fully whether or not the computer system would be successfully used by the people concerned'. The same exploration might be judged full if the use were successful, not full if the use were unsuccessful.

Section 8.2

1 Lack of objectives: e, f, v.
Lack of controller: j, u.
Lack of control actions: a, c, x, bb.
Susceptible to disturbance: k, aa, dd.
Insufficient information for feed-forward control: b, m?, t, y, cc.
Inaccurate prediction model: g, h, i, n?, p, q, s.
Feed-forward control not exercised: j, l, w.
Feedback control not exercised: ee.
   I had to make an assumption about the precise meaning of the stated cause in several instances, and I see no reason why your assumptions should be the same as mine. I put j in two places because I didn't know whether the project leader was being prevented from exercising the duties he understood because of detailed tasks assigned to him, in which case the problem is that he is not exercising control; or whether he had assigned himself to the tasks in ignorance of his control duties, in which case the project apparently lacks a controller! The causes d, o, r and z were not classified on the grounds of being too general or too vague. I would prefer to take z as a symptom; its cause could be lack of objectives, lack of controller, lack of control action or insufficient information.
   It might be better to consider p, and possibly q, to be 'causes of the causes' in the present context. In effect they are claiming that the weakness of the prediction model is caused by failings in the personnel. See section 8.4.

2 Reduce the reporting delay, reduce the report period so it covers a shorter time, reduce the report interval by increasing the frequency of production. (See Systems Analysis, section 4.5.)

3 The extent to which the project can get out of control, i.e. the amount of variance, between desired and forecast objectives, that might arise between reviews. If the prediction model, control information and control actions are good, this will depend on the amount of disturbance that can arise between reviews − the more disturbance possible, the more frequent should be the review. A weak prediction model, poor control information or restricted control actions also call for more frequent review.

4 Bias. The size of the estimated resources and the distance of the estimated completion date may determine whether or not the project is authorised. The estimator may have invested a lot of himself in the project and may be anxious to see it authorised. Especially when estimates are not measured ones, it is open to the estimator to make assumptions favourable to the project.

Section 8.3

1 (a) Yes.
(b) Yes.
(c) It reduces risk (see also Systems Analysis, section 1.3).

2 Encourage an experimental, or perhaps I should say experiential, approach to the proposed change through the construction of prototype or pilot systems, trial use of specimen forms and documents, dummy running of new procedures. These trials should be as realistic as possible and sufficiently long to enable a user to get over the effects associated with **any** change. It is to be hoped that users can give a more reliable statement

of their reactions after some experience of the proposal than if they try to make forecasts built on unsubstantial foundations.

3 Probably not. Firstly because committee and team membership is not doing much more than providing the opportunity for participation; it does not ensure that sincere participation takes place at a personal level. Secondly because only a proportion of users may be selected for (or elected to) committee and teams. They become the Analysts and the Innovators as far as the residue of users is concerned. There is still a need for participation with the residue and no guarantee this will take place. In other words, the horse may have been led to the water but this does not mean it will drink.

Some form of at least passive participation can be ensured through presentations, newsletters, group meetings and other 'official' attempts to keep people informed. However, what counts as much as anything is what actually happens at the grass roots level of analyst–user contact; how the analyst handles his dealings with the users.

4 Yes.

Section 8.4

1 Not a lot. I have discussed Targets at the level of the organisation, the department and the project. The Targets are objectives of a **group** of people, but they are also the **individual** objectives of the manager of the group. This prescription is trying to point out that every person in a group must understand what is individually expected of him if his contribution is to be effective.

2 It is not only the personal qualities of the jobholder that influence the need to spell out the objectives; it is also the nature of the job. The more complex the job, the more variety there is possible in interpreting the aims of the job, so the more need there is to clarify objectives. Systems analysis, and to a lesser but still important extent programming, are jobs whose aims and priorities are open to interpretation.

It is hard to accept the proposition that the talent and ability of even above average analysts and programmers give them sufficient natural insight into the objectives they should have on behalf of the organisation.

3 When I did this I put every cause except ff into 'Failure of guidance and training'. A lot also went into 'Failure to agree what is expected', mainly because this is also a form of guidance. Then came 'Lack of opportunity to perform', picking up particularly j, t, aa, ff, gg, hh, mm. Some went into 'Failure to let know how getting on' and none into 'Reward according to results'. Most of the ambiguity arose because it was not clear who is the management referred to in the question, nor how far one should consider the failings of the managers of the managers.

REFERENCES

The following items are recalled as sources of some of the ideas in this chapter.
(1)   Benjamin, R. I., **Control of the information system development cycle**, Wiley-Interscience, 1971.
(2)   Gildersleeve, T., **Data processing project management**, Van Nostrand Reinhold, 1974.
(3)   Mumford, E. , Implementing EDP systems – a sociological perspective, **The Computer Bulletin**, January 1969, pp.10–13.

9 Project phases and plans

9.1 PROJECT CONTROL PHASES

The solid lines of Figure 9.1 opposite show a ladder network describing the dependences involved in developing a new system. The system is assumed to be one which does not require building a pilot or prototype system. The rungs of the ladder show the activities that best describe the process.

The LEAD activities making up the left side of the ladder show that a lower rung activity cannot start until some time after a higher rung activity has started. Definition of requirements cannot start until some fact-finding has been done – the first LEAD activity can be interpreted as 'get enough facts to begin defining requirements'. Specification of programs cannot start until at least some requirements and procedures have been defined. Reliable estimates of the costs and benefits cannot be made until programs and procedures are known at least in outline. Programming and procedure training cannot start until one program or procedure is ready to be tested.

The LAG activities making up the right side of the ladder show that a lower rung activity cannot be completed until some time after the rung activity above has been completed. The network asserts that requirements cannot be finalised until enough relevant facts are known. Program specification cannot be completed until all requirements and procedures are determined. Programming and procedure training cannot be completed until all programs and procedures are specified. Testing cannot be completed until all programs and procedures are ready. Costs and benefits cannot finally be determined until after the project is completed and the new system is operational (if then).

The LEAD and LAG dependences are not very clearly observable in practice, so the validity of the ladder network for describing a project should be questioned. Take the 'requirements' of a system as an example. The requirements are not clearly observable in the scientific sense. You could say the requirements, or some of them, are often known before the feasibility study is authorised. On the other hand, you could argue that the requirements, or some of them, are still a matter of debate after the project is completed. I can only retreat into a rather tautological corner and say that the requirements spoken of in the network are the sort of detailed and firm requirements that emerge after a certain amount of fact-finding, and are the requirements that are eventually frozen in the requirements report. The form, and words, of this model seem to be readily recognised in practice.

Returning to the fact-finding, 'enough relevant facts' was written rather than 'all relevant facts' because it is unlikely in practice that **all** relevant facts can be found. The relevant facts are not a stable and objective set of facts; they change as the design features and requirements of the system change. These in turn change with people's preferences or knowledge, and as a result of pressures from the environment. To look for all relevant facts would be a never-ending task. The pragmatic systems analyst draws the line at the point where he judges that enough facts have been gathered to enable agreement to be reached on the requirements of the system. This point is the 'freeze' and after this time the system requirements are considered frozen.

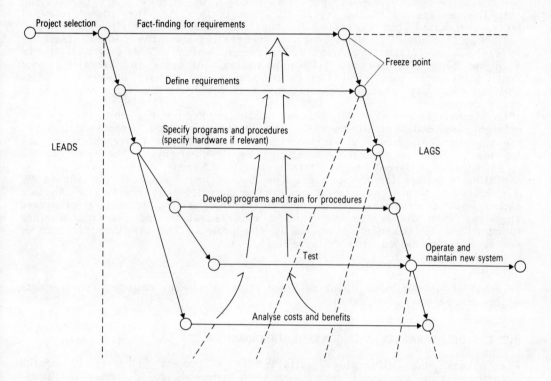

Fig. 9.1: The system development process – activity precedence network

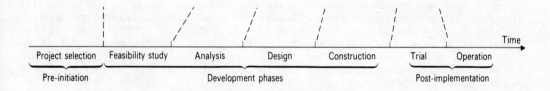

Fig. 9.2: The system development process – project control phases

This human attempt to crystallise the objectives is not mirrored in the real world. As system specification, programming and so on go forward towards completion after the freeze, unsuspected facts have a perverse habit of proving relevant as the design is made in greater detail and new problems are met. Also, the requirements, as desired by the users, may change as new business possibilities or pressures emerge, or as new users replace the old. The declaration of the freeze does not in fact stem the tide of relevant facts. The dotted line continuing the top rung of Figure 9.1 illustrates this.

Although the flow of dependence is generally down the ladder, there is a feedback of information, from lower rungs, which may modify activity in a higher rung. For example, although analysis of costs and benefits cannot begin until after some requirements are known, preliminary analysis of costs and benefits may change expectations and result in changed requirements being defined.

The dashed lines map the network model of Figure 9.1 onto the simpler straight-line model of Figure 9.2. The latter shows the project on a time-scale, split into phases which have been chosen as the conventional phases for the purpose of exercising control over development of the new system. In practice, different organisations adopt different conventional phases, or different names for the phases. The end of each phase is punctuated by a checkpoint, where the project monitoring committee can review the tangible evidence of achievements, and the control information, to assess progress. They can then decide, in the light of expected costs and benefits, whether to continue, to abandon or to modify the project. The tangible evidence of achievements is called 'the deliverables'.

Question

1   What should be done about relevant facts or new or changed requirements which emerge after the freeze?   (10 min)

9.2 THE DELIVERABLES AND CONTROL INFORMATION

The phases and deliverables suitable for a project of 3 to 12 months duration, using a project team of 1 to 6 members, could be as in Figure 9.3 opposite. For a longer or more substantial project, it is desirable to specify additional phases or deliverables so that suitably detailed control can be exercised over project development.

The longer or more substantial projects seem to bring an exponential increase in complexity or risk. Increased team size increases the amount of inter-communication and increases the difficulty of coordination. Longer duration increases the risk of disturbance. With any large project it is worthwhile, if humanly possible, to find a subset of the project which can be separated out and implemented on its own over a shorter time-scale. This subset should become a project in its own right, with its own Targets, checkpoints and deliverables.

In Figure 9.3, the Analysis phase can be omitted in a small project if the desired level of detail about requirements is attained in the Feasibility Report. The project timetable will show the target dates, checkpoints and deliverables identified for the particular project. An analysis of project tasks, and therefore required resources, up to completion will be required to support the timetable and to estimate the cost of development. The detailed plan and budget will show who is to do what in what time and at what cost. A budget is not essential for this control if virtually the only cost is analyst and programmer time. In this case, for budgetted and actual expenditure in Figure 9.3 substitute budgetted and actual analyst and programmer time.

Phase	End-of-phase deliverables	End-of-phase checkpoint control information
Project Selection	Terms of reference.	Detailed plan and budget for Feasibility Study.
Feasibility Study	Feasibility report.	Overall project timetable detailing checkpoints and deliverables. Forecasts of MOEs, i.e. project Targets. Detailed plan and budget for Analysis phase.
Analysis	Requirements report defining inputs, outputs, business procedures.	Revised project timetable. Revised forecasts of MOEs. Actual expenditure, Analysis phase. Detailed plan and budget, Design phase.
Design	Program specifications. Database definitions. Training materials and manuals. Hardware specification, where relevant.	Revised project timetable. Revised forecasts of MOEs. Actual expenditure, Design phase. Detailed plan and budget, Construction phase.
Construction	Documented programs. Test data and results. Supply of consumables. The working system.	Revised forecasts of MOEs. Actual expenditure, Construction phase. Detailed plan and budget, Trial phase.
Trial	Post-implementation evaluation report.	Estimates of actual MOEs. Actual expenditures, Trial phase.

Fig. 9.3: Phases, deliverables and control information of a typical project

Questions

1   If there are n members of a project team and each team member must communicate with every other team member, how many two-way channels of communication arise?   (5 min)

2   The probability of a disturbance (depending only on time) arising during a particular month is p. What is the probability that a project of n months duration will escape disturbances of this type?   (3 min)

3   Suppose that the probability of overlooking a given important task is 0.05. What is the probability, in a project involving n important tasks, that an important task will be overlooked?   (3 min)

4   What would you put in a post-implementation evaluation report?   (5 min)

5   Is it possible that applying more resources to a late project will make it even later?   (3 min)

9.3 CHECKPOINTS AND PLANS

Following the 'feed-forward control' analogy of project planning, checkpoints should occur more frequently as the probability and size of variance between forecast and actual MOEs increases. The more high-risk factors (Figure 3.2), the more checkpoints needed. The greater the size of the project, in terms of duration or resources, the more checkpoints needed.

The risk of variance can be considered to arise because of imperfections in information about what has to be done or what obstacles might arise. If the project manager had perfect information, he could in theory make a perfect plan. The perfection of knowledge improves as the project progresses – to be more exact, there is probably a negative exponential type of relationship between uncertainty and project progress, uncertainty being greatest at the outset. Thus the early activities in project development require more checkpoints than later ones, other things being equal. Figure 9.4 illustrates one way in which these variables can be put together.

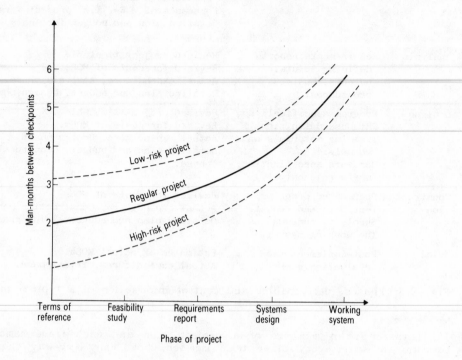

Fig. 9.4: A guide for choosing extra checkpoints. The illustration is purely intuitive on the author's part

At the checkpoint, a review should be made by the project monitoring committee. One of the objectives of this review should be an audit in the old-fashioned sense, i.e. the project monitoring committee wants to 'hear the evidence', in the form of the deliverables and other control information, on behalf of the interest groups they represent. This is one of their opportunities to participate by offering criticisms or suggestions, although if participation is otherwise working well there should be few surprises at the review. A further objective is to support, or overrule, the control actions proposed by the project manager. A control action which affects another project adversely, e.g. by drawing resources away from it, may need referral to the higher-level steering committee.

At each checkpoint, except the last, at least two plans must be drawn up. One covers the entire period remaining to the end of the project and is necessary in order to revise the forecast of system development cost and resources required, and to show the revised target dates of the remaining checkpoints and deliverables. The other plan spells out who is to do what, and when, during the next phase.

Further plans in the form of a project and phase budget will be required if budgetary control is being exercised.

Questions

1 Analysts often speak as if they were using the 'feedback' model of control in connection with their projects. For example, they might talk of 'getting feedback about project progess'. Is there any difference likely, in practice, if the analyst thinks in terms of feedback rather than feed-forward? (5 min)

2 A different argument for checkpoints is that they are needed as a motivator of action. The deliverables and review dates give intermediate targets which spur people on. Do you think this is a good argument? (5 min)

3 This chapter has emphasised exercising control over:

progress made towards target dates;
costs incurred towards target costs;
resources used towards planned resource usage.

This leaves out exercising control over the quality of the work done. Use the feed-forward or feedback control model to define the essential components of quality control. (10 min)

ANSWER POINTERS

Section 9.1

1 If the new facts or requirements do not materially threaten the Targets or introduce side-effects, account for them forthwith by changes in the design as necessary.

If the new facts do materially alter the Targets or introduce side-effects, try to get the sponsor's agreement to postponing the changes required until the end of the project, when they can be dealt with as part of system maintenance. This will avoid complicating or disturbing existing plans for the sake of non-essential changes.

If changes cannot wait, revise the forecasts of MOEs and side-effects and get the sponsor's re-authorisation to continue.

Section 9.2

1 1 member - no communication.
2 members - one two-way channel of commmunication.
3 members - a and b, b and c, c and a - three channels.
4 members - a and b, b and c, c and d, a and c, a and d, b and d - six channels.
n members - $\frac{1}{2}n(n - 1)$ channels.

2 Probability of no disturbance in a month = $1 - p$.
Probability of no disturbance in two months = $(1 - p)(1 - p)$.
Probability of no disturbance in n months = $(1 - p)^n$.

So, for example, if $p = 0.05$, a two month project would have 0.9 chance of escaping disturbance; an eight month project, 0.66.

3 $1 - 0.95^n$.

These three hypothetical questions cannot be taken too seriously, but they do illustrate the kind of ways project size might increase risk.

4 Discussion of project features and things learned which might help future projects;
measured versus target MOEs;
experienced versus forecast side-effects;
projected MOEs or side-effects if they are not yet stable;
review of maintenance projects completed or scheduled;

suggestions for improvement.

5   If the resources concerned are additional men, this could or does occur if the additional complexity in coordinating the efforts outweighs the extra contribution. This suggests that a better strategy is to get more resource out of the men you have, by overtime working or by increased motivation. This is not without its problems, either. Systems analysis and programming are not like digging potatoes, where twice as many hours worked means twice as many potatoes. Beyond the first two or three hours effort by development staff in a day, there is a quickly diminishing return from further effort. There are often more obstacles to progress outside normal hours because of the non-availability of other people inside or outside the organisation.

All this points up the difficulty of accelerating a project which has got behind, and reinforces the need for feed-forward planning and control. The best hope for acceleration may be to get more productive use of the resources available by increased method guidance and supervision. This calls for top calibre managers.

Section 9.3

1   Using the feedback model requires regarding the checkpoint status of cost of development and the deliverables as some sort of target. This is fair enough; they are targets. But when the checkpoint is reached, there is no control action which can correct any variance between, say, planned and actual cost of development to date. All that can be done is to predict, in the light of this information, the status of the next lot of targets at the next checkpoint or later. Control action might be possible to permit these future targets to be hit, but nothing can be done to change the past.

My motive in promoting the feed-forward model is to emphasise the need to forecast the eventual status: the state of cost of development and the other MOEs at completion of the project. Maybe the analyst who thinks in terms of feed-forward is encouraged to pay more attention to prediction of eventual status than one who thinks in terms of feedback. Feedback might be a more appropriate monitor of progress **between** checkpoints.

Incidentally, with all this talk of revision, I do not wish to imply that the revised forecasts are necessarily different from the original forecasts. They might simply be a vindication of the original estimates.

2   It seems to me that having to worry about 'What do we have to do to deliver the Requirements Report next week?' sharpens the mind wonderfully compared with 'What do we need to do to deliver the system next year?'. So I certainly think that the checkpoints are a motivator, overcoming a tendency to put things off until they are due.

Despite this, I doubt if they are a **sufficient** motivator. Deadlines that are two weeks, a month, six weeks away are still distant to me; at some stage, I want to know what are my targets next week, tomorrow, this afternoon.

3   Standards of quality performance, e.g. a standards manual giving standard methods and standard documentation.
Control actions for improving quality, mainly guidance and training, assistance.
A quality controller such as a supervisor.
For feedback control:
methods of checking quality, information about variance between target and delivered qualities.
Feed-forward control would require an advance forecast of the quality that will be delivered. This means the involvement of the supervisor while the work is being progressed, not just when it is thought to be completed.

10 Estimating

10.1 TASK IDENTIFICATION

Making a plan entails:

a   identifying the tasks that have to be performed;
b   determining the dependences, i.e. any necessary ordering of the tasks dictated by one task being a prerequisite of another.

For a specific plan, covering the next phase, the plan entails:

c   allocating personnel to the tasks;
d   estimating the time required to complete the tasks done by those personnel, and estimating other resources required;
e   making allowances (provisions) for contingencies such as sickness, delivery delays;
f   translating the result into a timetable of tasks, showing how available manpower and other resources will be utilised.

For an overall plan, looking towards the end of the project, planning entails:

g   estimating the manpower time required to complete each task in the remaining phases, assuming they are to be done by standard people, and estimating other resources needed;
h   making allowances for contingencies (reserves and provisions), such as the tasks being completed by non-standard persons, or an unexpected obstacle or overlooked task arising;
i   translating the result into a timetable of phases and checkpoints, and deliverables and a project budget.

A **reserve** here is an allowance for something that is not specifically contemplated. You cannot say what the reserve is for, except in vague terms, e.g. something overlooked. A **provision** is an allowance for a task or expense that can be nominated but which may or may not occur, or whose magnitude is in doubt. You can say what is being provided for.

What is a task is not an objective fact. A task is a unit of work that is convenient for making a plan. You do not want tasks so small that the plan becomes unwieldy. But you do not want a task so large that it might lead to over-simplification and lack of attention to the complexity of what has to be done. For a specific plan, covering the next phase, I like to deal with tasks that are between $\frac{1}{2}$ man-day and 15 man-days in size. If I deal with a task over 1 man-day, I like to be confident that I could break it down into smaller components, to be satisfied there is no hidden complication. So with these larger tasks, I like to think them through, back-of-an-envelope fashion, before committing them to the plan.

For an overall plan produced at the end of the feasibility study, it is often necessary to include larger tasks, say of 20 or 30 man-days. Again, it is desirable that these are thought through at a lower level of detail.

Figure 10.1 overleaf gives a short checklist of tasks in a project as they might be seen at an overall plan level. This is an illustrative list only - for a comprehensive list see, for example, Hice, Turner and Cashwell (1).

Activity	Phases to which the activities are most relevant (F = Feasibility, A = Analysis, D = Design, C = Construction)			
	F	A	D	C
Initial briefing	X			
Read background material	X			
State project objectives and scope	X			
Prepare overall plan	X	X	X	
Prepare detailed plan for next phase	X	X	X	X
Prepare end-of-phase report	X	X	X	X
Make end-of-phase presentation	X	X	X	X
Agree plans with sponsor/users/steering committee	X	X	X	X
Research similar systems	X	X		
Investigate object system	X	X		
Read existing system documentation	X	X		
Interview users	X	X		
Collect sample forms	X	X		
Collect statistics of volumes and usage	X	X	X	
Observe present processes	X	X		
Document existing system	X	X		
Check out existing system documentation with users	X	X		
Analyse requirements	X	X		
Develop alternatives in outline	X			
Select from alternatives	X			
Build data dictionary		X	X	X
Build data model	X	X		
Check out data model	X	X		
Design system of codes and user controls	X	X	X	
Specify clerical procedures	X	X	X	
Design clerical forms	X	X	X	
Design interactive dialogues	X	X	X	
Develop clerical system test plan		X		
Specify computer inputs	X	X	X	
Specify computer outputs	X	X	X	
Specify computer hardware and system software	X	X	X	
Define database files and records			X	
Choose file organisation			X	
Define computer runs, workfiles and access methods			X	
Define security and recovery procedures	X	X	X	
Write computer program specifications			X	
Develop system test plan			X	
Develop conversion plan	X	X	X	
(Note – all activities may apply equally to the conversion system in its own right)				
Prepare program component designs				X
Write program components				X
Test program components				X
Prepare user manuals and job aids				X
Test user manuals and job aids				X
Train users				X
Build system test files/conduct system test				X
Prepare site/install computer				X
Review system test results				X
Complete operating manuals				X
Train maintenance team				X
Hand over system				X

Fig. 10.1: Short checklist of typical tasks

The illustrative list in Figure 10.1 will do for many small projects, provided that the items on the list are seen as potentially subdivisible into further tasks by any convenient classification: department; subsystem; person; site; etc. So we may choose to define tasks as, say, Fact-finding department 1; Fact-finding department 2 ...; Interview User 1; Interview User 2 ...; Write Program 1; Write Program 2 ...; and so on. The list as it stands could be the tasks foreseen for a simple project with one user that required one small program to be written.

Questions

1 Suppose, at the end of the feasibility study, the overall plan includes an item Write Report Program. This is a simple, straightforward program and it is estimated that the task will take 15 man-days to complete – this includes program testing by programmer and analyst, program documentation and production of program operating instructions. How could this task be broken down into tasks suitable for the specific plan of the construction phase?   (10 min)

2 Suppose, at the end of the feasibility study, you have identified a program that will take more than 30 man-days to complete. How can this be broken down into tasks suitable for the overall plan?   (5 min)

10.2 ESTIMATION

The estimates made for overall plans and specific phase plans are of different types. With overall plans there is less certainty about what has to be done, the tasks conceived are larger and there is less incentive, or need, to invest time in making a precise estimate. Estimating for overall plans could be called coarse estimating, whereas estimating for phase plans is fine estimating.

Whether coarse or fine, the idea of making an estimate of the resources required to complete a task is wrong if it is thought of in the same way as estimating the length of a given piece of string. The piece of string pre-exists and its length is a matter of reasonably objective fact. The string cannot change its size to try and fulfil the estimate. Systems analysts and programmers, on the other hand, can and do modify their behaviour in the light of the estimates of time to complete the tasks. Estimates of resources required for project tasks tend to be self-fulfilling. It is not just a question of Parkinson's Law, 'Work expands to fill the time available for completion', although no doubt this sometimes plays a part. The estimate affects expectations of the quantity and quality of work to be done – how thorough testing is to be, what rarity of exception is to be handled by the system, what amount of idiosyncrasy is to be allowed for, and so on. The estimates we are speaking of tend both to **describe** the resources required and to **define** the work to be done. As the nature of the task is less objectively defined, so the self-fulfilling content of the estimate increases. It might be proper to speak of allocations rather than estimates, but the latter term seems universal.

The idea of a scientific approach to estimating is that regression analysis of previous times to complete a task will allow the derivation of a prediction formula which takes into account those variables which have a significant effect on task completion time. The argument in the preceding paragraph suggests that this approach can be valid only in a rather mature organisation with standards sufficiently well defined to allow a task to be conceived of as an objective thing. The organisation would also need to be large enough to have experienced a representative sample of tasks and, of course, completion times would have to have been reliably recorded. Pope (2) reports the US Army analysis, of 20 projects, which came up with a formula for very coarse estimates:

> total project man-months (project manager, systems analysts, programmers, operators) = (2.57 x number of output formats) + (5.1 x number of record types in database or files) + (0.12 x number of input transactions monthly).

Walston and Felix (3) at IBM identified 29 variables which significantly affected programming effort, in their analysis of 60 completed projects, of which the most significant was 'Customer Interface Complexity', subjectively rated as being less than, equal to, or greater than normal complexity. The projects involved generally look large and complex compared with projects typically undertaken by medium-sized data processing departments.

In the absence of large-scale analysis of objective tasks reliably recorded, estimators have little choice but to use intuition and experience to come up with an estimate which is at once predictive and prescriptive. This guesswork will be helped by a systematic record of the past kept in an estimators' log. In this, all estimators will record the estimates they make, the actuals experienced and the presumed reason for any variance. The estimates should be classified by type of task – fact-finding, interviewing, etc. The idea is that the estimator, facing a new estimate, can quickly review past instances to help him formulate the estimate for the present case.

Questions

1   You are undertaking your first project and have been asked to come up with a quick global estimate of total project costs. Should you use the US Army formula as a basis for your estimate?   (10 min)

2   Does the US Army formula have good face-value validity in context?
   (20 min)

3   One estimating rule of thumb for program development is '1 programmer-day per module plus $\frac{1}{4}$ day per module for link testing'. What question does this beg?   (2 min)

4   Testing the program takes as long as preparing it to the point of clean compile. Is this a plausible rule of thumb?   (5 min)

5   Brandon (4) proposed the following estimating rules.

> Analysis of existing system: 1 analyst-day per report or form in the existing system and 4 analyst-days per file in the existing system.
> Interviewing: $1\frac{1}{2}$ days per person, management or clerical staff;
>   2 days per person, supervisors;
>   3 days per person, technical staff.

Do these look as if they could be plausible in context? Can they be taken out of context?   (5 min)

10.3 INTERNAL CONSISTENCY

When making an estimate, should the estimator assume that analysts and programmers will apply themselves to their tasks without interruption, or should he make some allowance for sickness, holidays, training? If the latter, should these allowances swell the estimated time for each task, should a specific time be allocated to them, should they swell 'contingencies' or should they be accounted for in some other way, e.g. by assuming a four-day week when in fact a five-day week is worked?

The short answer is that any course of action is admissible providing the estimator keeps his various plans and estimates consistent with one another

TASK ANALYSIS

PROJECT: *SOE*

TASK: *Prepare Requirements Report*   EST. START DATE: *1·6·80*

EVENT NOS: TOTAL FLOAT: EST. FINISH DATE: *16·6·80*

DESCRIPTION: MAN/DAYS

Prepare appendices	*5*
Draft body of report	
⁻ *System description*	*2*
⁻ *Specimen inputs and outputs*	*3*
⁻ *summary and conclusions*	*1*
⁻ *contents and introduction*	*½*
Type report in duplicate	*3* *(typist)*
Proof-read draft and resubmit errors	*1*
Re-type errors	*1* *(typist)*
Collate two copies	*1*
Final check and submit	

EST. RESOURCES (PROJECT TIME): *14 analyst/days : 4 typist/days*

ACT. RESOURCES:

REASON FOR VARIANCE:

EST. DURATION: *11 days (2 analysts for 7 days, 1 typist for 4 days)*

ACT. DURATION:

REASON FOR VARIANCE: (ACT. START DATE: FINISH DATE:)

COMMENTS: *Much of the drafting work can be done as we go along must arrange typist availability.*

Fig. 10.2: Example task analysis. If forms like these are used, filing them in 'start date' order makes a reminder file for the project manager. After project completion, they can be filed under task name, along with forms from other projects, to make the estimators' log described in section 10.2

by making adjustments where necessary. Overall plans are usually made in ignorance of the specific persons who will undertake the tasks. There is usually no question of making specific provision for known holidays etc. and the estimator must assume that the work is to be done by fictitious 'standard' analysts and programmers. Plans for the next phase, by contrast, are usually drawn to allocate the work among the known project team, some of whom may have holidays or training scheduled to arise during the project. It will be essential to take these known absences into account when allocating the work, and to make allowances if any of the personnel concerned are expected to perform significantly differently from the standard. One workable way for organising for this problem is to:

  divide the team members' time into project and non-project activities;
  base overall plans initially on project time only, afterwards adding general provisions for non-project time and non-standard personnel;
  base phase plans on project time, adjusted for non-standard personnel, and known non-project activities;
  assuming the costing rates used for estimating the Cost of Development have been loaded for 'overhead', and therefore allow for non-project activity, calculate Cost of Development on project time only;
  get reports of actual time divided into project time and non-project time, using the same criteria for classification as was used in the original estimates;
  base calculations of actual Cost of Development for post-implementation evaluation etc. on project time only, using the same overhead loading factor as the original estimate (unless additional information has come to light which has caused you to believe that some other overhead factor would better reflect reality).

There is still plenty of scope for double counting or error in this scheme, but I think the project manager applying it can be reasonably sure he has avoided the worst pitfalls. The sponsor will also be given a reasonably fair view of estimated and actual cost of development.

If inflation is material, this should be allowed for in a manner agreed with the sponsor when formulating the project budget. If the estimates are to be the basis of the project manager's spending authority, they will probably need enlarging to allow for estimated inflation. If Cost of Development is estimated without allowance for inflation, then the actual Cost of Development should be calculated after discounting for inflation so that like is compared with like. Whether the actual inflation rate or the original inflation rate is used for this discounting will decide whether or not the project manager is accountable for inaccuracy in estimating inflation.

Question

1 Should a scheduled training course for a programmer working on a project be counted as project time or non-project time?   (5 min)

10.4 ELAPSED TIME AND CONTINGENCIES

With some estimates it may be envisaged that the resource cannot be applied continuously to the task, so the elapsed time to complete the task (i.e. the duration of the task) will be longer than the estimated man-days. For example, compiling and testing a small program may be thought to involve half-a-dozen test shots. If a programmer has unrestricted use of a computer for online testing, he might complete this task in one day. But if he is allowed only one batch turnaround per day, it will take him six days to complete the testing. For such tasks, the duration of the task must be estimated when making a plan. Of course, the corollary may be that only a portion of the resource is tied up for this extended time; in the example, it looks as though only one-sixth of a programmer need be allocated for the task duration.   However, programmers cannot be sliced up like cheese and it would be a mistake to assume that the programmer can manage six concurrent tasks on the batch turnaround in as little time as six consecutive tasks on the online turnaround. It would be sensible to plan for a maximum of, say, three tasks per programmer by allocating one-third of a programmer to the example task.

Probably the largest provision in an overall plan will be the provision for non-project time. This provision will probably lie between 25% and 50% of the estimated project time – the lower figure probably favoured by an in-house data processing department, the higher by a service bureau. Such provisions suggest that between 20% and $33\frac{1}{3}$% of an analyst's or programmer's time is not utilised by or chargeable to a project. The actual provision can be decided only after review of the particular data processing department, the type of projects undertaken and the method of recording project and non-project time.

How other provisions are treated will depend upon the project sponsor's attitude to risk. If he is prepared to take a 'swings and roundabouts' attitude to the project estimates, then provisions can be made on the basis of 'expected resources' (amount of resource that might be required, times the probability of the resource being required) or 'expected duration' (duration that might be required x probability of that duration). If the resource or duration is a continuous variable with a PDF, conceptually one is after the integral of each outcome times its probability; a weighted mean resource or duration – see section 11.3. If the sponsor is averse to risk and wishes to have secure estimates of project costs and duration, provisions must be made on pessimistic assumptions.

This leaves us with the question of reserves for unplannable contingencies. Some organisations choose not to permit such reserves in plans or budgets, on the grounds that it encourages sloppy estimating. On the other hand, it is a matter of common experience to project managers that unplannable events do occur, leading to unforeseen demands on resources. Depending perhaps on how much pessimism was built into the project estimates and, again, on the sponsor's attitude to risk, a small general reserve of 5–15% of time and cost seems proper. Beyond this, one must ask whether or not the project is sufficiently well understood to allow estimates to be made at all.

Question

1   Why might a service bureau expect their analysts and programmers to be only two-thirds utilised when an internal data processing department expects four-fifths utilisation?   (10 min)

ANSWER POINTERS

Section 10.1

1   The natural way to partition such a task depends on the available software – operating system, compilers and program development support utilities – and the usual programming practices and standards. The programming task might be partitioned into module (program component) tasks or into programming activity tasks, or into some combination of the two.

If program development is to be done by the construction of **small modules** – say, 20 or so source lines – which are to be separately compiled and tested before being linked together, then Write Module 1, 2, ..., n is a suitable set of tasks for detailed planning. This would leave such tasks as Make Detailed Module Plan beforehand and Link Test, Finalise Program Documentation, Prepare Operating Instructions and Final Review afterwards. Hypothetically:

Make detailed module plan	2
Write input formatting module	1
Write control module	1
Write report heading module	1
Write report detail line module	1
Write report footing module	1
Write page overflow module	1
Link test – programmer data	2
Link test – analyst data	1
Finalise documentation	1
Prepare operating instructions	1
Provision for difficult bug	1
Final review	1
	15 man-days

(To be sure I was on common ground with you, I have chosen a familiar example which is not very realistic unless perhaps this program is to be implemented on a microcomputer which has no high-level language; the program looks like a sitting target for report generating software such as RPG, Filetab, or COBOL Report Writer. In this case, 'Prepare Report Program Parameters, 2 man-days' could be a task replacing the module planning and writing.) On the whole, with the right support for this method of working, this is the approach I favour, since it leads to easily identifiable units of work and it is going to be clear whether or not each unit is completed.

If program development is to be in the monolithic style, the construction phase tasks could be entirely activity based: Plan, Code, Compile, Test, Finalise Documentation, Prepare Operating Instructions, Final Review, Provisions. There are in-between possibilities, too.

2   The answer to this question **could** be similar to the answer to question 1. However, my inclination is to find a large division of the program that can be made to split it into two or more smaller programs or program components (large modules).

Example   A validation program (over 30 man-days development effort) is to validate input prepared from a form which permits deleting, inserting or amending transactions. A deleting transaction is prepared on a card-type 1 (or card-image type 1), an inserting transaction on a card-type 1 followed by a card-type 2, an amending transaction on a card-type 1 optionally followed by a card-type 2.

This program is complicated because the physical structure of the input data does not match the message – the form. The validation program needs to check that the **form** is correct, but the physical limitations of the **cards** (or card-images) introduce new error possibilities that confuse the validation of the form (e.g. there may be a missing card-type 2 for an insertion, or a missing card-type 1 for an amendment).

I would divide this program into two, as follows.

a   A card validation program. This checks the sequence of card-types by transaction, reporting errors, and combines the valid cards where appropriate to produce a single record corresponding to the data on the original form.
b   A form validation program. This takes the records produced by **a** above and validates them for legal content.

If either of these programs were judged too large, they could be divided according to other criteria – e.g. program **b** could be split into validation of deletions, amendments, insertions respectively.

Section 10.2

1   Maybe. Imagine an estimator with no previous experience and no detailed insights into the project sufficient to allow him to formulate his own guess. For such an estimator, the US Army formula might make the best available evidence on which to base a prediction.

However, unless the estimator happens to have taken up employment with the US Army, or unless he has much more information about how their formula was derived than I have supplied, there is reason to believe that systematic differences may exist between the US Army and the organisation in the question. These differences may lie in the definition of a project, the definition or measurement of man-time, the definition of output format, record-type or input transaction, and so on. Some differences may be known - for example, the US Army formula does not account for the time of user personnel. The estimator who wishes to include such time in his estimate could make some adjustment in the light of the expected extent of user involvement. Other differences are unknown both in sense and magnitude. What the estimator does about this will depend on the sponsor's attitude to risk. This is discussed in section 10.4 on contingencies.

2   To have good face-value validity, the three variables in the formula should plausibly be the three principal determinants of project man-months.

Number of output formats seems very credible to me, since each output format calls for analysis, design and programming work. Obviously some output formats call for more work than others, so in applying the formula perhaps one ought to worry whether or not the particular output formats being dealt with are substantially unrepresentative.

Number of input transactions monthly is at first a little surprising since the complexity of a program, given that it has been defined, appears independent of the number of transactions processed by it. On the other hand, large volumes usually lead to more design problems in file storage and access method, and more need for tuning for efficient processing. Also, when large volumes are concerned, it is more likely to be decided that the computer system must deal with out-of-the-ordinary or exceptional cases, rather than leave them for manual processing. So on reflection, I warm to this variable.

Number of record types is not quite so plausible to me, since number of record types can be arbitrarily varied by the designer. Reducing the number of simple record types by the construction of a few large, complicated record types may actually increase the project man-months. A more credible variable to use would be the number of entity-types and relationship-types in a fully normalised data model. However, if there is a consistent relationship between these alternatives because of consistent design practices, 'number of record types' becomes more believable in context.

The last issue to discuss is whether or not we can think up a different variable which at face value has a greater effect than those analysed. One which comes to my mind is 'whether or not the system is an interactive, real-time one'. Interactive systems usually have more exacting design requirements - in the man-machine interface, in the technical design - than batch systems. I would not be surprised to find that an interactive system took twice as many man-months to implement as an equivalent batch system. Perhaps this concept is endorsed by the significance of Customer Interface Complexity, as found by Walston and Felix.

3   What is the definition of a module? An appropriate definition of a module for the purpose of this estimating rule is 'a piece of code which can be written and tested in a day'. This will be around twenty high-level language statements.

4   Considering a **given** program, it seems likely that testing time varies inversely with preparation time. In other words, the programmer can reduce testing time by increased program planning. A program can be cobbled together in quick and dirty fashion, but subsequent fault-finding and correction is likely to exceed initial preparation time. On the other hand, if attention is paid to good program structure, modularisation and desk-checking, testing will be less than preparation time.

One can imagine environments where programming habits, norms and standards are such as to make this rule of thumb plausible, but it is scarcely plausible for all environments.

5   They look plausible to me, but it would be necessary to understand what exactly is meant by 'Analysis of existing system' and 'Interviewing'. For the quoted time, I would expect 'Interviewing' to mean:

    plan set of interviews;
    arrange interviews;
    prepare interview guide;
    conduct interview;
    write up interview notes or discussion record;
    check back notes with interviewee;
    conduct follow-up interview if necessary.

Section 10.3

1   If the training given on the course is applicable to all projects, then the training is a general overhead and should be considered non-project time. This view may have to be moderated if programmer turnover was so high as to limit the chance of recouping the benefits of training on more than one project.

If the training gives a skill or knowledge which is useful only for the one project, it should count as project time.

If the training is particularly useful for this project but may be useful on others, then in principle it should count partly as project time and partly as non-project time in a suitable ratio. But few cases will call for such precision and it will be adequate in practice to count the training under the most relevant category.

Section 10.4

1   The service bureau does not have tame customers who will create projects or readily adjust their plans to accommodate the availability of analysts and programmers. When a service bureau analyst is 'between tasks' it is more difficult to find chargeable work for him to do than an in-house analyst.

Incidentally, it does **not** automatically follow from this that a service bureau quotation will be larger than an in-house one. Why not?

REFERENCES

(1)   Hice, G. F., Turner, W. S., and Cashwell, L. F., **System development methodology**, North-Holland, 1978.
(2)   Pope, D. J. M., Estimating the resources needed for ADP systems, in Frielink, A. B. (Ed.), **Economics of informatics**, North-Holland, 1975.
(3)   Walston, C. E., and Felix, C. P., A method of programming measurement and estimation, **IBM Systems Journal**, 16, 1, 54-73, 1977.
(4)   Brandon, D. H., and Gray, M., **Project control standards**, Brandon/ Systems Press, 1969.

11 Scheduling

11.1 NETWORK ANALYSIS

The purpose of the first three sections of this chapter is to explain some features of network analysis, not so much to impart any skill in this technique as to supply insights which are useful to the project manager.
 Although the value of network analysis is open to question, on balance I think it pays a project manager to sketch a network of his project or phase; and it is more worthwhile, the larger the project. Trying to draw the network is a good discipline for reviewing tasks and required resources, for identifying delays unconnected with consumption of resource and for getting a feel for the critical activities. On the other hand, having drawn a network it would be a mistake to believe it. Systems development projects are not a matter of putting together building blocks in some predetermined manner. A project, stripped of all the artificial structure we impose on it in order to explain, communicate and plan, comprises most of all a comprehensive exchange of ideas between sponsors, analysts, users, programmers, suppliers and operators. The tangible things such as stationery, program listings, user manuals and even hardware are not so much determinants of a project as incidental products of this exchange of ideas. Networks either emphasise the tangible or create unbelievably neat order. This order is based on a precedence requirement that exists mainly by convention or that is much more complicated than the project manager has the time or inclination to analyse. In spite of this, attention to precedence is essential for scheduling work, or we would risk asking for the system test to be completed before the feasibility study was started.

Question

1   The following activities have been precedence-ordered as in Figure 11.1.

A   Approve stationery (get users' approval of stationery design): duration 5 days.
B   Order stationery (call for stationery tenders, place order, await and check proofs): duration 20 days.
C   Await stationery: duration 20 days.

Is this precedence realistic?   (10 min)

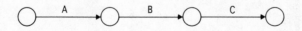

Fig. 11.1: Question 1, section 11.1

11.2 DRAWING UP A NETWORK

The activities in the precedence network comprise the tasks, which have an estimated resource requirement as previously explained, and the delays, which do not use resources.

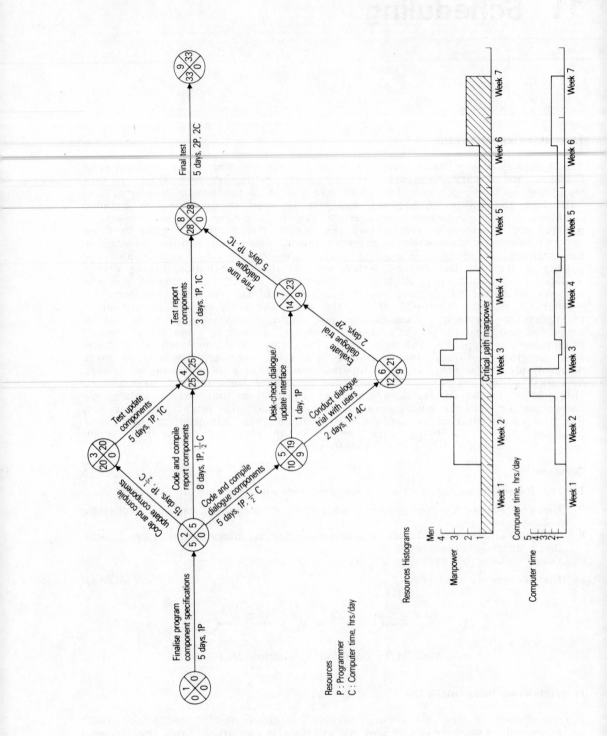

Fig. 11.2: Example network analysis

Features of network analysis are as follows (see example, Figure 11.2).

1   Give every network a single start event and a single end event. If necessary, a fictitious start activity should be created, e.g. 'Await authorisation'. Every activity will have this activity as a predecessor, so there will be no arrows unconnected at the tail, apart from this one. If necessary, a fictitious end event should be created, e.g. 'Final check'. Every activity will have this activity as a successor, so there will be no arrows unconnected at the head except this one. This avoids loose ends in the network.

2   The event circles can be segmented and annotated as in Figure 11.3.

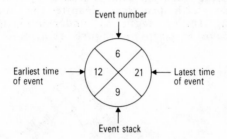

Fig. 11.3: Conventions for an event circle

Working from the start event, give each event a sequence number. The event at the end of an activity should be given a higher number than the event at the start of the activity. On a large network, this is not always easy to do by inspection alone. A systematic way is to assign the next number only to an event which is arrowed entirely from events already numbered. In other words, do not assign a number to an event that is arrowed from any unnumbered event. Should it prove impossible to follow this rule, then there must be a loop in the network; this is not allowed.

3   Assign zero to the earliest time of the start event of the network. Working in the direction of the arrows, add the activity duration to the earliest time of each event in order to give the earliest time of the successor event. Where a successor event is pointed at by more than one arrow, the latest of the alternative times should be entered (this is because the earliest time at which an event with several predecessors can be started is dictated by the completion time of the latest predecessor). Continuing in this way, the earliest time calculated for the end event of the whole network is therefore the earliest possible completion of the project.

4   Set the latest time of the end event of the network to equal the earliest time of the end event. Working now against the direction of the arrows, subtract the activity duration from the latest time of each event to give the latest time of the preceding event. Where a preceding event has more than one arrow emanating from it, the earliest of the alternative times should be entered (this is because the latest time at which an event with several successors can be completed is dictated by the starting time of the earliest successor). Continuing in this way, the latest time calculated for the start event of the network should be zero; if it is not, a calculation mistake has been made.

5   For each event, calculate the event slack by subtracting the earliest time of the event from the latest time of the event.

The total float of an activity is the amount of time it can be delayed, beyond its earliest start, without prejudicing the completion date of the whole project. Subtracting the earliest time of its start event from the latest time of its end event gives the maximum span for completing an activity. Subtracting the activity duration from this span gives the total float of the activity.

Activities with zero total float are therefore critical to completion of the project in the shortest possible time. Successive critical activities make one or more critical paths from the beginning to the end of the network, joining events with zero event slack. The project manager will wish to pay special attention to these critical activities, assigning them to the most reliable persons and reviewing methods for completing them.

Question

1   The explanation just given will no doubt have struck you as tortuous if you had little existing idea of what network analysis is about. Network analysis is easy to do, with practice, despite the apparent need to have a Ph.D. in legal English or logic to understand the explanation. Try applying steps 1-5 above to complete Figure 11.4, and identify the critical path. (30 min)

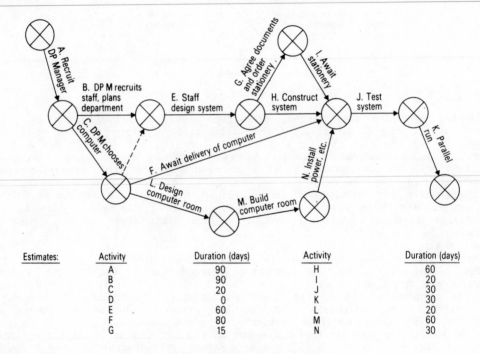

Estimates:	Activity	Duration (days)	Activity	Duration (days)
	A	90	H	60
	B	90	I	20
	C	20	J	30
	D	0	K	30
	E	60	L	20
	F	80	M	60
	G	15	N	30

Fig. 11.4: Question 1, section 11.2

11.3   UNCERTAIN ACTIVITY DURATIONS

In practice, few activity durations are as deterministic as implied by their use in network analysis. When we try to recruit the DP manager, perhaps we get our advertisement out within a couple of days, maybe we get a set of promising replies in five days, possibly we conclude the interviews and make our selection within a further five days and then the candidate accepts within three days, needing to give only one month's notice (say, 22 working days) to his present employers. If everything goes so smoothly, we could have the new man within 38 days. On the other hand, it may be that after advertising we find we have had no suitable candidate after ten days have elapsed, we re-advertise, the most promising candidate now responding cannot come for interview for another ten days as he is going on holiday, we eventually appoint him but he is on three months notice to his employers. The activity duration would have exceeded 100 days.

An approach to this problem is to model the distributions of the activity durations and to use this to derive the distribution of project completion times. A number of simplifying assumptions have to be made if this is to be easy enough to permit hand calculation, so the most that can be claimed for the method is that it allows the project manager to get some appreciation of the sensitivity of his project completion date to the uncertainty in the estimates.

The PERT suggestion is that the Probability Density Function (PDF) of each activity duration should be modelled by estimating the most optimistic duration (O), the most pessimistic duration (P) and the mode or most likely duration (M). The durations O and P should be judged so that there is only 1% chance that the activity duration will lie outside these boundaries. This will be aided if there are records of a large number of observations of similar activities. In the absence of such records, we may settle for an expert's guess of the duration (see section 7.1). If the durations are measured, we can conceive the model as describing objective reality; if guesses are used, we are on firm ground only if we claim that we are modelling the larger opinions the estimator ought to have if he were a logically consistent person. The practical difference is that in the latter case we must worry about the estimator's bias.

Provided that one or two activities do not swamp the whole network, the distribution of the network outcomes is not particularly sensitive to the shape of the PDFs of the activities, e.g. whether or not they are skew or normal. The total network outcome is sensitive to the mean of the activity durations and their variance (square of the standard deviation).

The PERT suggestion for estimating mean duration is

mean = $(O + 4M + P)/6$

This seems reasonable for dealing with activities which have a sharp peak in the PDF; indeed, it could be argued that M is not a bad approximation to $(O + 4M + P)/6$. I feel that most activities included in DP projects have rather flat PDFs, as well as rather skew ones, with the mode usually closer to O than to P. For this reason, I generally prefer the more cautious estimate of the mean $(O + M + P)/3$: a triangular distribution. When working by hand, there is nothing to prevent the analyst from estimating the mean for each activity duration by a fresh argument in each case, should he think this worthwhile.

PERT suggests estimating variance by assuming that the range O to P contains six standard deviations, so the variance is $((O - P)/6)^2$. This seems reasonable when dealing with measured cases. With guessed cases, there is some evidence that estimators, far from giving a range which contains 99% of cases, consistently underestimate this span and offer boundaries which in fact contain only about two-thirds of cases. For this reason, I prefer the more cautious assumption that the spread O to P is a biased estimate and contains only two standard deviations. This means that estimated variance is $((O - P)/2)^2$. Again, the analyst can argue each case separately should he so wish.

The analyst can now use the means to calculate earliest start times as before, and so determine the critical path of the project as if those means were fixed activity durations. This critical path is not deterministically the critical path; in fact, it is not even necessarily the most probable critical path. Let us call it the candidate critical path. If there is plenty of float or low variance on the sub-critical activities, the variance of the candidate critical path, found by summing the variances of all the activities on that path, is a fair estimate of the variance for the whole project.

If any sub-critical path does not have much float, or has a lot of variance, this will tend to increase the mean project completion time.

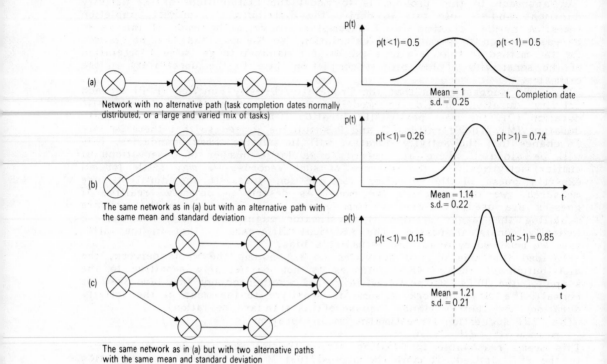

(a) Network with no alternative path (task completion dates normally distributed, or a large and varied mix of tasks)

(b) The same network as in (a) but with an alternative path with the same mean and standard deviation

(c) The same network as in (a) but with two alternative paths with the same mean and standard deviation

Fig. 11.5: Alternative paths in the network, even non–critical ones, tend to delay mean earliest completion and to change the standard deviation (usually by diminishing it, as here). Example figures are for independent alternative paths which share the same mean and standard deviation

Figure 11.5 illustrates this effect and shows how the presence of alternative paths makes it increasingly likely that the mean completion time of the candidate critical path will be exceeded. It is very difficult to propose a simple hand method for analysing these consequences in a network of any complexity, yet if they are not taken into account the mean project duration may be significantly under–estimated. One possible solution is to examine each segment of the candidate critical path, looking for alternative paths around that segment with little float or much variance. If an alternative path is found, the table in Figure 11.6 can be used to revise the mean and variance estimated for the duration of the candidate critical path segment.

Questions

1   The following estimates (guesses) have been made for the network of Figure 11.4, p.100 (O, M, P):

A   38, 60, 120   H   50, 60, 90
B   40, 62, 150   I   15, 20, 40

Standard deviation of the path with the shorter mean duration, as a multiple of that duration →

Standard deviation of the path with the longer mean duration, as a multiple of that duration

Ratio of the means of the alternative paths (longer mean over shorter mean)	SD shorter	2 x	2 s	1 x	1 s	1/2 x	1/2 s	1/4 x	1/4 s	1/8 x	1/8 s
1	2	1.6	0.7	1.5	1.1	1.5	2.0	1.5	3.7	1.5	7.4
	1	1.5	0.6	1.4	0.8	1.4	1.3	1.3	2.2	1.3	4.3
	1/2	1.5	0.5	1.4	0.6	1.3	0.8	1.2	1.3	1.2	2.4
	1/4	1.5	0.5	1.4	0.6	1.2	0.7	1.1	0.8	1.1	1.3
	1/8	1.5	0.5	1.3	0.6	1.2	0.6	1.1	0.7	1.1	0.8
0.8	2	1.6	0.7	1.5	1.1	1.5	2.0	1.5	3.7	1.5	7.2
	1	1.5	0.6	1.4	0.8	1.3	1.2	1.3	2.0	1.3	3.9
	1/2	1.4	0.5	1.3	0.7	1.2	0.8	1.1	1.2	1.1	1.9
	1/4	1.4	0.5	1.2	0.6	1.1	0.7	1.1	0.9	1.0	1.1
	1/8	1.4	0.5	1.2	0.6	1.1	0.7	1.0	0.8	1.0	0.9
0.6	2	1.5	0.7	1.5	1.1	1.5	1.9	1.5	3.6	1.5	7.2
	1	1.4	0.6	1.3	0.8	1.2	1.1	1.2	1.8	1.2	3.6
	1/2	1.3	0.6	1.2	0.7	1.1	0.9	1.1	1.1	1.1	1.7
	1/4	1.3	0.6	1.2	0.7	1.1	0.8	1.0	0.9	1.0	1.0
	1/8	1.3	0.5	1.1	0.7	1.0	0.8	1.0	1.0	1.0	1.0
0.4	2	1.5	0.7	1.5	1.1	1.4	1.9	1.4	3.5	1.4	7.0
	1	1.3	0.6	1.2	0.8	1.2	1.1	1.2	1.7	1.2	3.0
	1/2	1.2	0.6	1.1	0.8	1.1	0.9	1.0	1.0	1.0	1.3
	1/4	1.2	0.6	1.1	0.8	1.0	0.9	1.0	1.0	1.0	1.0
	1/8	1.2	0.6	1.1	0.8	1.0	0.9	1.0	1.0	1.0	1.0

Fig. 11.6: Table of factors for revising the estimate of a candidate critical path segment (results found by stochastic simulation). Table entries in the form x, s show the mean completion time if the two paths are independent, x, and the standard deviation of completion time, s. The factors x and s are to multiply the mean and standard deviation of the candidate critical path segment. Example: A candidate critical path segment has mean 20 and standard deviation 5. An alternative path around this segment has mean 16 and standard deviation 8. We enter the table at the column for 5/20 = 1/4. The row is dictated by 16/20 = 0.8 and 8/16 = 1/2, so x = 1.1 and s = 1.2. The revised estimated mean for the candidate critical path segment is 20 x 1.1 = 22, and revised standard deviation is 5 x 1.2 = 6. (In calculating the table factors, the activity durations were assumed to have truncated normal distributions. It should be noted that it is quite possible for the independence assumption to be defeated, e.g. by bad management.)

C	2, 15, 45		J	25, 30, 60
D	0, 0, 0		K	15, 25, 60
E	45, 55, 100		L	15, 20, 25
F	60, 80, 100		M	50, 60, 120
G	10, 14, 30		N	25, 30, 60

Accepting the assumptions of section 11.3, what is the mean and standard deviation of the project completion time?   (60 min)

2 Of what possible value is it to know the standard deviation of project completion time?   (5 min)

3 What target date for completing the project in question 1 above has 95%

probability of being reached? What is the probability of reaching a target of 362 days?   (5 min with tables of the normal distribution)

5   If uncertain activity durations have been allowed for in estimating project completion time, should a reserve for contingencies still be allowed when formulating the final target date?   (5 min)

6   Calculating project variance by summing activity variances contains the assumption that activity variances are independent. Is this reasonable?

(5 min)

11.4 BAR CHART

By systematically working through the network, histograms of week-by-week requirements for analysts and programmers can be built up (Figure 11.2) by tallying the resources assumed in the estimates. These histograms may disclose a need to use up some of the total float by rescheduling tasks so that peak resource requirements are avoided. Planning to use up the float in this way, by a late start of some activities, increases the likelihood that a sub-critical path will delay overall completion; the target date may need revision as discussed in section 11.3.

If a task is replanned so that it has negative total float, a new critical path is being created. If this replanning is at all complex, it may be desirable to redraw the network, this time taking account of the planned dependences caused by limited resource availability (computer packages exist to do this, of course, and their use may be worthwhile for a large project).

For a phase plan, the project manager will wish to assign the work to his team. A bar chart (Figure 11.7) is quite a good aid for communicating this plan and, if started and completed tasks are highlighted by colouring or similar, gives an at-a-glance record of actual progress made compared with that planned. On the whole, a bar chart is more easily constructed if one starts from the end of the project and works back, but where there is choice, any float remaining should be allocated at the end of the tasks involved so that they are planned for their earliest start. Specific non-availabilities of team members (vacations, training) should be catered for. Critical path tasks should be assigned to the most reliable personnel. Tasks assigned to junior and trainee staff should have their duration suitably increased - 50% and 100% increases respectively are commonly-used figures. Again, this re-estimating may affect the critical path and the expected phase completion time.

The bar chart aims to give personal targets for the team members. The idea is not to plan to use up reserves, so if there is any general reserve for contingencies, this should be allocated at the end in the overall plan. Similarly with provision for uncertain activity durations - it is impossible to say which activities will over-run, so the increased elapsed time attributable to uncertainty is just allocated as a block at the end of overall or phase plans. Other provisions may be best allocated where they fall - if provisions have been included in the original estimates of task duration, this will happen naturally.

The phase plans may therefore add up to less than the overall plan, the difference being the contingency allowances. In effect, this difference is attributable to the difference between the personal targets of team members, based on the expected (mean) activity durations - the project team's target - and the target which is acceptable bearing in mind the costs, benefits, uncertainties and attitudes to risk - the sponsor's target. This is **not** a question of setting 'challenging targets' to team members. If this is desired, shorter activity durations should be planned. But it is my opinion that analysts and programmers will have quite enough challenging targets in a project without the planner trying to make them more so.

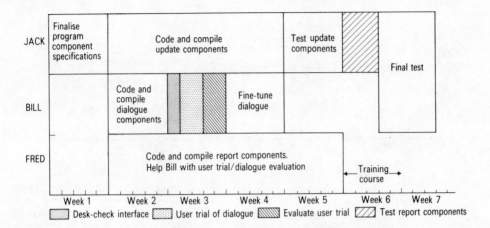

Fig. 11.7: A possible allocation of the network of Figure 11.2 to three programmers. The dialogue trial and evaluation has been delayed beyond the earliest start to smooth out the resource requirement. Jack is the senior programmer and has the critical activities. Fred is a trainee and has been allowed about double the originally-planned time to complete his assignment

Questions

1 Section 10.4 spoke of a provision for non-project time. Should such provision be added to the timescale of an overall plan, a phase plan, both or neither?   (10 min)

2 Suppose providing for inexperience of staff on the phase bar chart increases the elapsed time of the phase. Should the overall target date be revised to account for this?   (10 min)

ANSWER POINTERS

Section 11.1

1 Suppose you had asked users to approve the stationery design. After five days, four out of five users who should approve have given their OKs, but the remaining one has been called abroad and will not be available for three days. Suppose the timing of complete approval was critical to the project deadline and you had every reason to expect approval from the final user. Would you not at least prepare and perhaps issue the call for tenders, in the expectation that even if a change was required, a small change could be negotiated within the tender price? If so, the dependence of B upon A is not as clear-cut as suggested. However, the dependence of C seems reasonable; you cannot be 'awaiting' the stationery until the ball is entirely in the printer's court, i.e. until you have checked his proofs.

The dependence of B upon A is an example of a 'conventional' dependence which has to be fastened upon to treat the problem with a reasonable expenditure of effort, but which in fact disguises a much more complicated lead/lag dependence. The majority of dependences chosen for networks of systems projects, in my experience, are of this type.

Section 11.2

1

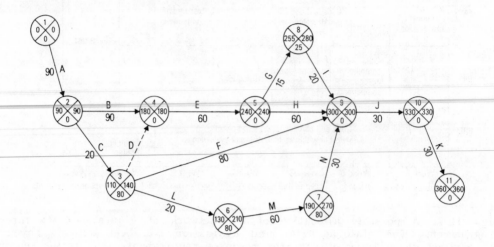

Fig. 11.8: Answer to question 1, section 11.2

Critical path: 1, 2, 4, 5, 9, 10, 11.
Critical activities: A, B, E, H, J, K.

Section 11.3

1

	O	M	P	(O+M+P)/3	s=(P–O)/2	s^2
A	38	60	120	73	41	1681
B	40	62	150	84	55	3025
C	2	15	45	21	21.5	462
D	0	0	0	0	0	0
E	45	55	100	67	27.5	756
F	60	80	100	80	20	400
G	10	14	30	18	10	100
H	50	60	90	67	20	400
I	15	20	40	25	12.5	156
J	25	30	60	38	17.5	306
K	15	25	60	33	22.5	506
L	15	20	25	20	5	25
M	50	60	120	77	35	1225
N	25	30	60	38	17.5	306

Mean project completion time without consideration of alternative paths: 362.
Candidate critical path: A, B, E, H, J, K.
Variance of candidate critical path: 6674.
Standard deviation of candidate critical path: 82.
Inspection suggests that the following alternative paths have negligible
effect: C, D as an alternative to B; C, F as an alternative to B, E, H;
G, I as an alternative to H. The path C, L, M, N, with mean 156 and
standard deviation 45, is an alternative to the critical segment B, E, H,
which has mean 218 and standard deviation 65. In Figure 11.6, this
corresponds approximately to the case where the two paths each have a
standard deviation about a quarter of their means, and where the shorter
path has a mean 0.8 times that of the longer path. This suggests that the

mean of B, E, H should be multiplied by 1.1, giving 240, and the standard deviation by 0.9, giving 58.5.
Revised mean project duration: 73 + 240 + 38 + 33 = 384.
Revised variance: 5915.
Revised standard deviation: 77.

2   The estimator can use it to predict the probability of reaching the target date or to pick a target date which has a given probability of being reached.
  The estimator can adjust his commitments to the sponsor, when discussing target dates, to reflect his understanding of the uncertainty.

3   384 + (77 x 1.66) = 510 days. 22/77 = .29; 1 - .6141 = .3859. Say 40%.

4   Perhaps such managers have discovered that the main benefit of network analysis, for them, is that it gives a basis for action by an orderly and logical arrangement of tasks. They are after 80% of the benefits of network analysis for only 20% of the effort. More power to their elbows.
  Although I am rather sceptical about the accuracy of the mean and standard deviation of a project, derived from estimates of uncertain activity durations, I like the way it reminds the project manager that things are not all cut-and-dried. It helps prevent over-optimism and glib promises. Nonetheless, it is not suggested that the methods advanced in this section are easy to put into practice; rather, it is the hope that this exercise will act as a moderation for the project manager who wishes to plan mostly by using his intuition.

5   Yes. The difference between the deterministic target date and that adjusted for uncertain activity durations is a provision, attributed to an analysed cause. A reserve may still be desired to allow for something else overlooked or unknown, i.e. an overlooked dependence or task, or an unplannable event.

6   Quite possibly not. For example, poor staff morale could be a systematic source of variance which tended to make all activies over-run; and high morale could have the opposite effect.

Section 11.4

1   Non-project time was a provision for vacations, training and slack time between tasks. The estimates were based on project time, so to get total man-days for scheduling, non-project time must be added; and to get total cost, non-project time must be allowed for by providing for overhead in the costing rates. However, vacations, training and slack time are catered for specifically in the elapsed-time phase plan, i.e. they are known and schedulable, so there is no need to provide for non-project time. Slack is also accounted for automatically in the elapsed-time overall plan, but maybe not vacations, training and unplannable events such as sickness. So the answer is that an overall plan should contain some provision for non-project time, but not that attributable to slack, since the slack element is accounted for in the total float. The phase plans should schedule the non-project activity and should not include extra general provision for non-project time.

2   Section 10.3 said 'Add general provisions for non-standard personnel' to overall plans. If this was done for elapsed time as well as man-hours, and the general provision was adequate, the specific provisions in the phase plan are drawing from this general provision. If these drawings are in line with what was expected, there is no practical need to revise the overall plan.
  If the drawings exceed what was expected, this may be a symptom of inadequate original provision for non-standard personnel. If for this or any other reason the provision is now thought inadequate, the overall target date should be revised.

12 Project control

Monitoring means getting information about the actual status of the project so that accomplishments can be compared with plans. Things to monitor are as follows:

actual versus planned achievements;
actual versus planned costs;
actual versus planned quality.

In addition, there is the less plain idea of actual progress-for-cost against planned progress-for-cost, discussed in the next section.

Actual versus planned achievements
This monitoring will be helped if all tasks that are established lead to the production of 'deliverables', i.e. tangible evidence of achievement. At a high level (overall plan) the products of the team's effort in a phase are considered deliverable to the sponsor or steering committee (see chapter 9). At a low level (phase plan), the product of an individual's effort could be considered deliverable to the project manager.

At the high level, progress reports should be submitted to the project steering committee at end-of-phase checkpoints. A written report from the project manager should cover:

accomplishments since the last report;
relationship to goals;
fresh problems encountered and proposed solution;
plans for the next phase;
revised overall projections, or confirmation of original projections.

At the checkpoint there should be a participative review (walkthrough) in which the project manager takes the committee through the project achievements. This is the committee's opportunity to audit the achievements and to question the assumptions behind the projections.

At the low level, there should be checkpoints at which the team members report their achievements, problems and projections to the project manager. These reviews may be weekly or scheduled to coincide with the planned completion dates of phase-plan activities.

On a large project, where there are frequent re-estimates of the project completion date, a trend may be revealed by monitoring a plot of estimated target date on one axis against the date of the estimate on the other.

Actual versus planned costs
The principal cost in a project is usually manpower. The principal problem in monitoring costs is getting reliable reports of manpower usage, or even getting any reports at all. Probably the best compromise is to try to establish a ritual that in the last few minutes of each day, all analysts and programmers record how they have spent their time, while it is still fairly fresh in their minds. A form such as the one illustrated in Figure 12.1 is suitable. In completing the form, team members should be aware that hours-per-day should add up to the standard hours in a day, except

TIME RECORD

Name.....J Smith........

Staff code ...1 0 5...

Week ending.........23 March.........

PROJECT	TASK	ACTIVITY	HOURS THIS WEEK							EST. HOURS TO COMPLETE TASK
			MON	TUE	WED	THUR	FRI	SAT	SUN	
SOP	DES	D	7	7	7	7	7			35

See over for project and non-project activity codes

Fig. 12.1: Analyst and programmer time record

in the case where the overtime is paid. Similarly, estimated hours to go is an estimate of the number of hours, as they will eventually be recorded on these forms, needed to complete the task.

From these time records, together with records of computer time used and records of other expenditure on the project, a total of actual expenditure on the project can be built up week by week for comparison with the budget. By costing out the estimated hours to go on tasks started but not completed, and adding on the cost estimates of tasks not yet started, a revised expenditure forecast can be made. This costing may be accomplished by a special manual system, or through the organisation's regular budgetary control system if suitable, or through a simple computerised time-recording system such as PROJECTMANAGER from MSP Ltd, or by some combination of these. An example of a project cost report from time records is given in Figure 12.2 overleaf.

Non-project time should also be recorded and reported as an aid to future estimating.

As with target date, a running plot of project expenditure forecasts against dates of forecast may reveal a trend.

Actual versus planned quality

There is also scope for review of the quality of the work done when the regular checkpoint reviews of achievements are made. Lack of time and lack of willingness to get down to a detailed level may limit the effectiveness of this type of quality assurance. Quality control by committees is quite widely advocated, presumably on the basis that review by many pairs of eyes is more likely to spot a fault. However, each committee member may hope that the **other** members have found the time to make the detailed scrutiny of the papers which is needed to gain the desired assurance of freedom from deep-seated faults. If none of the members read the papers in detail, the effectiveness of the committee review is diminished. Despite

TASK		THIS WEEK	TOTAL TO DATE	EST. TO GO	FORECAST TOTAL	ORIGINAL ESTIMATE	VARIANCE
ANALYSIS	MAN–HOURS	0	27	0	27	35	–8
	COST	0	405	0	405	525	–120
	EXPENSES	0	23	0	23	0	23
	TOTAL COST	0	455	0	455	560	–105
DES	MAN–HOURS	35	70	35	105	70	35
	COST	525	1050	525	1575	1050	525
	EXPENSES	0	0	0	0	100	–100
	TOTAL COST	525	1120	560	1680	1220	460
TOTAL	MAN–HOURS	35	97	35	132	105	28
FOR	COST	525	1455	525	1980	1575	405
PROJECT:	EXPENSES	0	23	0	23	100	–77
SOP	TOTAL COST	525	1575	560	2135	1780	355
FUTURE	TOTAL COST			7000	7000	7000	

COMPLETION COST   9135   8780

17% COMPLETED (TOTAL TO DATE/FORECAST TOTAL) AS AT WEEK ENDING 23 MARCH

Fig. 12.2: Example project cost report from time and expense records

this, there is something to commend a walkthrough before a committee when the quality assurance of the deliverable calls for several different types of expertise.

An alternative procedure, stressing individual responsibility for quality control, is to require that deliverables under control be approved by a quality inspector, possibly even to the extent of requiring his signature before work can go forward. Fagan (1) reports that detailed inspection of programs by an individual is probably more effective than walkthrough with a group. When a user is asked to approve the feasibility report or system specifications, he is in effect being asked to be an inspector in this sense. For technical quality, analysts and programmers within the data processing department may be designated inspectors for special purposes – finished program inspectors, program specification inspectors, file design inspectors, business procedure design inspectors, security inspectors, etc. – who can build up expertise in their specialism. The inspector should share with the original author responsibility for the quality of the work. Just how far this inspection is taken depends on what level of quality assurance is desired and the weaknesses in present practice.

Questions

1   If actual costs to date are less than budgetted costs to date, should the project manager be congratulated?   (1 min)

2   Should a post–implementation evaluation be done by a committee or an individual?   (5 min)

12.2 THE STATUS INDEX

If a project is behind schedule, the benefits are at risk of being delayed, and this is a serious matter. Nevertheless, it is less serious if the project is also under–spent; the sponsor might be getting value for money even though the timing is out.

If a project in progress is over–spent, this may be a serious matter. But if the project is also ahead of schedule the sponsor may yet get his value for money.

The Status Index is an indicator of project progress which tries to take both of these factors into account. It is useful as a broad concept, and possibly of practical value as a high-level indicator when budgetary control is exercised and projects are too large to permit frequent reworking of the forecasts of completion time and cost.

In essence, the index measures

$$\frac{\text{achievements relative to plan}}{\text{costs relative to budget}}$$

An index value of 1 means that achievements are in accordance with what was expected for the money spent. An index over 1 means that progress is greater than expected for the money spent. An index less than 1 means that less progress has been made than was expected for the money.

Measuring the actual total achievements relative to the planned achievements is difficult to do with precision. A simple but crude method is to measure project progress by reference to the tasks in progress in the phase plan. The task in the phase plan with the least total float is selected to represent overall progress. Positive float shows the number of days or weeks ahead of schedule; negative float the number of days or weeks behind schedule. If the phase plan was drawn up to start ahead of (behind) the original schedule, this gain (loss) of time should be added (subtracted) to give the total current float.

Of course, other tasks may have more float that the selected task, so this method will under-state achievements. It is probably better to err on the side of conservatism by letting this under-statement stand.

Measuring achievements relative to planned achievements to date,

$$\text{achievements relative to plan} = \frac{\text{duration to date}}{\text{duration to date less float}}$$

Considering how this formula will work at the end of the project, it will be seen that if the completion is early (duration to date is less than planned), relative achievements are greater than 1 (achievements exceed those planned). If completion is late (overall duration is greater than planned, so there is negative total float) relative achievements are less than 1.

Measuring actual costs relative to the planned costs to date,

$$\text{costs relative to budget} = \frac{\text{actual costs to date}}{\text{actual costs to date plus budget saving}}$$

If completion is achieved at less cost than budgetted, relative costs are less than 1; if at more cost, more than 1.

The Status Index can now be defined more precisely:

$$\text{Status Index} = \frac{\text{duration to date}}{\text{duration to date less float}} \times \frac{\text{actual costs to date plus budget saving}}{\text{actual costs to date}}$$

where float is measured relative to the overall plan (phase float plus float of the most backward activity in progress in the phase plan).

The Status Index can be calculated weekly and plotted as the project progresses. Figure 12.3 overleaf shows some possible interpretations.

Questions

1   The overall plan for project phases was as follows.

Day 0   Start analysis phase.
Day 30   Start design phase.
Day 70   Start construction phase.
Day 110   Start trial phase.
Day 130   Expected handover.

The construction phase started ten days late. The least advanced task in the construction phase plan was two days ahead of schedule when reviewed

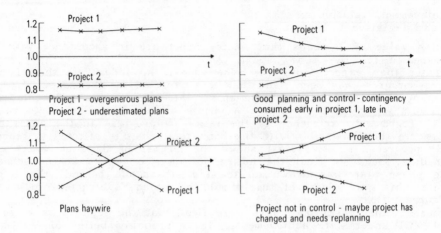

Fig. 12.3: Interpretation of Status Index plots. It is suggested that index values between 0.9 and 1.1 are considered to be within normal range, not requiring control action

20 days into the construction phase. Project expenditure at the time of the review was £76 540. Overspending totalling £5760 had been disclosed. What was the Status Index when the review was made?   (15 min)

2   The project in question 1 above was finally handed over on day 136 at a total cost of £107 400. The original budget was £96 000. What was the Status Index at project completion?   (5 min)

12.3 TAKING CORRECTIVE ACTION

The monitoring will be of little avail if there is no corrective action that can be taken, cancellation of the project being the only possibility. What can be done if the Status Index shows a gloomy trend, or if quality standards are not being met? Figure 12.4 shows some of the possibilities.

Rework plan

It may be some time since the phase plan was originally drawn up. Perhaps new information has come to light which opens up new planning possibilities for increasing the extent to which tasks may be undertaken simultaneously, reducing total duration, or which allow a reduction in non-project time or expense by, for example, rescheduling work, hiring alternative equipment or reducing travel requirements.

Reorganise individual priorities

The assignments of each individual should be reviewed to make sure that they are working on the most critical activities. Ensure that each team member knows his personal priorities.

Increase motivation

My experience has been that analysts and programmers are highly motivated when there is work to be done. Misdirected enthusiasm is more likely to be a problem than lack of it.

 If there are problems with motivation and they are long-standing, quick

Possible action \ Type of variance	Under-achievement on planned tasks	Overspending on budget	Poor work quality
Rework plan	✓	✓	—
Reorganise individual priorities	✓	—	—
Increase motivation	✓	—	—
Redeploy resources	✓	✓	✓
Increase method guidance or supervision	✓	—	✓
Draft in help to cover resource shortfall	✓	—	?
Draft in help above what was planned	—	×	?
Training course	×	×	✓
Revise targets	✓	✓	✓

Fig. 12.4: Possible corrective actions. A tick means the action is an apt counter-measure for the type of variance; a dash means that it is probably ineffective; a cross means that the action is probably counter-effective

reversal is highly unlikely. Particular obstacles or distractions, such as personality conflicts within the team or personal problems, may be amenable to treatment.

Redeploy resources
If time is the problem, are the critical activities allotted to the persons who will complete them soonest? If cost is the problem, are the tasks scheduled to the most suitable persons, the ones whose productivity is greatest on the type of work concerned? If quality is the problem, are sensitive activities to be done by the most skilled or conscientious people?

Increase method guidance
On-the-job supervision and advice from a knowledgeable project manager or specialist can quickly increase productivity, especially where junior or under-trained staff are concerned. Business procedures design, design of computer files and procedures, program design and testing are activities which can often be improved.

Training
Training through a more formal programme is a longer term solution and cannot usually be considered in mid-project unless there is time and cash in hand.

Drafting in help
Help from outside the project team may cover a shortfall of resources, but if the help is not suitably trained and ready to go the effect may be neutral or even counter-productive. Adding help to a fully-manned project with the aim of accelerating progress is a forlorn hope; unless, perhaps,

there is a great need for method guidance and the outsiders can provide it. The effect on work quality could be beneficial or harmful, depending on the calibre of the outside help relative to the insiders.

Drafting in outside help is a more plausible course of action when:

the DP department has a functional division between analysts and programmers, tending to discourage informal ways of working into which it is difficult to slot a newcomer;

the systems and programs are designed on a highly modular basis, leading to small, complete chunks of work which can be reassigned;

exacting standards of documentation are set;

quality monitoring and sign-off are practised;

popular and portable methods, languages and equipment are chosen;

systems are kept simple.

Revising the target

This step is, of course, an admission of defeat, but the responsible project manager faces this squarely, and early. Note that speeding a project through by reduction of planned quality control or testing is revising the target; requiring sign-off by inspectors may discourage project managers from falling prey to this temptation without declaring it. The revised targets of completion date, cost or quality will need the approval of the project sponsor. Failing this, the project must be killed off.

Questions

1   What can project managers do if projects keep over-running or exceeding budget?   (5 min)

2   What can project sponsors do if projects keep over-running or exceeding budget?   (2 min)

ANSWER POINTERS

Section 12.1

1   Is actual progress less than planned progress?

2   Such an evaluation is not only a sort of quality assurance. Judgements may be made about fault or blame which have political consequences in the organisation. In some respects, the evaluation may be like a trial, weighing conflicting evidence. I have heard lawyers say that they have more confidence that a trial before a Judge alone will arrive at a proper conclusion than a trial with a Jury. On the other hand, trial by Jury is more ostensibly fair. In rather the same spirit, I would personally back a post-implementation review made by a high-calibre individual in whom I had confidence. But where conflicting interests are present, a committee is more likely to be accepted by all parties.

Section 12.2

1   Duration to date $= 70 + 10 + 20 = 100$.
Float $= (-10) + 2 = -8$.
Actual costs to date $= 76\ 540$.
Budget saving $= -5760$.

$$\text{Status Index} = \frac{100}{100 - (-8)} \times \frac{76\ 540 + (-5760)}{76\ 540}$$

$$= \frac{100}{108} \times \frac{70\ 780}{76\ 540} = 0.86$$

It is more cautious to neglect contingency allowances, when calculating float, if the place in the project where the contingency was allowed has not yet been reached.

2    $\dfrac{136}{136 - (+4)}$ x $\dfrac{96\ 000}{107\ 400}$ = 0.92

Section 12.3

1 Review or revise estimating procedures and planning procedures for
   setting targets.
   Increase staff training; review or revise methods of analysis and
   programming.
   Change staff.
   Improve monitoring information or procedures.
   Improve potential to use outside help.

2 Train the project manager.
   Change the project manager.

REFERENCE

(1) Fagan, M. E., Design and code inspections to reduce errors in program
     development, **IBM Systems Journal**, **15**, 3, 182–211, 1976.

13 Personnel recruitment and selection

It is something of a truism that the quality and quantity of labour-intensive work done in an organisation is sensitive to the personal qualities and skills of the people employed. For many organisations, the largest single determinant of continued success is the calibre of their personnel. This is surely true of data processing departments. The recruitment and training decisions may therefore be the most important decisions made in the data processing department. The effects of a good or bad decision here will echo through the department, if not the organisation as a whole.

Unfortunately, recruitment decisions are not clear ones to make. The information needed to make good choices is not easily acquired and may be unreliable or misleading. A good decision calls for substantial personal efforts on the part of the present highest-calibre people in the department, yet these are the same people whose time is being called on for a hundred other urgent purposes. After the effort has been made, the recruiter who finds his carefully reasoned predictions or hopes dashed or denied - that high flier, full of potential, who left before he had contributed anything lastingly useful; that solid programmer of unpersonable appearance, destined for the back room, who has blossomed into the most reliable and respected analyst - may be excused for wondering if he might not just as well have chosen his staff at random.

I start from the premise that most people could do most jobs, if they wanted to badly enough and they were trained well enough. You do not have to be a genius to be an analyst or programmer; indeed, some managers have concluded that too much genius is bad for profits. At the other extreme, a person with much less than average intelligence has little hope of learning a skill such as programming within any reasonable time-scale. This leaves a lot of people in between who **could** do such a job well. The main difference between these people, from the point of view of their effectiveness in employment, is how badly they want to do a good job - their motivation; how much skill they bring with them - their attainments; and how quickly they can aquire further skills - their intelligence or aptitudes. Other factors, such as physique or disabilities, personal circumstances and remaining personality, are less important to their effectiveness. Personality may affect how much a man is liked, how pleasant he is to work with, but practically any personality can be effective at programming or analysis: a survey by the National Institute of Industrial Psychology (1) found only one personality trait - expediency - that seriously correlated with analyst success, and that not much; and in any case some personality traits in this sense can be learned, like a skill - a man can learn to be expedient, if that is what is wanted. In short, the prevalent idea that there is a particular stereotype suited to programming and analysis, with its corollary that the recruiter is seeking this special type of person, is not justified.

Does all this mean that the DP recruiter might as well throw dice and appoint applicants at random? Not quite; although on the score of motivation alone such a strategy has something to be said for it since it is supposed that any person who applied for and accepted a post would thereby self select someone with a more than average leaning to do the job. Applicants could be selected at random **if** the employer was prepared and able to 'motivate' them should they insufficiently motivate themselves; **if** the employer is prepared and able to train them to fill the gap between their present skills and those the employer desires; and **if** the employer is prepared to wait whatever length of time training takes.

Recruitment strategy and criteria for selection are best decided in the light of the employer's plans and capabilities for motivation and training. An employer with no such plans or capabilities needs fully skilled contractors or self-starters; and, of course, he must fish for these in a smaller pool.

Questions

1   What factors, would you suggest, should most influence an employer's decision whether to recruit skilled staff or trainees?   (10 min)

2   Define in your own words the following terms as used in this section: motivation; attainments; intelligence; personality.   (10 min)

13.2 JOB DESCRIPTION

Before searching for the right man to do the job, it might be worthwhile to have a good idea of what the job is. Later, having got the man, it might be desirable to review the job to make sure it is right for the man. (Lest there should be some awful misunderstanding, I should specify that the word 'man' is used in its widest sense of 'human being'. If a sexual distinction is intended, I shall make this clear in context.)

Perhaps the recruiter, as a result of his experience and knowledge (e.g. through having done the job himself), can describe the requirements of the job by introspection. This description will be most helpful if the recruiter can define the job in terms of clearly observable tasks, i.e. objective achievements which anybody can recognise. This **task analysis** is difficult to do without any prompts to memory or imagination; some comprehensive lists of tasks for data processing personnel can be found in books by Chandor (2) and Dickmann (3). In practice there is a limit to how far one can take objectivity, and the recruiter may have to be satisfied just to avoid the worst cases of vagueness.

Failing personal knowledge, the recruiter is obliged to call for expert suggestions for tasks, or to observe or interview people doing the job. Consideration should be given to the relative importance of the tasks in the sense of the extent to which ability to do each task contributes to the overall effectiveness of a person doing the job. This importance may be unrelated to the proportion of time spent doing the task. For example, an applications programmer may spend rather little of his time Planning Programs and Planning Test Data compared with, say, Coding Programs or Documenting Programs, yet the former abilities are more important than the latter. With a large-scale investigation, objective techniques such as principal component analysis or factor analysis may be used to sift methodically the tasks observed or proposed, but this is not usually feasible in the average data processing department.

Methods of describing jobs in terms of desired personality **traits** are dubious, especially in the present context of establishing job features as an aid to selection. This is for two reasons. Firstly, there is little convincing evidence that particular personality traits, of the type usually measured, give rise to particular job abilities in data processing. A list of desired traits for systems analysis or programming looks either like a list which could suit any job or a description of some impossible paragon. By comparison, ability to do the **tasks** is unquestionably required. Secondly, even if we knew which traits to look for, establishing whether or not they exist in a candidate is either difficult or error-prone. There is much more hope that we can discover the candidate's ability to do the **tasks**.

Questions

1   Criticise this job description:

Applications Programmer.
Tasks:
a   liaise with analysts and users;
b   understand specifications;
c   plan and code programs;
d   thoroughly test programs;
e   document programs;
f   supervise junior programmers;
g   assist with programmer recruitment.   (20 min)

2   Prepare a task analysis for a systems analyst (about 20 items expected).
                                                                 (20 min)

13.3 SEARCH

With the post defined, a search can be made for a suitable person. In the data processing job market, supply of labour has on the whole failed to meet demand. Thus for most jobs at most times, the DP manager's strategy should be to search extensively and to deter as few candidates as possible; an opposite strategy might apply if the market state were reversed. The number of candidates applying for a post is usually much more sensitive to the state of supply and demand than to any factor within the control of the recruiter. The recruiter's strategy is to counteract the prevailing state as much as possible.

Search **inside** the organisation should not be neglected. An insider has some knowledge of the company, knowledge which may be valuable for the work to be done and which will reduce or eliminate the induction period of orientation or training that an outsider would need. It is easier to get a reliable appraisal of an insider and it is more feasible to stipulate a probationary period with a promise of the previous job, or an alternative job, if things do not work out. Insiders are usually more cheaply recruited, are less likely to quit to take up posts outside and will often be satisfied with lower salary levels (although these are rather cheeseparing consider- ations: there is no point in saving on recruitment, turnover and salary costs if the person appointed is no good at the job). A policy of internal search can aid staff relations throughout the organisation by opening up additional career paths, but there may be some risk of envy of those selected or the creation of tension between department managers if they feel their best staff are being poached. Insiders may need more technical training than outsiders, of course. DP managers are sometimes wary of recruiting inside in case managers of other departments put forward their most dispensable staff for consideration. A climate where a user department manager advances his **best** men for work on data processing projects in his own department, because of a belief in the importance of the project, is a happy one.

Inside or outside, an advertisement may be required, for placement in the press, for internal circulation, or to go on notice boards. If it is to go in a place where people do not usually actively look for job advertisements, an eyecatching feature will be required, e.g. colour, illustration, typesize. For an advertisement in the 'situations vacant' columns, the type of job – e.g. systems analyst, programmer – is probably the right thing to emphasise to gain attention.

In the usual state of the job market, the advertisement should aim to avoid inessential discrimination against unsuitable candidates and should aim to encourage response. The following points may help.

Salary   Do not omit to mention a figure or range. Do not put it too low.

The job   Summarise the features of the work and any special prospects.

Location   State it. If not a major city, give information about the location. Give information about relocation assistance.

Attainments   State the minimum attainments or qualifications of the applicant in terms of what he should be able to do, or the training or experience he has had. Avoid stipulations which are more precise or ambitious than you really mean. If you are tempted to state the preferred or ideal attributes of a candidate, ask yourself if it would not be better either to make the attribute a firm requirement or to state that training will be given to candidates who lack it.

Response   Give a name and telephone number to contact for further information, being a manager or supervisor who has knowledge of, or responsibility for, the work. Anonymous employers, requests to deal in writing only or with a personnel department who do not have technical knowledge, demands for curriculum vitae, stipulation of artificial closing dates – all tend to discourage response.

There is another important but elusive quality of an advertisement which has a bearing on its effectiveness. This is the overall impression it makes on the reader; a blend of impact, clarity, aesthetics, credibility and warmth.

Questions

1 How could you get outside analysts and programmers other than by advertising?   (2 min)

2 Many advertisements emphasise the advanced technology – hardware or software – involved in the work, because this often proves attractive. Do you think it could be worthwhile to introduce advanced technology, which would otherwise be unnecessary, for the purpose of increasing the attractiveness of the work to potential analysts and programmers?   (5 min)

13.4 SELECTION

Details in an application form, apart from information about attainments directly relevant to a task in the job, are not helpful in determining how well an applicant may do a job. There has been no reliable relationship discovered between success in data processing employment and age, sex, marital status, location, general education level, interests. Some of these, for example sex, are related to staff turnover, but since it is not obvious whether staff turnover is a good or bad thing, since it is illegal to discriminate by sex, and since turnover may be much more sensitive to other factors such as management style, the relationship to turnover is somewhat academic. Even information about past achievements may not be entirely helpful since it is easy for an applicant to overstate or understate his achievements (for example, Dickmann reports how one US employer found that 30% of applicants taken on had overstated their previous salary).

This stresses the need to verify attainments by inspection of diplomas and by taking up references where these are pertinent to attainment. Referees should be telephoned, not written to, since written references tend to be bland or partial, and give the recruiter few clues as to the credibility of the referee. If the referee is not known personally or by reputation, and is not a present supervisor of the applicant, there can be little credibility attached to the reference anyway.

Judgements about attainment formed during interview are prone to bias. One well-known class of bias is 'halo effect' by which a single feature of an interviewee - good or bad - tends unfairly to colour the interviewer's overall judgement. This feature may be, for example, one question well (or badly) answered, one particular achievement or failure which stands out. Other biases may be based on subliminal clues; for example, people who wear glasses are subjectively judged to be more intelligent than those who do not. An articulate candidate may be favoured, but there is no objective evidence to support articulateness as an attribute which leads to success in data processing jobs. The interviewer may be blind to deficiencies in a candidate which are the same as his own, or place too much store on strengths which he has himself. Altogether, if an interviewer selects on the basis of his subjective feelings after asking general questions at interview, i.e. questions which do not test attainment, he might be almost as well off throwing dice to make his choice.

This is not to say that interviews are useless. They are an opportunity for the interviewer to sell the post and the corporation. If the interview is conducted by the intended supervisor, it may help to confirm the supervisor's authority. The supervisor's subjective feelings about the compatibility or sociability of the employee may be important, although such judgements made on short aquaintance are of course by no means infallible. Perhaps most of all the interview allows an exchange of information which helps both parties to adjust their expectations to reality: the employer was looking for an ideal candidate, the applicant was looking for an ideal job - better they understand reality sooner than later.

It seems that the best predictor of the future success of an applicant is his past achievements. The interview has the best validity, in the case of an experienced applicant, if the interviewer asks questions or gives tests which explore the applicant's achievements. The interviewer must weigh the evidence of achievement and value it according to its confirmation that the candidate can do the tasks required in the job.

Question

1   If experienced applicants are so hard to come by, is there much point in judging candidates according to what little experience they have? If not, should one bother to ask questions about past achievements?   (5 min)

13.5 APTITUDE TESTS

An aptitude test, such as the IBM Aptitude Test for Programmer Personnel, can be useful for predicting an inexperienced person's achievements on a programmer training course, although a general intelligence test would do nearly as well. Using an aptitude test is probably particularly valid if testing an unselected population with a view to training those who do well on the test, provided that they have other characteristics believed to augur well for their eventual performance in employment.

A programmer aptitude test must be considered less discriminatory when the candidates have already been selected according to other criteria, e.g. their intelligence or general or specific educational qualifications. An aptitude test which has a proven ability to predict success in training may give little help, or may even be counter-effective, in choosing those candidates who will perform well in their eventual employment. This is because the abilities and skills necessary to score well on a training course are not necessarily the same abilities and skills as are needed to do the job. An unproven aptitude test is a subjective assessment and has about as much (or as little) chance of picking out a good candidate as other subjective methods.

A recruiter who wishes to use an aptitude test should establish for himself the validity of the test for the purpose to which he wishes to put it. For example, if using a proprietary test to pick inexperienced candidates for posts as programmers, the following approach could be adopted.

a Check on the test's precision. Precision, or reliability, is the ability of the test to come up with the same answer each time it is administered to a particular candidate. Candidates' ability to improve scores slightly with practice is not considered important, but if there are wide differences between a candidate's score in one test session and another a fortnight later, or if there is inconsistency between his score on, say, even-numbered questions compared with odd-numbered questions, the precision of the test is suspect. The test documentation should report on the reliability studies made.

b Consider the face validity of the test. In other words, do the skills apparently called for in the test bear a close relationship with the target skills? The skills in business programming that are widely thought to be the most important are:

1   ability to plan a program;
2   ability to check out a program;
3   ability to understand the assignment given.

I have not seen an aptitude test which I thought had good face validity for item 1, except in the rather general sense that to make a plan is intelligent behaviour and most tests call for some sort of intelligent behaviour - but this is hardly specific enough to justify the particular forms of aptitude test which can be found. Checkout involves the hypothesis of bugs and the mental conception of data which would refute the hypothesis. Arithmetic problems or figure series or any test of precise mental reasoning or logic seem reasonable here, although there is an added dimension of persistence in checkout which perhaps is important. Tests involving long problem statements may test the same skill as is required for understanding of programming assignments.

Many tests were constructed at a time when more emphasis was placed on a programmer's ability to construct algorithms, his knowledge of the syntax and semantics of programming languages and his ability to do assembler language programming than is the case nowadays, and this does little for their face validity.

If a test lacks face validity, this does not rule it out completely since there may be some relationship between the tested skills and the target skills which is not understood by the tester. Under these circumstances, though, the tester should require other, very much more convincing, evidence of validity before having any faith in the test, and he should demand a higher standard of proof than that which might be acceptable if the test were face-valid.

c Check the validity studies reported in the test documentation. Do the testees who were used in the study come from the same culture as, and have similar education to, your applicants? Were they selected for the tests using similar criteria to those you use for selecting your applicants? Are the criteria used in the study, for deciding how successful were the subjects, the same as the criteria you will use for deciding how successful are your programmers? If the answer to any of these questions is 'no' - and with the tests I have inspected, at least one of the answers has been 'no' - then you must discount the published validity study and conduct your own.

A popular validity test is 'concurrent testing', whereby the test is applied to existing programmers who are placed in rank order of proficiency by their supervisors. The worst weakness of this method lies in the ordering by the supervisor, who is in effect being asked to give his judgement of overall utility when multiple criteria are present (see chapter 4). If this is accepted, it should also be accepted that a programmer may be valued **because** his strengths are different from those of other programmers; he fills a gap. The possession of such a strength could lead to halo bias in the supervisor's judgement. More importantly, an aptitude test which is validated according to a sole criterion such as supervisor's ranking is at best a blunt instrument since a low-scoring candidate may have a particular programming strength which should be highly prized precisely because it is complementary to the strengths of the existing programmers.

Questions

1   Should an aptitude test be applied to candidates applying for posts as experienced programmers?   (2 min)

2   'An aptitude test which has proven ability for predicting performance in training may be counter-effective in choosing candidates who will perform well in their eventual employment' (p. 120). Explain in your own words what this means.   (2 min)

3   It is often said that an aptitude test is just one item of information which should be considered along with other information about the applicant. Can you think of an argument for not taking aptitude test results into consideration?   (3 min)

ANSWER POINTERS

Section 13.1

1   The supply of skilled staff in the market.
   The urgency of the employer's plans, i.e. how soon the skills are needed or how much delay is permissible in system development.
   Employer's experience of, and facilities for, training.
   Availability of suitable outside training.
   Constraints on ability of employer to compete for skilled staff (e.g. rigid payscales).
   Constraints on ability of employer to compete for retention of staff he has trained.

2   **Motivation:** Willingness or drive to act or achieve.
   Attainments: The skills held by a person, resulting from his intelligence, training and experience. I would distinguish this from **achievements** by defining the latter as the things done by a person which call upon his skills. A person may have attained high skill but achieved rather little (because, for example, he has not had the opportunity); but if he has good achievements then he must also have good attainments.
   Intelligence: General learning ability or problem-solving ability. An **aptitude** can be considered a sort of specific intelligence; an ability to learn a specific skill or to solve a particular type of problem.
   Personality: The result of the collected and integrated components of a person's behaviour (including intelligence, aptitudes, attainments, motivation). The many components, when separately identified or measured (for example, thoroughness, sociability, resourcefulness, expediency, objectivity, dominance, curiosity, initiative, empathy ...) are called personal characteristics or personality traits. There is a vagueness attached to these words in everyday usage, and the (only?) reliable way of being more precise is to let the method of measurement define the characteristic. Hence the apparently cheeky definition of intelligence: intelligence is what is measured by intelligence tests.

Section 13.2

1   General criticism: insufficient detail, insufficient objectivity, no apparent attention to relative importance.

Points c, d and e are perhaps the most objective, especially if there exists a standard against which the quality of these activies can be judged. But, for example, does 'programs' mean 'all programs, of any type'?

Point b could perhaps be objective if there was a standard for specifications, and 'understanding' is revealed by lack of need for further explanation of the specification when the program is prepared.

Points a, f and g are particularly vague. Taking g as an example, does it or does it not mean that the applications programmer's duties will include:

drawing up recruitment and training plans (which classes of employee?);
writing job descriptions based on task analyses (which jobs?);
choosing search method:
designing advertisements;
corresponding with applicants to arrange interviews;
interviewing applicants;
testing applicants' attainments or aptitudes;
advising successful and unsuccessful applicants of the outcome of their applications;
agreeing pay rates and conditions of service;
etc?

2   a   Identify the participants in system development.
   b   Propose methods of participation.
   c   Find out system evaluation facts, user requirement facts, design decision support facts.
   d   Document existing or proposed systems to National Computing Centre standards.
   e   Prepare and check out a data analysis entity–relationship diagram.
   f   Design business procedures for processing data.
   g   Design interactive dialogues.
   h   Design input and output forms and displays.
   i   Design codes and business procedure controls.
   j   Define database file and record content and record layout.
   k   Choose file organisation and access method.
   l   Define computer runs and procedures.
   m   Design security and recovery procedures.
   n   Write reports for the participants describing feasibility, proposals, detailed specifications.
   o   Write user manuals.
   p   Prepare and give user training courses.
   q   Plan for conversion.
   r   Conduct system test.

This is of course just one possible list, for a rather general–purpose systems analyst. Which items are most important will depend a lot on the particular environment.

Section 13.3

1   By using an employment or staff selection agency, by poaching staff, by using contract labour.

Poaching (picking out a known person in another employment and making him an attractive offer) is generally frowned upon. Whether this is because of the tone of secrecy and enticement in such an action, or because employers believe that if the practice were widespread it would work to their collective disadvantage in the long run, or for some other reason, it is difficult to say.

labour is a viable alternative to recruitment provided that the contract management – choice of contractors, contractor standards, quality assurance, project control procedures – is taken seriously by the purchaser.

2 Some employers, to my knowledge, have decided that it is. If the staff obtained by this method make slower progress than normal because they are learning how to use the new technology, this is a counteracting factor.

There is an element of deceit in this which I am uncertain about. The dilemma is rather like that posed by the worst commercial advertisements; I do not condone the phoney product differentiation, the unwarranted fulsome praise from some personality prepared to prostitute himself, the weasel words and other widespread tricks of the advertiser, but I can hardly deny that they are effective.

Just where the border lies between honest persuasion and deceit is not clear (I am talking ethics, not law). I suppose we each have to decide for ourselves about this. I like to vote with my feet and systematically avoid products which are sold trickily; and I wouldn't apply for a job where I thought the advertiser was not wholly genuine.

Section 13.4

1 If all applicants have few relevant attainments, the differences of attainment between them do not amount to much. Questioning about attainments is a weak basis for selection in this case. However, the selected candidate will need training. Questioning about achievements, and other evidence of attainment, is helpful to determining the deficient skills for the tasks contemplated, and hence the training required.

Section 13.5

1 Only if it has been validated under those circumstances. As far as I know, none has. I have much more confidence in relevant attainments, such as is evidenced at interview or by referees, degrees or diplomas in relevant subjects, professional qualifications. If experienced personnel are in short supply, it is possible that the need to submit to any sort of test may discourage acceptance of jobs; but a sensitive interviewer should be able to counteract this.

2 The greater the score on the aptitude test, the worse may be the programmer. This is only a possibility, although Reinstedt (3) in his 1966 research into the IBM aptitude test of the day found an organisation with such a negative correlation, albeit on a sample size too small (10) to be considered reliable. He also found a more reliable relationship that those who scored very highly on the test tended to be ranked by their supervisors lower than those who scored only fairly highly.

3 The aptitude test is one of the few quantified measures that will be available and may receive undeserved weight. If the aptitude test result is middle range, it affects judgement little and the result might as well not have been obtained. If it is high or low, halo bias may lead the recruiter to have an unwarranted favourable or unfavourable impression of the candidate.

REFERENCES

(1) Crawley, M., and Morris, J., Computer personnel selection – 1: Systems analysts, NCC Publications, 1970.
(2) Chandor, A., Choosing and keeping computer staff, George Allen and Unwin, 1976.

(3) Dickmann, R. A., **Personnel implications for business data processing,** Wiley, 1971.

14 Performance planning and appraisal

14.1 PERFORMANCE PLANNING

The purpose of performance planning is to allow a manager and subordinate to reach agreement over what is expected.

From the manager's point of view, if he is concerned for results, he gains because a well-stated definition of what is expected will help ensure that the subordinate's efforts are directed to the ends desired by the manager. In the absence of such definition, it is more likely that the subordinate will misconceive the aim or have misplaced emphases. An example could be a programmer who spends much of his time tuning his program code, when the manager believes there is a surplus of computing resource; perhaps the manager is more interested in thorough testing, documentation or early completion. It is open to the programmer to change his behaviour somewhat to meet what is desired (see Weinberg, 1) but in the absence of an explicit agreement, there is every chance his actual efforts will be off-beam to some extent.

If the manager is concerned for the subordinate's development and training, systematically defining what is expected helps draw out those points on which the subordinate's abilities are deficient. Provided that the analysis of abilities is equally systematic, the gap between desired and actual performance provides a reliable guide to coaching and training required. This helps avoid unnecessary wide-spectrum training, which is both costly to the organisation and less interesting to the trainee when it covers old ground.

If the manager is concerned for the subordinate's humanity, well-stated objectives can increase the subordinate's self-reliance by giving him an opportunity to deliver the agreed performance satisfactorily, using his initiative and with minimal supervision. This method of working is likely to enhance or preserve job satisfaction, at any rate of personnel who invest themselves in their work.

From the subordinate's point of view, he stands to gain responsibility, and from this increased job satisfaction and an opportunity to demonstrate his abilities. If the targets are objectively stated, there is less opportunity for bias on the part of the manager when the time comes for appraisal. The analysis of his training needs may allow him to grow in the job, taking promotion should he wish.

Questions

1 What are the preconditions that would allow a programmer intuitively to deduce what is required of him?   (5 min)

2 Could a programmer have a better understanding of what is required than has his manager?   (3 min)

3 Would you say there is increased or reduced need for performance planning when the nature of the job dictates that the jobholder has a lot of discretion in his work?   (3 min)

14.2 AGREEING OBJECTIVES

If attention has been paid to quality standards and controls, to standard deliverables and to defining Targets for specific projects, a large part of analysts' and programmers' individual objectives will have been defined as a by-product. When assignments are given according to the project plan, it is plain that an individual's objective is to complete the assignment within the planned time, in accordance with standards, in such a way that the quality controls are passed and the Targets are reached. Since the idea is to **agree** the objectives, it is preferable for the personnel who are to execute the plans to have participated in drawing them up.

The terms of reference of such assignments should note any special objectives which are not covered by the standards or Targets. For example, a program specification should state the target source or object size and target execution time, unless any reasonable size or time is acceptable.

Many organisations, particularly larger ones, choose to have a more formal cycle of performance planning in which manager and subordinate meet periodically (e.g. yearly, half-yearly, quarterly) to review past performance and to agree the subordinate's targets during the coming period. This is an opportunity to define the subordinate's individual Targets in accordance with the defined KRAs for the unit (in the definition of which he has participated; see section 1.3). For system development staff, the major Target may be simply to carry out agreed assignments as they arise during the period. However, there may be other Targets which run across the boundaries of these assignments. For example, suppose Staff Productivity were a KRA of the data processing manager. The programming manager may see this enlarged into, say, Non-project Time and Program Development Time. The manager's Target for Program Development Time might be an average of 25 tested instructions per programmer per project-time day, to be reached in the last month of the planning period. In the programmers' performance plans, there may be included a Target for each programmer which aims to produce this overall average. The Target for a particular programmer will be agreed in the light of his present productivity, the language he uses, the type of work usually assigned to him and the expected impact of plans for improvement.

A record of these agreed Targets should be made so that an equitable review can be made when the subordinate is being appraised. Some organisations use a standard form such as in Figure 14.1 overleaf. This helps management training and increases manager mobility. It can form the basis of a personal record of employee performance which is helpful to senior management, particularly in large organisations, for making systematic objective reviews when looking for candidates for promotion, training, reassignment, etc. For development staff, individual project assignments and achievements should be systematically recorded. These assignments should form part of the performance plan and appraisal.

Questions

1 When a person participates in the definition of his assignment and target date, this is conducive to personal commitment to meeting the targets. Should the manager accept the subordinate's idea of suitable performance, assuming he (the manager) would find such performance acceptable?   (5 min)

2 What factors should influence the lapse of time planned between successive performance planning/review sessions?   (5 min)

3 What conditions should be met to ensure the objectivity of the Program Development Time MOE mentioned in the text?   (5 min)

4 It has been said of public administrations that promotions are governed too much by seniority and paper qualifications and too little by true ability

PERFORMANCE PLAN

For ... J. Smith ...   Position ... Programming Manager ...   Period ... 6 months to 1st Nov ...

Key Result Area (in priority order)	Target (in priority order within KRA)	Exceeded	Met	Partly met	Little done	No action	Notes
Staff	Reduce programmer turnover from 40% to 20% during period		X				35% turnover
	Introduce team programming by 1st September			X			Had to postpone own training
Program development costs	Reduce program development costs to 20p per tested instruction in next accounting period	X					19p
Production program efficiency	Reduce average test shots to 2.5 per module by 1st October without reducing test rigour	X					
	Reduce run time of customer ledger update by 20%, by end October	X					
	Eliminate sort transfer files - all programs with run time over 10 mins to be own-coded by end October						
Program quality assurance	Introduce program design and code Inspection and sign-off procedures by end August	X					40% reduction

Fig. 14.1: Example performance plan

in the job. Discuss possible reasons for this being said.   (10 min)

14.3 PERFORMANCE APPRAISAL

It is natural that a subordinate should link his appraisal with pay and prospects. In my opinion this is very proper – a person's rewards should be (partly) governed by the results he achieves. However, it might be best to put those matters aside when counselling a subordinate on his perform- ance, since there are determinants of rewards other than results – corporate or departmental profitability, government policy or guidelines, time since last review, relativities within the department or corporation or in the local or national environment.

A humane approach to appraisal is for the manager to hold no secrets from his subordinate. This is a more difficult policy for a manager to execute than one of secret appraisal. It is a prerequisite of open appraisal that a manager has the confidence of his subordinate.

A suitable procedure for open appraisal is for the manager to invite the subordinate to an appraisal discussion. At this interview, the performance plan and project assignments for the past period can be reviewed, noting and discarding any obsolete objectives, and the subordinate's achievements can be graded (see right-hand side of Figure 14.1). The manager should encourage the subordinate to analyse his own performance, reaching agreement if possible. Specific strengths and weaknesses should be identified.

The causes of any failed performance should be analysed. Maybe the subordinate was at fault. Maybe the manager was at fault, by failing to declare explicitly what was required; by failing to give the subordinate the required authority or opportunity; by failing to give him supporting information or method guidance; by failing to supply suitable training or by failing to give suitable reward. Maybe neither party was at fault; the failure was beyond prevention because of external factors. The manager should encourage the subordinate to analyse causes, reaching agreement if possible. Specific causes should be identified.

The performance, and the causes of it, are in the past. There is no point in delving unnecessarily into history. The main thing about appraisal is to improve the future, so the major part of the appraisal session should be taken up with discussing possible actions and coming up with a definite plan; see section 14.1.

Questions

1 Many performance planning and appraisal schemes in large organisations require the manager to write his overall appraisal on the form. There is also a requirement for the subordinate to sign the form and a space for him to give a dissenting opinion if he desires. What are the pros and cons of this arrangement?   (10 min)

2 Should the subordinate be given a copy of the plan and appraisal form when it is completed?   (1 min)

3 The 'possible actions' in the text are cast in the context of possible cures for lack of performance. How would you see 'possible actions' if the subordinate has no lack in his performance?   (2 min)

4 Should the appraisal cover personality weaknesses?   (5 min)

ANSWER POINTERS

Section 14.1

1 What is 'required' of the programmer is not an objective fact but is

determined by the manager, and the manager's manager, and so on up a hierarchy, ultimately to all the powerholders or stakeholders in and around the organisation. So if the programmer is to deduce all that is required, without being told by his manager, he would have to gain intelligence of all the plans and intentions of the organisation. He could deduce some of what is required by having intelligence about some of the plans, of course.

2 Yes, possibly. If one accepts that 'what is required' is defined by the requirements at the top, then a programmer who receives intelligence equal to that received by his manager, and has powers of insight or deduction at least equal to his manager's, may have a better understanding. However, one must count this as unlikely. Firstly because the manager has probably been selected at least partly for the sake of his above average insight or deductive powers; and secondly because a subordinate usually receives or seeks less intelligence for objective-setting than does his manager. So the probability is that the manager has a better understanding of what is required than the programmer.

3 Increased need. The objectives of a job which has little discretion, e.g. keyboard operating, are quite patent. They do not need spelling out because there is little scope for misconception. The objectives of a job with much discretion, e.g. systems analysis, are obscure. There is plenty of scope for misconception.

Section 14.2

1 If the manager has more experience than the subordinate, he may be able to form a more realistic performance target. If the manager accepts the subordinate's estimate, achievement on this target is more at risk. This may have repercussions on overall targets.
  People differ widely in their attitudes to setting themselves targets. Some people are over-ambitious and will set themselves such demanding targets that they have little chance of reaching them, or at least they have a good chance of regretting their suggestion. Some people, who are perhaps averse to risk, make self-assigned targets which are so easily within their compass that they do not explore their potential. I think it a proper use of a manager's judgement that he should try to persuade or encourage either type of person to adopt more realistic targets.

2 (1) The rate at which objectives/plans are likely to change and need revision.
  (2) The expectations of the subordinate, his age and experience in the job. To a school-leaver, three months between reviews may seem a long time. A trainee needs more guidance and review than an experienced man.

3 The terms 'tested instruction', 'programmer', 'project-time day' should be defined. The MOE should be measured. 'Tested' could mean tested in accordance with a standard, or tested sufficiently to pass quality-control inspection. 'Instruction' could mean an executable source line, provided that some standard of coding exists if the language permits multiple statements per line or multiple lines per statement. If there is a distinction between, say, systems programmers and applications programmers, or if there are analyst/programmers, the basis for finding the average should be determined beyond dispute.

4 It might be said because it is true. It is a tenet of many public administrations that not only should fair decisions be made, they must be seen to be fair. If the only objective evidence to support a promotional decision is seniority and paper qualification, then completely defensible decisions can be made only on this evidence.
  It might be said even though it is untrue. In this case, the critic is

biased or misinformed. In the absence of objective evidence of attainments, though, it is impossible to refute convincingly the suggestion that ability plays insufficient part.

It may be partly true. For example, promotion may be governed not by seniority etc. but by the subjective opinions of selection boards and referees. Bias may mean that these opinions misjudge the true abilities. Again, if there is no recorded measurement of performance, the truth cannot be found and the suggestion of bias is hard to refute.

This is not to say that performance measurement will remove all these difficulties at a stroke. Faced with objective evidence, it is quite possible that boards or referees will decide that the only thing proved is that the wrong MOEs were chosen in the first place. All one can hope for in this case is that in the long run refinement of the chosen MOEs through debate will make things better for all concerned.

Section 14.3

1 It makes the manager's appraisal clear – a purely verbal appraisal is open to misinterpretation or even subsequent dispute. It means the employee's opinion is available in any review behind closed doors – otherwise only the manager's opinion is apparent. It is a check that policy concerning performance appraisal is being carried out by the manager.

The main disadvantages are that it might encourage dispute or 'bush lawyer' attitudes, or that heightened formality makes for awkwardness and deters a genuine appraisal effort. The success of any sort of performance planning and appraisal scheme is determined most of all by the personal relationships and mutual confidence between manager and subordinate. This climate must be right before the appraisals can work.

2 If open management is the policy, clearly 'yes'.

3 Possible ways in which the subordinate can realise his potential for greater responsibility or more skilled work.

Many appraisals will concern part of each; partly cures, partly realisation of potential.

4 Only if the personality weakness manifests itself in objective behaviour which can be exemplified and which tends to defeat the achievement of results as previously agreed. There will be little point in dwelling on it if there is no improvement action in contemplation.

REFERENCE

(1) Weinberg, G. M., **The psychology of computer programming**, Van Nostrand, 1971.

15 Staff development, training and organisation

15.1 PLANNED DEVELOPMENT

A top-down approach to planning individual development and training starts with a **succession plan.** In this plan, personnel in the unit are reviewed in order of seniority of position, starting at the top, and a forecast is made of their expected date of leaving their present position. The idea is to choose a successor for each leaver, especially of course for those leaving soonest, and thence successors for the successors until eventually a recruitment possibility is found. Forecast date of leaving is of course a problem in the absence of specific clues such as retirement, promotion or transfer.

Successors may be chosen in the light of the present position they hold and their performance in it, as well as age, length of service, time in present job and abilities. The gap between the abilities, knowledge, skills and attitudes required for the next job and the successor's present abilities etc. shows the succession training required.

From the review made of the **performance plan**, as in the last chapter, a gap may have been identified between the jobholder's present abilities etc. and those required to carry out the job with the desired proficiency. This gap reveals the present job training required.

A further influence on training may be **corporate** or **unit plans** which involve changed technology, changed organisation or changed methods of work or standards. The training for change that results from these plans will probably disclose a general training need of many employees.

The **recruitment plans** will identify newcomers. In addition to possible training for their intended jobs, new recruits may need induction training to introduce them to the organisation, its philosophy, its objectives and attitudes, and the methods and structure of the unit.

It should be recognised that not all desired training can be identified from such a neat process of deduction. If training is based only on such well-defined needs, there is a risk of stagnation caused by insufficient fresh input of ideas from outside. There is a case for a certain amount of training which amounts to foraging in the environment in the hope of finding new opportunities.

Each person's training is therefore individually defined by:

    induction training;
    job training;
    succession training;
    training for change;
    possible foraging training.

Induction training and training for change may be predictably applicable to certain classes of personnel. Other training requirements will only by chance be the same for different personnel. To make the most effective plans for training, each individual's personal training and development should be considered separately.

Questions

1 Who does not need training?   (1 min)

2 Is training patronising?   (2 min)

15.2 TRAINING

If the word 'training' has so far suggested a formal, classroom operation, this is far from what was intended. Probably the most effective forms of training for day-to-day work are on-the-job coaching of a subordinate by his manager, and interplay and exchange between peers. Formal training can lay the foundations, but coaching and exchange coupled with self-discovery are needed to turn this to effective use.

Coaching, to be effective, calls for the manager to be skilled both in the work and in teaching. The learner must see high standards set by his tutor and his colleagues if he is going to consider it important to master a new skill. Teaching and learning are aided if what is expected is specified in terms of objective behaviours or achievements, as in project and personal Targets, quality standards and documentation standards.

There should be opportunity for healthy exchange between peers. 'Ego' programming, as described by Weinberg (1), where a programmer considers his program his own property, not to be exposed to the criticism of peers, is not conducive to this exchange. With egoless programming, a program is considered group property suitable for group discussion, criticism and improvement. Which style of work exists is as much a matter of attitudes as it is of organisation, and the attitudes of the opinion leaders of the programming group (who should include the programming manager among their number) are a considerable influence on group attitudes.

Questions

1 Is the periodic performance appraisal the best time to consider training needs?   (5 min)

2 In his famous Hygiene theory, F. Herzberg proposed that the components of work should be divided into Motivators and Hygiene factors. A Motivator, such as the sense of achievement that comes with accomplishment of a task, promotes a persistent state of well-being that enhances the worker's satisfaction. A Hygiene factor, such as company administration, is not a positive satisfier but is something that may give rise to dissatisfaction. People may complain if the company administration is bad, but they hardly jump for joy because it is good.

In considering the applicability of this theory, one must allow that the important motivators and hygiene factors may be different in different kinds of work and with different kinds of worker (or different individuals or even the same individual in different moods), and that most components of work are part motivator and part hygiene factor. For systems analysts and programmers, it is likely that achievement, recognition, advancement and work itself are motivators. The competence and friendliness of supervisors, company policy and administration are probably hygiene factors. Pay is probably more of a hygiene factor than a motivator.

Would you guess that training is more of a motivator, or more of a hygiene factor, for systems analysts and programmers?   (5 min)

3 What should a manager do if he feels incompetent to coach his subordinates?   (5 min)

15.3 ORGANISATION

About half of data processing departments are formally organised with basically functional divisions, as with Figure 15.1(a), and about half with project division as with Figure 15.1(b).

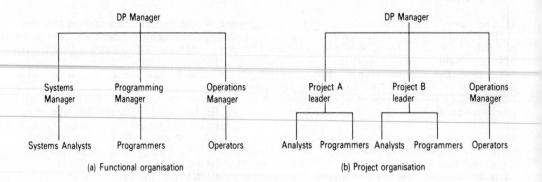

Fig. 15.1: Functional vs. Project organisation

There is no clear net advantage of either arrangement, perhaps because, whatever the form, alternative organisations are going to emerge in practice. In the functional organisation, there is going to be a need for temporary links across functional boundaries in order to enable projects to be furthered. In the project organisation, there will be permanent links across projects concerned with standards, quality control, supervision and training of analysis and programming functions (unless projects are so large that these can be replicated within each project).

A matrix organisation as in Figure 15.2 is a possible way of giving more formal recognition to the practical organisation that is likely to be needed.

An advantage of the matrix organisation is that it increases the recognised positions of authority, giving more places for people to go to and permitting more advancement and recognition. It also encourages the development of project and functional management specialists; the other organisations tend to diminish the status of one or other of these for no good reason that I can see. In a small department, one person may be both a functional manager and a project manager.

Further positions of responsibility, and interplay between peers, can be promoted by teams or committees with special responsibilities – a standards committee who agree and promote standards and give training; a quality assurance team who inspect all deliverables; a review team who supervise or contribute to all post-implementation evaluations.

Many organisations choose to increase functional divisions, tending to divide labour so that each individual can develop and contribute a special skill. A distinction between systems analysts and systems designers is common, the former looking towards the user, requirements determination, business procedures, conversion and user training; the latter looking towards the computer, database design, computer runs and procedures, recovery, etc. Similarly the chief programmer team (Baker, 2) may divide programmers into program designers, coders and documenters, program testers.

Some firms choose to play down functional specialisation, tending to promote all-rounder analyst/programmers who can carry a project through from initiation to implementation. In such firms, individuals may be encouraged to develop expertise in a specialism, but this does not prevent them from contributing to any aspect of system development.

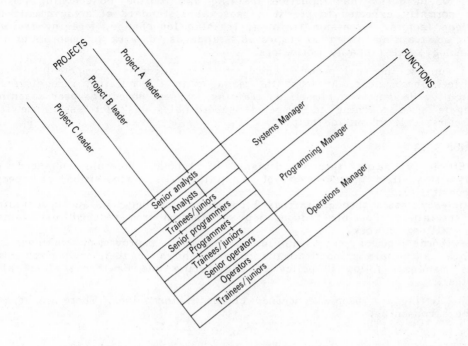

Fig. 15.2: Matrix organisation

Questions

1 What factors should be taken into acount when considering organising for increased functional specialisation?   (5 min)

2 How can one ensure that the chosen organisation is conducive to commitment to making it work by the people in it?   (1 min)

ANSWER POINTERS

Section 15.1

1 An inducted employee, competent in his job, not being prepared for succession or organisational change, who has no need for or is not suitable for foraging training.

2 If patronising means 'to give encouragement to', yes. If it means 'to be condescending towards', not necessarily.
 Patronism can also have a sense of protection, particularly protection of someone who could protect himself, given the chance. One could argue that training is patronising if the trainee is capable of learning or developing himself. But then one could argue that all employment is patronising if a person is capable of self-employment.

Section 15.2

1 The best time is some time before the training is to be put to use, in the case of formal training, or at the time it is needed, in the case of ad hoc coaching.
 This is not to say that training should not be reviewed at appraisal time.

2   I would guess that induction training and routine job coaching, of the sort normally expected to permit a reasonable standard of achievement, are hygiene factors. Succession training, training for change, foraging training and job training aimed at improved standards of work or embracing new technology, are probably motivators.

3   I suppose the real problem arises if the manager **is** incompetent but does not **feel** incompetent. At least the manager in the question recognises his difficulty. He can send himself on training courses, encourage peer coaching, delegate some coaching to competent subordinates, ask for assistance from superiors, call in outside help.

Section 15.3

1   Efficiency gains through division of labour. Possible enhanced job satisfaction from development of special skills, acquisition of special responsibility.

Efficiency losses through increased communication between, and coordination of, specialists. Possible reduced job satisfaction from reduced task variety or deskilling of work.

'Hawthorne' effect may lead to a temporary improvement whatever the change, as people respond to the interest shown in their method of work. Some managers follow a policy of engineering one Hawthorne effect after another.

2   By letting the people concerned choose it themselves. There would need to be a consensus.

REFERENCES

(1) Weinberg, G. M., **The psychology of computer programming**, Van Nostrand, 1971.
(2) Baker, F. T., Chief programmer team management of production programming, **IBM Systems Journal, 11,** 1, 56–73, 1972.

16   Case studies

16.1 INTRODUCTION

These cases, which are all to some extent drawn from real life events but which I have fictitiously collated or embellished, are intended for classroom discussion, personal analysis or simply interest. It is hoped that by speculating about the ins and outs of these cases, the manager will improve his abilities to recognise potential trouble in practice.

A systematic line to take to the cases is to ask first of all: is there a problem or are there problems? If so, what exactly is it or are they? What are the causes of the problems and how could they have been avoided? What should be done now?

In considering these questions, I like to inspect each of the actors in the case in turn. What mistakes (if any) have they made? What good actions have they done? What positive action could they have taken to avoid the problem? What should each person do now?

Another tack is to ask: what decisions were taken in the case? By whom? Was there sufficient information to support the decision? Was the right decision taken?

Alternatively one can ask: what sections of this book are relevant? Would the participants in the case have acted differently if they had followed the precepts of the section? What would you have done?

There are no cut-and-dried answers to the cases; no hard solutions; plenty of opportunity to bring personal experience and opinion to bear. Some are so open-ended as to be little more than a starting-point for what could be a very wide-ranging discussion.

The analyst should not be satisfied with the first, and most obvious, point he identifies. Few practical problems involve a single cause or faulty party, although managers often try to diagnose them as if they did.

16.2 THE LONG-TERM PROJECT

A real-time multi-access system was proposed to help the designers of large vehicles. The initial specification related only to outline descriptions of the sort of applications the system should support. However, it was sufficient to show that the system must include:

i)   a special language interpreter;
ii) a database (relational);
iii) interactive graphics.

Financial provision was made for the first two years of an anticipated 5-10 year development program and a steering committee was set up. After this decision, recruitment started of software designers, systems analysts and operators and, within a year, the team had about 20 people. Early in the year, however, there were problems with recruiting the right people, so consultants were brought in to help with the design of the special language interpreter. This forced a decision to be made concerning which language the interpreter should be written in. There were four candidates:

BCPL, ALGOL 68, CORAL 66 and RTL2. Since the hardware had not been selected or bought, it was decided to evaluate the languages over a three-month period using an available computer.

After three months a decision was taken to use RTL2 and a training program was initiated for all the recruited staff. The consultants started to design the special language, but the clients felt that the consultants were trying to force their opinions on them. After a short time, the consultants were paid off and it was decided to use the internal staff. Meanwhile, because the annual budgetary cycle was approaching, a decision on hardware had to be taken.

The decision was taken on economic grounds to purchase hardware for development and then reconfigure it for the final system. A tender was drawn up on this basis. The steering committee enforced their view that the hardware must be maintained by manufacturers and that the system software should be portable. After a month or so the decision was taken to buy IBC hardware in the belief that suitable software was available.

An RTL2 compiler was obtained for the IBC hardware but it was found that it was not portable to other machines. Therefore a re-appraisal was made and CORAL 66 was chosen. This changed

i)   the training scheme;
ii) the specification of the special language interpreter.

Moreover, it was found that CORAL 66 was not fully supported on the purchased machine and many enhancements had to be made.

Serious managerial problems now appeared because trained and expert staff started to leave for new jobs. The senior management responded by re-organising and promoting within the project. This created further problems since the managers had to design software as well as manage.

After two years, at a steering committee meeting to review the project, some committee members said that every large project met teething troubles and that it was important not to lose sight of the long-term gains. Others said they were being asked to throw good money after bad. On a vote, it was decided to withdraw support at the previous level, and the debate centred on how the project should now proceed.

16.3 THE CONSULTANT'S VISIT

As sales order office manager of Mail Order Sales Ltd, Charles Frame supervised 24 employees who were taking orders, and processing and filing associated paperwork. The General Manager had rung him to say that a firm of systems consultants had been hired to streamline, possibly to computerise, procedures and would he (Frame) give them any assistance or information they wanted.

When the consultants came, they spent three days interviewing Frame and his employees and studying clerical operations in detail. They said they wanted to measure work volumes and time taken for the tasks involved, and that these measurements would start the next day and continue for two or three days. The next day, Frame discovered that six of his employees were absent and the consultants complained that their measurements would not be reliable because the work force present was not typical. When Frame telephoned some of the absentees, he received excuses ranging from 'feeling unwell' to 'exhausted after answering all those questions'. The following day, eight employees were missing. Expecting to be blamed for the failure of the consultants' work, Frame began to wonder if he should absent himself as well...

16.4 PARTICIPATION I

Fred Arnold, chief systems analyst at the Light Engineering Works Ltd, had recently attended a course at the Midland University on user participation in system design. Fired with enthusiasm, he decided to try this idea on the production scheduling system he was currently working on. He persuaded the Works Manager to allow him to call a meeting of the 20 operatives involved and to give them the opportunity to discuss and design their own system for short-term schedules. At this meeting, Arnold pointed out that the main defect of the present system was that too much time was wasted waiting for related jobs to finish, and the resultant low throughput was threatening the firm's competitive position. When he left the meeting, he was sure the men would come up with ideas which would be more effective and acceptable than anything he could propose himself.

When the operatives later explained their plan, about which they were unanimous, Arnold realised with dismay that it would actually increase the time wasted. When he challenged them on this, they said they had decided that this time provided an essential rest between periods of intensive work and, furthermore, there was insufficient rest opportunity in the present system.

Arnold knew the Works Manager would not accept this, but it would be extremely embarrassing, to say the least, if he had to remove from the work force the licence of self-determination previously granted.

16.5 PARTICIPATION II

John Simmons was a newly-appointed analyst in a large engineering works where there were entrenched attitudes in both management and shop floor. The management in the past had ruled out participation by shop-floor workers, even at consultation level, mainly because they feared that an invitation to participate would be taken as an invitation to negotiate. Equally, the trades union shop stewards' main contacts with the management were in the reconciliation of disputes or making bargains.

John had been assigned to design a new system for collecting job progress information from the shop floor operatives. This system would affect only a small portion of their duties, but John believed they should at least be consulted about, and preferably encouraged to design for themselves, their own part of the system.

John made this point to the chief systems analyst, Robbins, who agreed whole-heartedly. Robbins said that when he had joined the company, five years earlier, he had felt exactly the same and had crusaded to change attitudes. However, he had got nowhere and he had felt he was banging his head against a brick wall. He now felt the only way he could keep sane was to accept the attitudes of the management and the unions as given, and try to work within that.

While they were having this conversation, Robbins was perusing his morning mail. 'Good Heavens!' he exclaimed 'Look at this.' He held up a memorandum from the General Manager. It read:

'You are probably aware that the company has recently appointed Dr Eric Muffet to act as consultant to top management on development of new systems.

Dr Muffet has recommended, and the management have fully accepted, that a more participative approach to systems design should be adopted. Employees at all levels are to be more fully consulted about the design of systems they are to operate, and preferably they are to be encouraged to design their own systems for themselves.

The management is committed to this philosophy and to give it impetus have arranged for Dr Muffet to give a three-day residential seminar

on participatory methods of system design at the Lux Plaza Hotel. Selected representatives of the work force, the management and data processing staff are being invited to attend this seminar and you have been chosen to represent your section. Further details are attached.'
'Well, well, well,' said Robbins, somewhat crestfallen. 'That's almost exactly what I was arguing for. I wonder why they didn't accept the idea from me.'
'Yes,' said Simmons, 'I'd like to know that. And I'd also like to know - will this proposal work out as well as they hope?'

16.6 INTRODUCING DOCUMENTATION AT INERT SLUDGE LTD

Inert Sludge's data processing department had 17 staff comprising DP manager, secretary, 1 senior programmer, 2 programmers, 1 senior analyst, 1 analyst, 1 operations supervisor, 3 operators and 6 data preparation staff. The DP manager had just left to further his career with a new company; Tom Taylor, previously Projects Supervisor in the data processing department of Smooth Oils Ltd, had been appointed to take his place. Although Smooth Oils was a much larger operation than Inert Sludge, Tom Taylor's progress there was blocked and he felt his new appointment was an opportunity to broaden his experience in general DP management.
On Tom's first day, Peter Pleasant - the senior analyst - met him and showed him round the shop.

In the computer room, Tom stopped to observe the shift leader running Sludge's daily suite. He asked to see the operating instructions for the sales analysis that was running. He was shown to a loose-leaf book which had a half page entry for the sales analysis program. 'Are these the only two programmed halts?' he asked. 'One for invalid date card and one for the data error?'
'Oh yes,' said the shift leader. 'At least, they were the only ones in the original program. Of course, the Graticula Filters patch added last year has changed this job quite a lot.'
'Graticula Filters patch?' queried Tom.
'Yes, you know, Sludge took over Graticula two years ago and we had to accommodate their special requirements on the sales analysis. In addition to the regular reports, they have a fancy system for getting ad hoc reports based on historical data, which is retained on about 40 reels in the library. The program works out which files and years are required, tells us, we look up the reels in the file register over there and basically its just a big tape reel loading job. There's the stationery change as well, of course.'
Taylor decided not to follow up the stationery change. He asked, 'If you didn't get replacement operating instructions, how did you get to know how to run the changed job?'
'Man, how could we **not** get to know it! The heat was really on for that job - the programmers practically slept in the computer room and we had so many runs trying to get things right while the patch was being added that all the operators got to know it backwards. I don't know why they were in such a hurry - rumour had it that Sludge management had made fancy promises to Graticula, to show how slick they were, without consulting your predecessor. Anyway, the program messages are pretty helpful, now we've got used to them.'

In the programmers' office, Tom Taylor noticed the generally cluttered appearance, desks piled high with listings and card trays.
'What are you working on now?' he asked Robinson, the senior programmer, after being introduced.
'Well, I do the new development work, while the other mainly do maintenance,' said Robinson. 'At the moment, I'm working on a new system for the

Hydrolising Department's recycling operation. The old system we did for them has run OK for a number of years, but now they've changed the requirements quite a lot.'

'Changed requirements? So it's maintenance, not new development?' queried Taylor; but Robinson just looked blank. Tom decided not to pursue this line. Instead, he asked 'What language are you using?'

'Assembler. It's much more efficient on our machine. We use assembler mostly.'

Indicating a particularly full tray of cards, Tom asked 'What's this one?'

'That? Oh, that's the sales analysis source. At least, part of it – the rest is down here,' indicating behind his chair, 'and a right so-and-so that one's been over the years too.'

'Ah yes, I saw it running in the computer room. Why have you got it on your desk?'

'Well, it's mine – that is, I wrote it in the first place.' There was a pause.

'May I see the documentation?'

'Well...yes...OK,' said Robinson, defensively, reaching into the bottom right-hand drawer of his desk and retrieving a large folder, 'but I'd better warn you that we're not so proud of this one. It was a rush job, especially the Graticula patch. And at the same time the Catatype Separator program was blowing up like mad and fancy documentation was the last thing on our minds.'

In the folder Tom Taylor found the original typed specification, somewhat scribbled on, three small specifications of changes, a three page narrative specification for the changes required for Graticula Filters, altered in ink in several places, a rather neat flowchart of the original program on which the three small changes were annotated, another obviously hastily-drawn flowchart of the Graticula patch, together with a listing of the source, again with some pencilled comments. 'Is this documentation up to date?' he asked.

'Oh yes,' came the reply. 'And I've marked on the listing all the patches we did through the console.' (Patching through the console = changing the object code in memory by using the facilities provided at the computer operator's console.)

Back in Peter Pleasant's office, Tom asked to see the sales analysis documentation. He found the program specifications in a much neater condition, unsullied by any pencil or ink markings.

'When I saw this job running,' Tom challenged, 'the operators didn't seem to have any revised instructions to cater for the Graticula Filters amendment.'

'Didn't they?' frowned Pleasant. He thumbed deeper into his folder. 'Well, we certainly prepared them, because here's the copy on file. And look at this handwritten note 'Sent to ops June 20'. They must have forgotten to insert it in their instruction manual.'

'How much did the Graticula amendment cost to implement?' asked Taylor, on an impulse.

'Cost? I'm sure I don't know, and I don't think we could find out, now. I could make an estimate for you though, if you'd like.'

The following week, the analysts, programmers and operators received the following memo:

From: Tom Taylor, DP Manager

To: All staff   Re: Documentation Standards

Effective immediately, we are adopting NCC standards for system and program documentation. Standards manuals for each staff member accompany this memo. All systems currently being developed will be documented to these standards. The possible need to re-document past-developed projects will be reviewed at a later date.

Time records will be submitted weekly by all development staff. A supply of all the required forms has been lodged in the stationery cupboard and new cabinets are being delivered. One of these will be for development files, the other for library files. In future, production source decks will be stored centrally in card racks - J. Smith (Junior Programmer) is hereby appointed librarian.

Three months later, the following memo was sent.

From: Alan Active, Finance Director

To: Peregrine Paternal, General Manager   Re: Data Processing Dept.

Dear Perry,

  This is the memo you asked me for to confirm my conversation with you yesterday over lunch.

  A week ago you asked me to investigate what was going on in the data processing department to find out the reason behind the hold-up in project development and the current chaos on the Sales Analysis system. I have interviewed all the senior staff and this is my inter-pretation of the facts.

1 Shortly after Tom Taylor was appointed he introduced a new, and elaborate, system for documenting the work of the department. This system was widely resented by the staff - and still is, by most of them - who claim that documenting is now taking up most of their time and doing the work has to take second place.

2 As a direct consequence of the new documentation system, Robinson, the senior programmer, quit to take up a post at Smooth Oils. His reason seems to have been that the documentation was making his work too rigid and constrained (whereas previously he had scope for personal freedom in how he did his work) and he resented being made to fill in time sheets to account for how he spent his time. Taylor says in his opinion the work produced by Robinson was sloppy and he was so ingrained in his ways he couldn't change.

3 Whatever the rights or wrongs, Inert Sludge could ill afford to lose Robinson, who knew more about the detailed workings of the computer-ised systems than any other person in the company. Probably the loss even of Taylor would have been less serious.

4 Four weeks after Robinson left, Graticula Filters management discovered that the Sales Analysis report figures had a big error in them which could only be explained by improper computer processing. Robinson wrote the Sales Analysis program, and without his expertise and knowledge, Taylor has not been able to locate and correct the fault, even though practically the entire department is now flat out on it. Taylor is talking about rewriting the system entirely as being more fruitful than carrying on down the present path.

5 Partly because of Robinson's quitting and the time it has taken his replacement to orientate himself, partly because of the increased time spent on documenting and partly because of the time spent looking for the Sales Analysis fault, work on other projects ran behind schedule and is now virtually at a standstill. The departments affected have all got their noses out of joint.

6 Taylor is adamant that his demands for documentation were the right decision. I am not expert enough to comment on this, but it's the view of Pleasant, the senior analyst, that 'filling in all those forms' as he puts it has not improved knowledge or records about the systems by much. Certainly, it's plain that the short-term consequences are diabolical. The only way I can see out of the Graticula mess immediate-ly is to hire a small army of clerks to do an emergency job by hand.

7 Taylor seems to have precipitated this state of affairs and I think he should carry the can for it.

                                        Alan

16.7 THE IDLE PROGRAMMERS

Every time the Data Processing Manager passed through the programming section, half the programmers seemed to be doing crossword puzzles.

16.8 THE INDISPENSIBLE PROGRAMMER

Dave Diamond, Systems Programmer, had complained to Frank Parker, DP Manager, that maintaining the manufacturer's software and other systems utilities did not keep him fully occupied. Parker had accepted this and had resolved to find a further outlet for Diamond in due course.

Parker was also concerned that Diamond had unique and vital knowledge and expertise, and the department was vulnerable should Diamond quit or have an accident. He decided to appoint an Assistant Systems Programmer to learn something about the software. A keen recent graduate, Arthur Freshman, was appointed to understudy Diamond.

Parker was surprised when Freshman tendered his resignation, after only two months, on the grounds that he (Freshman) had been made such an attractive offer from another company that he couldn't refuse. During his exit interview with Parker, however, Freshman blurted out: 'It was Diamond; he didn't give me any help or advice at all. He didn't cooperate. He hardly gave me anything to do. I was bored and couldn't see any way I could make progress.'

16.9 OPEN DOOR

Bill Jones, Chief Programmer at the Op-time-um Corporation, approached Jack Edwards, the Data Processing Manager, and handed him an envelope.

'Sorry about this, Jack,' said Jones awkwardly. 'It's my resignation – I've just accepted a post at Southern Polytechnic as manager of their new computer centre.'

Edwards was shocked, open-mouthed. 'I – I had no idea' he stammered. 'Why – I thought you liked it here?'

'Oh, I like it fine here, but there doesn't seem to be anywhere for me to progress to. Besides, Southern Poly will pay a lot more.'

'But, Bill, if only you had told me, I'm sure we could have talked through your prospects here satisfactorily. You know my door is always open to you. And you know how much we value your work – I bet the directors would have matched your offer from Southern Poly.'

Jones shrugged his shoulders. 'Well, it's done now. Anyway, if you thought I was worth more, why weren't you paying me it?'

16.10 METHODS

A consultant had been called in for a small technical assignment to one of the plants of a very large multi-factory heavy engineering company. The company had local DP centres at each plant. In his final interview with the local DP manager, he said 'I couldn't help noticing that your COBOL programmers are writing unstructured programs. Don't you think you ought to train them in structured programming?'

'I don't know about that,' replied the DP manager. 'All our training is arranged from Head Office in London. If they don't say we need it, we don't need it. Besides, I'm only interested in whether or not their programs work, not how they wrote them.'

16.11 ALPHA STANDARDS

The Alpha Corporation's data processing activities had grown quickly, and they now had a large staff of analysts and programmers headed up by Stan Vrakow, Systems and Programming Manager. Most of the major applications had been implemented and the workload was now more maintenance, tuning and improvements than new applications.

In preparing his own performance plan, Vrakow identified 'staff morale and motivation to produce desired quality and quantity of work' as a Key Result Area. James Hunt, his DP manager, pointed out that staff needed to know what was expected of them as regards quality and at the moment there was no published quality standard. If there was such a standard, assignments given to staff could require results 'according to Alpha standards' as well as time and quantity targets.

In the ensuing discussion, Vrakow and Hunt agreed that one of Vrakow's Targets would be to introduce a standards manual within three months. A list of analysis and programming tasks to be covered in the manual was also agreed.

Vrakow felt it would require too much effort by his best men to write such a manual from scratch, so he gave the assignment to a firm of consultants, who delivered an impressive document. Vrakow personally ensured that each analyst and programmer received a copy, was asked to read it and was informed that future assignments would require work 'to Alpha standards' where applicable.

In reviewing the results later with Hunt, Vrakow felt that quality was to a certain extent improving, but that morale generally had not. Indeed, a couple of important resignations suggested otherwise. 'But that wasn't anything to do with the new standards,' declared Vrakow. 'They were both going for promotions outside. I think the problem is more that the type of work we have on now is not as challenging or varied as it used to be.'

Glossary

Bayes' Theorem   This permits a revised calculation of the probability of a phenomenon after a symptom or symptoms connected with it have been detected.

Budget   A financial plan.

Budgetary control   Monitoring a process by comparing incurred money amounts with those planned.

Checkpoint   A point in a plan at which a review of progress is to be made, e.g. by a **project monitoring committee.**

Chief programmer team   An organisation in which a chief programmer and a backup chief programmer design the programs and code key modules, other team programmers developing the other modules. A librarian-cum-secretary coordinates effort and maintains information about programs, testing and project status in a development support library.

Close MOE   A MOE which is determined entirely by the system development project (cf. **Distant MOE**).

Consensus   A form of participation in which every affected user is involved.

Construction   A phase in a project during which the system is brought to operational status, starting from program and procedure specifications.

Consultation   A form of participation in which the analyst proposes a design and invites criticism or suggestion from users.

Contingency   An event, in a plan or budget, which may or may not happen and against which a **reserve** or **provision** may be made.

Cost-benefit analysis (financial)   The money valuation of project costs and benefits and evaluation by **payback period, yield, internal rate of return** or **net present value.**

Cost-effectiveness analysis   Evaluation by stipulating a level of cost or a level of **effectiveness.**

CPM   Critical Path Method.

Decision tree   A technique for decision making in which a complex decision is broken down into alternatives and sub-alternatives. Actions which the decision-taker can choose are shown with a square node (see Figure 7.3), and alternatives which are outside the decision-taker's control are shown with a circular node. By back-calculating **expected monetary values** (or expected **utilities)** from the leaves of the tree, the action expected to be most beneficial can be found.

Deliverable   An ostensible evidence of achievement of a **task** or set of tasks.

Designation   A form of participation in which the **sponsor** decides who is to be the participant.

Discounted cash flow   A **cost-benefit analysis** using **NPV** or **internal rate of return.**

Distant MOE   A MOE which is influenced by variables outside but which is hypothetically also influenced by the system development project (cf. **Close MOE**).

Division of labour   An attempt to improve **efficiency** by simplifying complex work so that separate persons can work on separate components of it.

Effectiveness   The success with which a system meets or furthers the aims of the organisation; the results.

Efficiency   The ratio of the inputs to the outputs of a production system; the ratio of resources used to results achieved. Inverse of **productivity**.

Election   A form of participation in which an affected group with a common interest vote to decide who will represent them.

Electronic office   An office in which traditionally manual or secretarial work, such as reminding, filing, mail and message distribution, retrieving information and reporting are undertaken by computers, perhaps in addition to word processing and calculator facilities.

Expected Monetary Value, EMV   A financial benefit times its probability of occurrence.

Expected Value of Information, EVI   The **EMV** attributable to the receipt of a new message which contains **information**.

Feasibility study   A phase in a project, following project initiation, during which systems analysis work is done to produce a feasibility report.

Feedback   Provision of messages about the output status to the controller of a system.

Feed-forward   Provision of messages about the input status to the controller of a system.

Formal message   A message whose content is predefined as regards the entities and relationships, and their attributes, alluded to.

Hawthorne effect   The effect noted by E. Mayo in his Hawthorne studies (1927-32) in which productivity of workers was temporarily increased following any change in their working conditions; attributed to the employee responding to the interest of the management.

Inflation   An increase in the supply of money in an economy without a corresponding increase in the production of goods and services.

Information   Specifically, the ability of a message to discriminate a meaning from all the possible meanings that may have been sent; the surprise value of the message. Loosely, a message.

Insider   A participant who is a member of a project team.

Internal rate of return   An interest rate which brings the **NPV** of a project to zero.

Key result area, KRA   An identified, important facet of an organisation or unit, its activities or its environment, by which its managers subjectively judge its **effectiveness**.

Linear programming, LP   A technique for maximising the extent to which some objective is met when all the constraints on achieving it can be expressed in terms of linear equations.

Long-range steering committee   A group, consisting of representatives of interest groups affected by long-range DP plans, who make long-range plans, translating them into medium-range plans and monitoring the results.

Lumpy MOE   A **MOE** whose **utility** does not have a regular relationship with MOE values: a graph of the MOE values against their utilities would show a peak, valley, kink or discontinuity.

Maslow's hierarchy of needs   An explanation of human behaviour which draws attention to the fact that attention is turned to higher-level needs, such as realisation of potential or social contact, only when lower-level needs, such as food or shelter, are largely met.

Management by objectives, MBO   A process by which the managers of an organisation participate in the setting of goals and the making of plans for achieving them. Successive participations at lower levels of a hierarchical organisation serve to propagate the higher goals throughout the organisation. Each manager's responsibilities for furthering the plans are agreed and each is judged primarily on results.

Management style   The way a manager influences the actions of his subordinates. Different styles emanate partly from different beliefs about subordinates; see **Theory X and Theory Y**. In the 'tell' style, a manager decides what needs to be done and instructs his subordinates to do it. In the 'sell' style, the manager decides what needs to be done and gets his subordinates to do it by emphasising the benefits to them. In the 'consult' style, the manager proposes what should be done, invites comments and criticism, revises his proposal as appropriate and instructs subordinates to implement. In the 'participate' style, the manager shares the problem with his subordinates and they jointly agree upon a course of action.

Measure of effectiveness, MOE   An objective measure by which success or failure in achieving the results will be recognised.

Net present value, NPV   A sum of money which if received at the present moment would be judged equal in value to a cash flow or flows postponed in time.

Non-project time   Staff time which is deemed not to have been used in connection with any particular project.

Object system   The system referred to by the **formal message** system.

Orthogonal   Neat and tidy; providing a place for everything and everything able to go into just one place.

Outsider   A participant who is not a member of the project team.

Payback period   The time taken for the income of an investment to exceed the initial outlay.

Personal probability density function, PPDF   A hypothetical **PDF** which expresses the subjective likelihood a person gives to an event.

PERT   Programme Evaluation and Review Technique.

Policy   An organisational rule which no one seeks to cost-justify; an element of a long-range plan.

Productivity   The ratio of the results achieved to the resources used. See **Efficiency**.

Probability density function, PDF   A function which describes, for a continuous variable depicting a state of nature, the probability that it will take a value within a particular range.

Project initiation   The event that starts a **feasibility study**; the point at which **terms of reference** are given to the study team.

Project monitoring committee   A group, consisting of representatives of interest groups affected by a project, which reviews project plans and progress.

Project selection   A phase preceding **project initiation** in which the project is prioritised, e.g. by the **long-range steering committee**.

Provision   An allowance for a specified **contingency**.

Regression analysis   The technique of estimating a function which describes a set of observations.

Reserve   An allowance for unspecified **contingencies**.

Sensitivity analysis   Investigation into the effect that a change in the inputs or assumptions of a model would have on the results produced by the model.

Side-effect   An effect on a goal which is not described by the **MOEs** chosen for a particular project.

Smooth MOE   A MOE whose **utility** has a regular relationship with MOE values (cf. **Lumpy MOE**).

Sponsor   The person or body authorising the project and to whom the project team are principally responsible.

Surrogate   One who stands in for another.

Target   A value of a **MOE** which, if hit or exceeded, will be evidence of success of the project.

Task   An item of work convenient for planning.

Terms of reference   An initial briefing given to a study team.

Theory X and Theory Y   After D. McGregor, alternative theories which may be held by managers to explain subordinate behaviour. The manager's belief may be self-fulfilling by inducing subordinate behaviour which confirms it. A Theory X manager believes that the average person needs to be directed and to be motivated by persuasion, reward, punishment; to be controlled to ensure that his behaviour fits the needs of the organisation; that the average person is passive about or resistant to the organisation's needs, works as little as possible and dislikes responsibility. A Theory Y manager believes that most people are not naturally like this but are often made to behave that way by Theory X management; that potential for development, willingness to direct behaviour towards organisation goals and to undertake responsibility are widely to be found; that management should not so much direct and control as to provide the conditions under which people can grow by directing their own efforts towards organisational goals. A Theory X manager gets things done through other people. A Theory Y manager gets other people to do things through delegation, participation, self-set objectives and self-appraisal.

Utility   A personal, internal valuation which explains or is defined by a person's preferences.

Yield   The rate of interest earned by an investment.

Annotated bibliography

Akhurst, B. A., **Assessing intellectual abilities**, EUP, 1970.

Alter, S. L., How effective managers use information systems, **Harvard Business Review,** Nov/Dec 1976, pp.97–104. Survey of 56 computerised decision support systems, discusses user involvement and factors in success or failure.

Alter, S. L., **A study of computer–aided decision making in organisations,** Ph.D. Thesis, Sloan School of Management, MIT, 1975. Decision support system as tool of persuasion of other departments, in takeover credibility, defensive arguments. The EDP–style assumption that systems should always be justified in monetary savings terms does not suffice in the area of decision support systems. Examples of successful strategies – impose gracefully (find useful subsystems), active involvement through workshops, use a prototype, make user responsible, sell the system.

Anderson, J. C., **Decision–maker response to probabilistic information in the capital investment decision process,** Ph.D. Thesis, U of Minnesota, 1973. Cited in Davis (1974): decision makers were given mean, mean and range, probability distribution; those with all three were more confident but less consistent in decsion making than when they received only the mean.

Andrews, W. C., The business system proposal, **Journal of Systems Management,** 29, 2, 39–41, February 1978. Executive summary, identification of the business problem, business scope and objectives, information requirement, system concept, implementation strategy, justification and cost evaluation, alternatives, risk assessment, project management.

Archibald, R. D., and Villoria, R. L., **Network–based management systems (PERT/CPM),** Wiley, 1967.

Aris, J. B. B., Quantifying the costs and benefits of computer projects. In Frielink (1975), pp.15–24. Resource–level decisions not closely connected, temporally or causally, with project–oriented decisions of go/no go. Two types of appraisal: macroscopic and close focus. Argues all indirect expense should be allocated according to 'contribution'. Projects should be marginally costed. Believing 25% chance of £1000 000 does not allow us to claim benefit of £50 000. There is no such thing as an intangible. Valuation by: market price, substitution, highest possible value, bracketing, global effect of several intangibles, ask several people and average the results, opportunity costs (e.g. profit foregone by not hiring out programmers on open market), management time.

Bally, L. and others, Information system design and development, **Information and Management (Nederlands),** 1, 1, 21–6, November 1977. Development styles: linear; loopy–linear; plug–in (subsystems implemented in sequence); prototype (crude version). Prototype advantages: copes with fuzzy situation, less protracted study. Apparently more expensive.

Banbury, J., The concept of information system effectiveness. In Frielink (1975), pp.28–36. Defines decision maker; purpose; decision situation, environment, decision process, action, outcome. Likelihood of particular choice opportunities being recognised by decision maker is a function of his perceptual set. Alternatives generated is a function of his perceptual set. Decision–making skill requires judgement, intuition and creativity.

Barefield, R. M., The effect of aggregation on decision–making success: a laboratory study, **Journal of Accounting Research, 10,** 2, 229–42, Autumn 1972. Review of literature on information processing. Subjects receiving disaggregated data performed slightly better than subjects receiving aggregated data. Conservatism – subjects extract less information from data than would be extracted by applying Bayes' theorem. Pitz Downing and Penhold, Sequential effects in the revision of subjective probabilities, **Can J Psych,** Vol 21, 1967, pp.381–93: more conservatism when data does not confirm subject's present beliefs.

Bedford, N. M., and Mohamed Onsi, Measuring the value of information – an information theory approach, **Management Services,** Jan–Feb 1966, pp.15–22.

Bell, T. E., Money-saving EDP questions, **Financial Executive (USA),** December 1977, p.18. Anbar: computer department may provide an un-necessarily expensive service to humour the users.

Benjamin, R. I., **Control of the information system development cycle,** Wiley-Interscience, 1971.

Bennis, W.G., Benne, K. D., and Chin, R. (Eds), **The planning of change, readings in the applied behavioural sciences,** Holt Reinhardt and Winston, 2nd ed. 1969. Comprehensive surveys of sociologists' views. Chin and Benne, General strategies for effecting changes in human systems, pp.32–59: three groups of strategies, empirical-rational (rational appeal to self-interest); normative re-educative (develop changes in attitudes, values, skills, relationships); power (to enforce/command compliance). Empirical-rational: dissemination of knowledge, personnnel selection/replacement, systems analyst as change agent. Normative re-educative: improving problem-solving capabilities of a system, releasing/fostering growth of persons in system. Power-coercive: nonviolent means (civil disobedience), political institutions, recomposition/manipulation of power elites.

Bishop, D. J., and O'Farrel, W., Project cost control, **The Accountant,** August 25 1977, pp.218–20, and September 1 1977, p.249. Uncertainty indicated by allowance for contingencies of experienced estimator so need to know (a) amount which is represented by firm/quoted prices (b) estimated cost of other items and what has been added for contingencies (c) how much has been included for cost escalation.

Blumenthal, S. C., **Management information systems: a framework for planning and development,** Prentice-Hall, 1969.

Bonney, M. C., Some considerations of the cost and value of information, **The Computer Journal,** Vol 12, 1969, pp.118–23. The majority of published work consists of general discourse and case studies. Six common assumpt-ions: managers manage better with more information, information is of greater value if produced more quickly, give a manager what he wants or what he thinks he wants, more inter-departmental communication improves performance, manager does not have to understand how a MIS works, make information logically consistent, e.g. reporting performance against plan.

Bower, J. B. and Sefert, J. B., Human factors in system design, **Management Services,** 2, 6, 220–55, November–December 1969. Lists of factors by top management, middle management, non-supervisory managers.

Boyd, D. F., and Krasnow, H. S., Economic evaluation of management information systems, **IBM Systems Journal,** March 1963. Reprinted in McRae.

Brooks, F. P., **The mythical man–month,** Addison-Wesley, 1975.

Burton, B. J., Manpower estimating for systems projects, **Journal of Systems Management, 26,** 1, 29–33, January 1975. Based on own personal judgement.

Butterworth, J. E., The accounting system as an information function, **Journal of Accounting Research, 10,** 1, 1–27, Spring 1972. Relationship between level-of-detail of information and its benefits: any information system which has at least as much disaggregation of account balances as another must be at least as valuable as another.

Canadian Institute of Chartered Accountants, **Computer control guidelines,**

Auerbach, 1971. Comprehensive planning and control checklists.

Canning, R., Overall guidance of data processing, **EDP Analyzer, 6,** 8, August 1968. Project selection: set general goals and objectives, represent company's overall viewpoint, no gaps or overlaps in data processing programme, stimulate local initiative, review proposals from functional units, achieve integration, consider proposals for feasibility studies as well as implementations, recommend priorities, schedules, logical sequences. Example of Lockheed Aircraft, steering committee made up of branch heads, reviews proposal submitted. DP budget may be small but impact large. Current methods foster competitive spirit, do not force over-worked executive management to be trained in computer technology. Better guidance from intelligent risk taking (high gains from high risk projects?), recognition of where main problems lie, insistence on searching for alternatives. Alternative organisations: strong executive; new function with own executive; liaison personnel; steering committee. Steering committee has most merit.

Carter, D. M., Determining system success, **Journal of Systems Management, 27,** 7, 24-7, July 1976. 100-person survey ranked ten most important factors in planning and control phase of system development: 1 control over needed resources, 2 determination and justification of requirements, 3 management involvement in planning phase, 4 manager/user attitudes towards system development, 5 allowance for change and priority considerations, 6 allowance for appropriate planning time, 7 even identification and work assignment, 8 user expertise in making wishes known, 9 steering committee composition and place in organisation, 10 cost consciousness of EDP/user/management personnel. Proposes method of prioritising.

Chandor, A., **Choosing and keeping computer staff,** George Allen and Unwin, 1976.

Chervany, N. L., and Dickson, G. W., An experimental evaluation of information overload in a production environment, **Management Science, 20,** 2, June 1974. Reprinted in Davis and Everest. Decision makers given data summarised through simple descriptive statistics made higher quality decisions than those getting standard formats; had less confidence in the quality of their decisions; took longer to make their decisions.

Cloot, P. L., Management information systems – can computers help?, **The Computer Bulletin, 11,** 4, 276-81, March 1968. Ground rules: put people first, minimise outputs, do not insist on conversational computing, expect errors in data and decisions, involve line management, identify decisions and their value, work on small sub-systems, use a simple model of the management problem.

Conway, B., The information system audit, **Management Review,** March 1968. Reprinted in Sanders. Checklists for planning stage and others.

Cooke, J. E., and Kuchta, T., Feasibility studies for the selection of computer systems and applications, **Cost and Management** (Canada), September–October 1970, pp.11–19. Reprinted in Li. The methods of assessing economic feasibility are comparatively primitive and unreliable. Often difficult to measure true return on investment even after it has occurred. Typical problems: wrong system selected in first place, implementation took longer and cost more than was predicted, resultant savings in staff did not materialise, operating managers won't use the new information provided, the new application never did work properly, new application works well but costs more than old method, new application is OK but wish we had done this instead, turnover among computer staff too high. Frequently the fault of top management, not computer staff or computers. Despite simplicity and theoretical correctness of NPV, not widely used or understood. Perhaps also unable to cope with uncertainty in costs and benefits. Principles to reduce chance of failure: identify key objectives and likely progression of the company, set up high-level steering committee, involve operating managers, list all potential applications looking particularly for applications in areas of high company expenditure or revenue, assess profit potential by present value analysis, draw up long-range plans for successive implementations, review progress and profitability regularly, appraise each project and estimates after completion, be prepared to revise the plan.

Cotton, I. W., Cost-benefit analysis of interactive systems, **Computer Networks**, 1, 6, 311-24, November 1977. 32 refs.

Crawley, M. and Morris, J., **Computer personnel selection – 1: Systems analysts**, NCC Publications, 1970.

Damodaran, L., User involvement in system design – why? and how? In Parkin (1977), pp.13-19.

Davis, G. B., **Management information systems: conceptual foundations, structure and development**, McGraw-Hill, 1974.

Davis, G. B., and Everest, G. C., **Readings in management information systems**, McGraw-Hill, 1976.

Dew, R. B., and Gee, K. P., **Management control and information**, Macmillan, 1973.

Dewhurst, R. F. J., **Business cost-benefit analysis**, McGraw-Hill, 1972.

Diebold, J., Bad decisions on computer use, **Harvard Business Review**, Jan-Feb 1969, pp.14-28. Cost displacement not enough. Need to evaluate computers in terms of contribution to entire management process: cost of development, operational gains, intangible benefits. Payback or ROI that does not take into account intangibles is obviously pointless. People costs often underestimated.

Dickmann, R. A., **Personnel implications for business data processing**, Wiley, 1971.

Ditri, A. E., and Wood, D. R., The project management process, **Tempo (Touche, Ross and Co)**, September 1969, pp.31-5. Reprinted in Li. Extent of planning should vary with amount involved/risk involved. Steps: 1 first user/systems encounter, discuss anticipated change, technical feasibility, broad benefits, approximate costs; 2 preliminary systems study, the real need for such a project in the user's area, the business benefits the application would provide to the user's department, can it be implemented in time to provide the benefits required, the risks involved versus the dollar and non-dollar benefits involved; 3 systems planning study, technical feasibility, costs and benefits, number of man-months of programming and preparation required, complexity of conversion, impact on user's departments and amount of training needed to convert to new system, monthly cash flow that will result.

Drucker, P. F., **The practice of management**, Harper and Row, 1954.

Dujmovic, J. J., **The preference scoring method for decision taking – survey, classification and annotated bibliography**, U of Belgrade, Department of Electrical Engineering, 1977.

Dunn, D. A., The statement that computer costs are dropping at 25% per year is reasonably correct, **Datamation**, October 1969.

Dzielinski, B. P., A guide to financial planning tools and techniques, **IBM Systems Journal**, 12, 2, 126-44, 1973.

Eason, K. D., and Corney, G. M., The evaluation of a small interactive management information system, **Proceedings of the conference on man-computer interaction**, IEE, 1970, pp.113-20. Before and after experiment but had to assess means of decision taking rather than the decisions. Information searching and calculating time successfully transferred to the computer, but new inactivity due to waits due to computer, queries (studying user manual) and errors may have exceeded time saved. Hypothesis that interactive system enhances management decision taking not confirmed by this study.

Eason, K. D., The manager as a computer user, **Applied Ergonomics**, 5, 1, 9-14, March 1974. Survey of 200 computer users. Managers complain about inaccurate information, too much irrelevant information, service not complete to their requirements, terminal hardware, response time, terminal software. Clerks complain difficult to read.

Efstathiou, J., Hawgood, J., and Rajkovic, V., **Verbal measures and inseparable multidimensional utility in system evaluation**, Science Laboratories, U of Durham.

Ein-Dor, P., and Segev, E., Implementors of management information systems, **Management Datamatics**, 5, 6, 251-9, December 1976. Knowledge of MIS comes from case studies, field studies, field tests, laboratory studies. Mostly first two categories. Dearth of hard data, abundance of position papers, conceptualisations. Based on first hand experience, so kind of evidence. 70 refs.

Elliott, C., and Haynes, J., The conflict between management and computer specialists, **University of Michigan Business Review**, March 1977, p.9. Anbar: examines different frames of reference of managers/computer specialists; nature of gap in terms of functional, informational and spatial separation; stresses need for top management involvement.

Emery, J. C., and Morgan, H. L., Management and economics of data base management systems. In Jardine, D. A. (Ed.), **SHARE working conference on data base management systems**, North-Holland, 1974.

Emery, J. C., Can we develop cost-effective information systems?, **Management Informatics**, 1, 6, 243-9.

Emery, J. C., **Organisational planning and control systems**, Macmillan, 1969.

Emery, J. C., **SMIS workshop report volume 1: Cost benefit analysis of information systems**, Society for Management Information Systems, Chicago, Illinois.

Exley, M., and Hardinge, N., Computers for people – designing human systems, **Data Systems**, February 1977, pp.16-19, **Management Services in Government (UK)**, November 1976, pp.206-8. Path lab system to save doctors time in chasing up results; but doctors used to go to path lab to provide break in very long shift; expected savings in time probably not materialised as other reasons for going found. Automated GP/consultant referral system; GPs still preferred informal telephone discussion, bypassing computer system, upsetting queues etc. Design system to meet formal and informal ways of working, consider effect of changed supervision methods, reduced task variation/limited responses are less satisfying, identify core satisfiers/dissatisfiers for group. Does system provide operational benefit for data inputting required? Job discretion? Job control? Are staff just to be a data input machine?

Fagan, M. E., Design and code inspections to reduce errors in program development, **IBM Systems Journal**, 15, 3, 182-211, 1976.

Farmer, R. S., Evaluation of the effective data processing shop. In Gruenberger, pp.64-80. Seven phase/28 milestone/165 task checklist. Two-tier steering committee.

Feltham, G. A., The value of information, **Accounting Review**, October 1968, pp.684-96.

Foundation for research on human behaviour, **Managing major change in organisations; an undeveloped area of administrative and social research**, Ann Arbor, Michigan, 1964. Management should seek benefit of employee participation through real (actual) not apparent (psychological) participation. Coch, L., and French, J. R. P., Overcoming resistance to change, **Human Relations**, vol 1, 1948, pp.512-32: participation in decisions concerning how a change in production procedures is made relates to the rate of recovery of production rates and the level of production following the change; Tannenbaum and Vroom both show that the effect of psychological participation varies with the personality of the participant (egalitarians, more effect). French, J. R. P., and Raven, B., in Cartwright, D., **Studies in social power**, Institute for Social Research, U of Michigan, 1959: legitimate power, reward power, coercive power, expert power, referent power. Strategies for managing change considered on grid:

management's estimate of impact on individuals (incompatible with personal goals, don't know, compatible) versus individual's estimate (incompatible, don't know, compatible).

Fredericks, W. A., A manager's perspective of MIS, **MSU Business Topics**, Spring, 1971, pp.7–12. Reprinted in Li. Nine management questions: what are we selling, where are we selling it, what will we be selling and where, what do we own, where is it, what are we producing for sale, when will it be ready for sale, what will it cost us, what should we be producing and selling tomorrow? Five tests of relevance of systems project: 1 will system help to answer one or more of the nine questions; 2 has the system been cost-justified by the operating area which is to use it; 3 are the systems people working with and for the staff of the sponsoring operating area; 4 are there explicit time targets for systems people to meet to finish project; 5 does top management know and recognise where this system will fit into total information system needs of company?

Fried, L., The post-implementation feasibility study, **Datamation**, 1966, pp. 47–50. MOEs: number of transactions processed in given time, average time required, average age of data being processed. Case cited where post-implementation review cost ½% of yearly operating cost of system.

Fried, L., How to analyze computer project costs, **Computer Decisions**, August 1971, pp.22–6. Reprinted in Li. Case study of Title Insurance and Trust Co. Implementation cost worksheet, operating cost worksheet. Five year cash flow analysis, present versus alternative, and payback analysis.

Frielink, A. B. (Ed.), **Economics of ADP**, North-Holland, 1965.

Frielink, A. B. (Ed.), **Economics of informatics**, North-Holland, 1975.

Garrity, J. T., and Barnes, V. L., The payout on computers: what management has learned about planning and control, **Management Review**, 53, 12, 4–15, December 1964. Identify key objectives, the 80% of the benefits areas; list potential applications, catalogue benefits; draw up long-range applications plans; analyse profit potential (pitfalls: crediting the computer with efficiencies that could be achieved with a manual system and overestimating future growth in clerical costs – can seldom be accurately estimated on a percentage of sales or cost per transaction basis); prepare implementation plans; review progress regularly; post-appraise completed projects.

Gilb, T, **Controlling the computer**, Studentlitteratur, 1974.

Gildersleeve, T. R., The time-estimating myth, **Datamation**. Is failure due to mis-estimation or mis-management?

Gildersleeve, T. R., **Data processing project management**, Van Nostrand, 1974.

Glaser, G., Plain talk about computers, **Business Horizons**, 10, 3, 33–8, Fall 1967. Reprinted in Sanders. A basic decsription of technical economic and operational feasibility.

Glass, R. L., Computer failure: a learning experience, **Proceedings of the software quality and assurance workshop, Performance Evaluation Review**, 7, 3 and 4, November 1978. Lighthearted anecdotal discussion of failure.

Gorry, G. A., and Scott Morton, M. S., A framework for management information systems, **Sloan Management Review**, vol 12, Fall 1971, pp.55–70.

Gordon, R. L., and Lamb, J. C., A close look at Brook's law, **Datamation**, June 1977, pp.81–3, 86.

Gottfried, I. S., Justifying data processing, **Data Management**, 15, 1, 60–1, January 1977. Cites **Infosystems** September 1974: DP success criteria in rank order – 1 meeting deadlines; 2 accuracy and completeness; 3 rapid response to user requests; 4 budget performance and cost control; 5 operational tranquillity.

Graham, J., **Making computers pay**, Unwin, 1976.

Grindley, K. and Humble, J., **The effective computer: an MBO approach**, McGraw-Hill, 1973.

Grindley, K., Justifying computer systems, **Computing Europe**, March 10 1977, p.17. Anbar: consider computer as means of achieving objectives that could not be achieved otherwise, not just cost reduction; all objectives must be quantified.

Grodman, L. K., and Kerr, E. F. (Eds), **Data base management systems,** QED Information Sciences, Wellesley, Massachussetts, 1973. Ranking criteria for database projects: low risk, probability of success, utility, visibility.

Gruenberger, F. (Ed.), **Effective vs efficient computing,** Prentice-Hall, 1973.

Hall, P. G., and Lincoln, T. J., A cost-effectiveness study of production and engineering systems within a tightly integrated manufacturing environment, **Management Datamatics,** 5, 6, 261–73, December 1976.

Hanna, W. E., A case study in procurement. In Frielink (1975), pp.156–70. Programmer works on five programs at a time with 2.3 in testing stage. Moving to time-sharing for program development reduced machine cost per test from $35 to $7, program delay cost per test from $22 to $6.

Harrison, H. J., and Mackie, P. J., **The comparability of cost-benefit and financial rates of return,** HMSO, 1973, 17pp. Government projects are appraised some by financial some by social cost-benefit – can they be equated in seeking to invest until returns are equal at all margins? No simple rule connects financial rate of return to investing organisation to social cost-benefit return.

Hawgood, J., Quinquevalent quantification of computer benefits. In Frielink (1975). Customer service benefit = –difference in average time per visit x (number of visits with unchanged policy + $\frac{1}{2}$ difference in number of visits). Job satisfaction benefit = proportion of contractual areas with predicted improvements. Financial benefit = difference in total income – difference in total running costs. Flexibility benefit = weighted proportion of cases with positive benefits in other categories.

Haynes, R. J., The evaluation of management information systems, **Proceedings of the conference on man–computer interaction,** IEE, 1970, pp.24–8. Information for confirmation should only exist if results in action or decision. Systems analysts responsible for system could not answer some of: who receives this report? what is his task? for what decisions is he responsible? what is the value of those decisions? what information does he use in those decisions? Three firms, 45 managers, 232 reports – 45% reports monthly, only 12% on request, no exception reports, only one graph. MIS can only be evaluated in terms of the improved effectiveness of managers who use it. This can only be done by senior management.

Hayslett, M. S., **Statistics made simple,** W. H. Allen, 1971.

Head, J. G., Estimating the costs and benefits and monitoring the effectiveness of large government installations. In Frielink (1975), pp.181–90. DCF using 10% discount rate laid down by UK Treasury. Intangibles included if reasonably objective estimate is possible, otherwise considered separately.

Herzog, J. P., System evaluation technique for users, **Journal of Systems Management,** 26, 5, 30–5, May 1975. Define problem, assign improvement priorities, define objectives, assess against objectives, assess reliability. Points system.

Hice, G. F., Turner, W. S., and Cashwell, L. F., **System development methodology,** North-Holland, 1978.

Hicks, H. G., **The management of organisations: a systems and human resources approach,** McGraw-Hill, 1972.

Higham, P., The real cost of business forms, **Data Processing,** March 1978, p.29, 31. Acquisition costs estimated at 15% of supplier's price; purchase cost about 5% of total cost of using form; therefore improvement in efficiency of form can far outweigh price.

Hirsch, R. E., The value of information, **Journal of Accountancy,** June 1968. Reprinted in Davis and Everest.

Hofstedt, R., The processing of accounting information: perceptual biases. In Burns, T. J. (Ed.), **Behavioural experiments in accounting,** Ohio State University, 1974, pp.285–315. Do people process non-accounting information differently from accounting information? Probably. Bias of psychological involvement, recency, sensitivity to variance, scepticism. More confidence with relatively less information.

Holland, W. E., et al., Socio-technical aspects of MIS, **Journal of Systems Management**, 25, 2, 14-6, February 1974. Systems did not evolve in carefully planned stages, despite agreement on the 'steps'.

Hoos, I. R., When the computer takes over the office, **Harvard Business Review**, **38**, 4, 102-12, July/August 1960. Two year study of 19 firms San Francisco. For every five jobs eliminated, only one is created. EDP stimulates recentralisation. Resistance affects upward flow of communication. EDP specialists fail to recognise workers' point of view. Personnel department devalued by do-it-yourself DP managers.

Hoos, I. R., Can systems analysis solve social problems?, **Datamation**, June 1974, pp. 82-92. Systems analysis techniques not appropriate to social problems. Best service would be to let society understand true limits of technology.

House, W. C., **The impact of information technology on management operation**, Auerbach, 1971.

Institute of Cost and Works Accountants East Anglia and North London Study Group, How to judge the success of an EDP installation, **Management Accounting**, 45, 6, 244-6, June 1967.

Jacq, J-F. and Jehanin, L., **La rentabilite des systemes informatiques dans l'entreprise**, Presses Universitaires de France, 1974.

Jedamus, P., and Frame, R., **Business decision theory**, McGraw-Hill, 1969.

Johannsen, H., and Birch, S., **Achieving computer profitability: a survey of current practice in 102 companies**, British Institute of Management, 1971, 43pp. Key factors: 1 look at business not computer; 2 don't rush; 3 spend as much time as possible on feasibility study; 4 ensure top management support; 5 train and educate all staff; 6 involve/participate; 7 recruit first-class DP staff; 8 recruit a DP **manager** not a technician; 9 don't underestimate time and cost for development; 10 analyse systems and potential applications ensuring that databases are reliable and comprehensive; 11 keep systems simple; 12 lay down standards for systems and programming. Reasons for installing: twice as many offered improved management information as reduced costs.

Joslin, E. O., **Analysis, design and selection of computer systems**, College Readings, Arlington, Virginia, 1971.

Kanter, J., **Management guide to computer system selection and use**, Prentice-Hall, 1970. Activity thresholds for potential in computing to give instant feasibility study. Sales orders, 75 per day; purchase orders, 40 per day; inventory items, 2000; etc. High potential if two at threshold or one at double threshold. Looking for applications: high volume, repetition, common source documents, mathematical processing, quick turn around time. Should study team be individual or group? Group. Full time or part time? Full time. What capabilities required? Experience plus personal. To whom should study team report? Steering committee or chief executive. Should outside resources be used? No.

Kaufman, G. M., and Thomas, H., **Modern decision analysis**, Penguin, 1977.

Keeney, R. L., and Raiffa, H., **Decisions with multiple objectives: preferences and value tradeoffs**, Wiley, 1976.

King, J. L., and Schrems, E. L., Cost-benefit analysis in information system development and operation, **Computing Surveys**, 10, 1, 19-34, March 1978.

Kintisch, R. S., and Weisbord, M. R., Understanding between EDP specialists and users, **SAM Advanced Management Journal (USA)**, Spring 1977, p.4. Anbar: suggests why differences occur and how they can be managed through use of joint-project teams.

Kliejnen, J. P. C., **Computers and profits: quantifying financial benefits of information**. In preparation.

Kriebel, C. H., The evaluation of management information systems, **IAG**

Journal, 4, 1, 1971.

Kruger, I., and Miller, J. R., MIS: success or failure, **Atlanta Economic Review**, November/December 1976, p.10. Anbar: most failures due to human factors (personnel competence, organisation and man-machine interaction). How to avoid.

Lamberton, D. M. (Ed.), **Economics of information and knowledge**, Penguin, 1971.

Land, F., Criteria for the evaluation and design of effective systems. In Frielink (1975) pp.239-50. Survey.

Land, F. F., Evaluation of systems goals in determining a design strategy for a computer-based information system, **Computer Journal**, 19, 4, 290-294, 1976.

Lasfargue, Y., Les facteurs de la rentabilite d'un systeme d'informations, **Direction et Gestion**, Numbers 3 and 4, 1969.

Lave, L. B., The value of better information in the raisin industry, **Econometrica**, 13, 1-2, 151-64, 1963. A supply curve is fitted to Californian raisin growing, the equation containing a constant plus adjustments for the number of degree days, price two and three seasons before and a random fluctuation factor. Weather most significant factor. Build pay-off table: grower can under-crop or fully-crop, nature can rain earlier or later. Decision tree extended from probability of rain in six ten-day periods. Forecast allows better choice of path through tree.

Leitmann, G., (Ed.), **Multi-criteria decision making and differential games**, Plenum Publishing, 1976.

Li, D. H., **Design and management of information systems**, Science Research Associates, 1972.

Litchfield, J. W., Hansen, J. V., and Beck, L. C., A research and development decision model incorporating utility theory and measurement of social values, **IEEE Transactions on Systems, Man and Cybernetics**, SMC-6, 6, 400-10, June 1976.

Lucas, H. C., A user-oriented approach to systems design, **Proceedings of the 1971 ACM Annual Conference**, pp.325-38. Questionnaires and interviews to gather design data and attitudinal responses to help plan implementation, forecast impact on work groups and sensitise design personnel.

Lucas, H. C., The problems and politics of change: power, conflict and the information services subunit. In Gruenberger. Cites Ackoff, managers may suffer from overload of information, may not know what they need, more communication may not lead to better performance. Mechanical quality of system: provide filtered information; do not overload with data; examine decisions and data flows; be sure system works. Physical user interface: design for flexibility; use understandable error codes, be polite; provide educational feedback; use appealing terminals; experiment with interface; test exhaustively; implement gradually. Impact on organisation: relations among sub-units; locus of decision-making; socio-technical system; avoid reassigning successful work groups; encourage group participation in changing tasks; forecast impact; develop implementation strategy; encourage participation.

Lucas, H. C., Measuring employee reaction to computer operations, **Sloan Management Review**, 15, 3, 59, 1974. Favourable user attitudes towards EDP staff and user ratings of computer potential correlate with user's perceptions of quality of EDP service and management support.

Lucas, H. C., **Information systems concepts for management**, McGraw-Hill, 1978.

Lyman, T. R., Performance evaluation of a criminal justice information system: a transferable methodology, **Urban systems**, 2, 2-3, 63-73, 1977. NCC: Scoring.

McDonough, A. M., **Information economics and management systems**, McGraw-Hill, 1964.

McFadden, F. R., and Suver, J. D., Costs and benefits of a database,

Harvard Business Review, January/February 1978, pp.131–9. Hypothetical case discussing advantages of DBMS: performance improvement; cost avoidance and reduction.

McFarlen, F. W., Management audit of the EDP department, **Harvard Business Review,** May–June 1973, pp. 131–42. Excessive preoccupation with detail by steering committees; encourage intelligent initiatives at lower level; informal as well as formal procedures; balanced portfolio of EDP proposals from risk point of view. Is there a complete periodic inventory of hardware and software? How efficiently is the inventory being used? Is there a concise objective performance reporting system (turnaround time, rerun time, component utilisation, user complaints)? Are users satisfied with speed of service? Has problem of project control been systematically addressed? Is there a formal procedure for coping with problems of restructuring a project? Is there a formal process for performing post-audit? Are post-audit results used to improve the management of other projects? Have key project managers been exposed to project management training? Does management reward effective project management?

Macintosh, H. G., and Morrison, R. B., **Objective testing,** U of London Press, 1969.

McKinsey and Co, **Unlocking the computer's profit potential; a research report to management,** McKinsey, 1968. Reprinted in McRae, Sanders and Computer Automation, Vol 18, April 1969, pp.24–33. Choose applications with greatest potential, get top management support, test technical economic and operational feasibility. Lack of success correlates with lack of planning and lack of user involvement.

McLean, E. A., Assessing returns from the data processing investment. **In** Gruenberger, pp.12–25. Type 4 error: doing right thing too late. Most companies have little idea of costs or benefits. EDP experts understand precision but not accuracy. System life cycle = unwarranted enthusiasm, uncritical acceptance, growing concern, unmitigated disaster, search for the guilty, punishment of the innocent, promotion of the uninvolved.

McLean, E. R., and Soden, J. V., Strategic planning for MIS – a conceptual framework, **Proceedings of the National Computer Conference,** 1976.

McRae, T. W., **Management information systems,** Penguin.

Mann, F. C., and Williams, L. K., Observations on the dynamics of a change to EDP equipment, **Administrative Science Quarterly, 5,** 2, 217–56, 1960. Case study of electric power and light company.

Marschak, J., Decision making II: Economic aspects, **International Encyclopaedia of the Social Sciences,** Macmillan and Free Press, pp.42–54.

Mitutinovich, J. S., and Schellenberger, R. E., Countdown to more efficiency, **Data Management, 14,** 9, 24–8, September 1976, and **14,** 11, 16–9, November 1976. Establish decision making responsibilities and authority; establish missions and goals; determine constraints; identify ROI; consider effective system design; seek innovation; recognise characteristics of products; set priority of tasks; consider human factor; measure performance against objectives.

Mockler, R. J., Developing a new information and control system, **Michigan Business Review, 20,** 2, 13–19, March 1968. Reprinted in Sanders. Appoint corporate executive to head systems development group; define scope of project early; include someone from each affected department; define major decision-making areas and information needed; top management should participate; machinery order should be withheld until very firm idea of what is needed; plan for change in organisation structure and personnel; realise side benefits of education and coordination.

Moore, P. G., and Thomas, H., **The anatomy of decisions,** Penguin, 1976.

Morris, J., and Martin, J., **Computer personnel selection 2: Programmers,** NCC Publications, 1972.

Mumford, E., and Ward, T. B., **Computers: planning for people,** Batsford, 1968.

Mumford, E., Implementing EDP systems – a sociological perspective, **Computer Bulletin**, January 1969, pp.10–13. Reprinted in Li. Uncertainty rests on existing instability of user group and user's perception of change. Resistance rests on how the innovating group's role is perceived and their strategy for change.

Mumford, E., **Job satisfaction – a study of computer specialists**, Longman, 1972.

Mumford, E., and Pettigrew, A., **Implementing strategic decisions**, Longman, 1975.

Mumford, E., and Sackman, H. (Eds.), **Human choice and computers**, North-Holland, 1975.

Mumford, E., Towards the democratic design of work systems, **Personnel Management**, September 1976, pp.32–5. Ideas on industrial democracy: giving workers say on board; joint consultative system, employee representatives; consultative committees; hand responsibility for design of work system over to employees who work it. Expert role is to help. Argues morally right, managerially advantageous, employee advantageous, organisationally advantageous.

National Computing Centre, **Economic evaluation of computer-based systems**, NCC Publications.

Neu, C. W., Small EDP shop risks, **Journal of Systems Management**, 27, 6, 36–9, June 1976. Underhardwared (bottlenecks at peak volumes); resistance by employees; wrong EDP manager appointed; long term dependence on one individual at core of MIS effort. Turnkey postpones risk of wrong person, may intensify risk of underhardware.

Nolan, R. L., The plight of the EDP manager, **Harvard Business Review**, 51, 3, 143, May/June 1973. DP manager must be provided with a career; subordinates think of him as a manager, but boss thinks of him as a technician. Case anecdotes.

Nolan, R. L., and Knutsen, K. E., The computerisation of the ABC Widget Co., **Datamation**, April 1974, pp.71–6. Comparison of 1963 and 1973 attempts to computerise. Lessons: payoffs from computers do not come at the press of a button; if you need medecine ask a doctor not a pill company; development is complex and requires trained staff; it's expensive to be on the cutting edge of technology; management support is vital; planning and estimating must be flexible; benefits are difficult to estimate, insistance on full quantification and ROI criteria absurd.

Owen, J., A criterion for investing in information, **Management Science**, 14, 12, B715–20, August 1968.

Parkin, A. (Ed.), **Computing and people**, Edward Arnold, 1977.

Parkin, A., Attainment testing of experienced programmers. **In** above.

Parkin, A., Critique on multi-criteria utility analysis applied to alternative data processing systems, **Computer Journal**, 21, 2, 188–90, May 1978.

Parkin, A., **Systems analysis**, Edward Arnold, 1980.

Payne, J., Knitting needles to key tape: technical and social change in a data processing department. In Parkin (1977) pp.36–40.

Pearson, B., Controlling MIS, **Management Today**, March 1978, p.17. Value analysis applied to MIS for evaluation. Who needs to know? Why? When and how often? What actions and benefits will result? Would a simpler analysis produce the same result? Would approximate/estimated figures available sooner be useful? What would happen if the information was suppressed?

Peffers, J. E., Computer feasibility studies – standards for presentation, **Cost and Management**, 34, 9, 387–97, October 1965; **Journal of Data Management**, July 1966, pp.24–9. Study should be work of company-oriented personnel. Report: procedures and operations to be computerised; capability of selected equipment; computer housing needs; cost of computer; personnel problems in designing, implementing, operating; personnel disruption in affected areas; flexibility; involvement of users; plans for implementation; summary of benefits.

Podolsky, J. L., Horace builds a cycle, **Datamation**, November 1977, pp. 162, 164–6, 168. Plan to throw one away; you will, anyhow.

Penney, G., Applying knowledge to reducing recruitment costs. In Parkin (1977), pp.72–5.

Pope, D. M., Estimating the resources needed for ADP systems. In Frielink (1975), pp.304–13.

Post Office Department, **Report to congress: Need to evaluate and improve postal source data system before further expansion**, US General Accounting Office, Washington, 1971. Abridged in Li. Case study of inadequate feasibility study. Feb 1966 estimates: total cost $33M, fully installed in 75 largest post offices by Nov 1968, $36M saving in first five years of operation. Feb 1971 actual: total cost $44.5M, not operational in several post offices. 1966 operating salaries estimate 740 employees, $5.5M p.a., equipment $9.1M p.a.; 1970 actual operating salaries 1857 employees, $19.6M p.a., equipment $17M p.a. Inadequate study before installation, only limited testing of prototype, and that different from system adopted. Feasibility of nationwide system not adequately demonstrated, sufficiently detailed system specifications not prepared, site surveys at most of 75 locations not made, so unrealistic estimates of equipment and costs. Prototype system not fully tested nor proved successful; specific problems not identified; no alternatives considered. System specification not prepared prior to purchase of equipment; if had have been, would have had more realistic requirements and target date, might have selected different equipment.

Pruzan, P. M., Is cost benefit analysis consistent with the maximisation of expected utility? In Lawrence, J. R. (Ed.), **Operational research and the social sciences**, Tavistock, 1966. Only in special cases.

Quinn, R. E., Overcoming resistance to EDP, **Public Productivity Review (USA)**, Autumn 1976, p.5. Anbar: outlines factors contributing to resistance, many refs.

Rees, R., **The economics of investment analysis**, HMSO, 1973, 41pp.

Reichenbach, R. R., and Tasso, C. A., **Organising for data processing**, American Management Association, NY, 1968. Importance of computer responsibility locations. Interviews with 91 executives in 16 companies. Sample policy statements, project requests and authorisation forms.

Reps, D., Choosing a hospital computer system, **Hospital Financial Management**, January 1977, p.31. Anbar: describes feasibility study, thorough.

Rodger, A., **The seven point plan**, National Institute of Industrial Psychology, 1972.

Rodgers, Le R., Getting the right results from your data processing investment — the DP shop view. In Gruenberger, pp.39–46. What is the right job? – larger concern than DP department's. DP responsibility is to provide technical facilities to support desired applications, minimise total investment made to provide those facilities.

Ross, J. E., Computers – their use and misuse, **Business Horizons**, April 1972, pp.55–60. Clerical and accounting systems transformed, but real payoff lies in impact on operating problems of management. MIS no substitute for MS. Lack of operational applications implies that the management process is not being performed well. Chief executive involvement emphasised. Communications gap between analysts and programmers leads to abdication of the operation to the technician. Organise for MIS; if controller or secretary has responsibility, emphasis will be on accounting systems. Systems more likely to work if you design them yourself. Average breakdown of costs: hardware 35%, staff 30%, updating present system 15%, new applications 20%; spend more on new development. Do not let computer salesman or DP manager take the decisions. Build MIS on top of MS. If the system doesn't work, scrap it. Inclination of systems people is to underestimate costs and time by a factor of 50–90%. Get management involved. Eyeball the output. Upgrade clerical systems. Establish technical, economic and operational feasibility. Plan thoroughly.

Rue, J., Power, politics and EDP, **Datamation**, December 1976, p.51. All user departments are not created politically equal. Personal purposes take precedence over organisational ones every time. Where the power lies is where the data processing goes.

Sanders, D. H., **Computers and management/text and readings**, McGraw–Hill, 1970. Common pitfalls: lack of top management support, failure to specify objectives, excessive reliance on vendors, lack of awareness of past estimation error patterns, crash programs through failure to appreciate magnitude of task/neglect of old system until urgent solution needed/ desire to get immediate benefit/hardware delivery date used to arbitrarily set system implementation date, hardware bought first – think afterwards what to do with it, improper priorities, piecemeal approach simply converts manual system, inadequate staffing. Some common feasibility study goals: expense reduction – clerical labour, supervisory and non-clerical labour, equipment, space and overhead, supplies, inventory carrying; revenue raising – shorten processing time, increase processing capacity for expansion, more accurate/comprehensive information, improve control, improve customer service, get new information, better planning; other – prestige, meet clerical labour shortages, prepare required government reports. Advocates DCF evaluation.

Saville, P., and Simpson, D., Selection and testing for computer staff, **Data Processing**, September/October 1973, pp.318–23.

Schewe, C. D., and Wiek, J. L., Guide to MIS user satisfaction, **Journal of Systems Management**, June 1977, p.6. Anbar: systems implementation as a marketing exercise.

Schlaifer, R., **Probability and statistics for business decisions**, McGraw–Hill, 1959.

Schwartz, M. H., Computer project selection in the business enterprise, **Journal of Accountancy**, April 1969. Reprinted in Li. Selection requires criteria for decisions, a methodology. Criteria are (a) dollar impact on profit (or cost–effectiveness in goverment departments) (b) qualitative factors (c) institutional criteria. Cost figures should be painfully comprehensive. Use rate of return or NPV for evaluation on tangibles, weigh against intangibles. Convenient relative measure is present value of net earnings per present value outlay in project costs. Mentions possibility of using ranges in costs and earnings, probabilities assigned to figures or ranges, OR models. Project selection system needs selection criteria, project generation and formation through research, documentation to convey the possibilities to management, organised review and analysis in the light of long-range plans, project decision by top management. Results should be shared through steering committee chaired by DP manager or superior. Project documentation in four parts: objectives, financial overview, qualitative and institutional considerations (high/low value checklist), plans (for development, conversion and operation).

Seiler, K., **Introduction to systems cost effectiveness**, Wiley, 1969.

Seward, H. H., **Measuring user satisfaction to evaluate information systems**, Thesis, Harvard Business School, 1973.

Shaw, J. C., and Atkins, W., **Managing computer system projects**, McGraw–Hill, 1970.

Shidal, J. G., Long-range DP plan, **Journal of Systems Management**, 29, 4, 40–5, April 1978. Let users project their requirements, attach a technical summary, don't assume understanding, evaluate current system, construct a philosophy of operation, analyse user requirements, develop your resource, don't forget costs, present plan.

Shio, M. J., New look at MIS, **Journal of Systems Management**, May 1977, p.38. Anbar: causes of failure.

Simmons, J. K., and Barrett, M. J., A behavioural and technical investigation into the utilization of accounting reports by middle managers. In Burns, T. J. (Ed.), **Behavioural experiments in accounting**, Ohio State U, 1971, pp.351-414. Are reports prepared by accountants used by those receiving them? Hypothesis: utilisation of internally generated accounting reports by middle managers varies according to (1) the reports (2) selected personal characteristics of the users (3) certain background factors in the organis-ational setting.

Smith, W. A., and Wechsler, B. L., **Planning guide for information system evaluation studies**, Computer and Information Systems Division, AIEE Inc, Norcross, Georgia, 1973.

Soden, V., and Tucker, C. C., Long-range MIS planning, **Journal of Systems Management**, July 1976, p.28. Survey of 20 MIS executives in large mature organisations. LR objectives exceeded: identify internal MIS improvement opportunities, cancel marginal development efforts, decrease cost of computer operations, increase visibility of MIS effort in the overall organisation. LR objectives not attained: improve user communications and cooperation, improve top management support, improve resource requirement forecasting and allocation, identify new or higher payout applications, gain better understanding of overall organisation. Ideal content of LR planning document: statement of objectives, system development plan, personnel and facilities plan, projection of possible future MIS environ-ment, projection of possible future user environment, expenditure plan, recommended implementation timetable, organisation plan, education plan, projection of possible future industry environment, alternative MIS strategy definition/evaluation, evaluation of past performance against plan by MIS, summary of strengths and weaknesses of MIS staff. Five year planning horizon usual; median effort two man-years on LR planning. Discusses pitfalls.

Somers, G. G., Cushman, E. L., and Weinberg, N. (Eds), **Adjusting to technological change**, Harper-Row, 1963. Taft: case studies of effect on organised labour. Burbash: management's perception of technological change is producing an offensive strategy, the union's perception is in general producing a defensive strategy; automation may promote strikes and strike-resisting power of management. Weber: transfer rights of displaced employees - preferential hiring rights at other plants etc.; attrition rights; transfer of operations (shift with operations); interplant bumping rights (displaced senior can displace junior at other plant). Levitan and Shephard: skilled employees replaced by unskilled employees in e.g. textile mills; college trained technicians replaced mill operatives in the ladder of promotion; outcome was an emphasis on the difference between labour and management.

Staff of Business Management, How to make sure your computer pays off, **Business Management**, vol 95, 1965, pp.37-41, 96, 98. Reprinted in McRae.

Staff of Computer Management, EDP pioneering by ICI, **Computer Management**, May 1971, p.32. Anbar: ICI Pharmaceuticals as first time user, why and how feasibility study undertaken.

Staff of EDP Analyzer, The economics of computing, **Data Processing**, April 1977, pp.21-4. Nederlands bank: future plans, 9-person executive level steering group (meeting monthly) plus task/working groups, some on functions (securities, payments), some technical (internal control, emergency and recovery). Top tier committee: goals, timescales, priorities, investigations. Now top-tier function taken by chief general manager. Three groups report to CGM: automation committee, user interface (methods and procedures), system building department. Only the president can answer the question 'is this the right mix of products?'. Project selection, implementation at two levels, division and corporate. Natural resources case: time-sharing terminals placed at various points in company has encouraged use of quantitative methods, company executives believe this will deliver even greater benefits than the $3M from consolidation of three centres into one.

Staff of EDP Analyzer, Planning for multinational EDP, **Data Processing**, September 1977, p.13, 15–16, 19. Main influences on multi-national DP: type of enterprise, make to order or make for stock; expansion policy, monolithic growth or acquisition; headquarters orientation, line versus staff; division characteristics, size, location, commonality, relations; country characteristics, laws, customs, labour relations, language and character set, technological differences, vendor support. Reviews European state computer guidance organisations.

Staff of EDP Analyzer, What information do managers need?, **EDP Analyzer**, **17**, 6, June 1979. Critical success factors/key result areas.

Staff of Management Review, Consultants: how to know what you're getting and get what you pay for, **Management Review**, **52**, 12, December 1963. Assess consultant's competence: 1 education and experience; 2 knowledge in the specific field; 3 technical skills; 4 forthrightness and courage; 5 common sense.

Stamper, R., **Information in business and administrative systems**, Batsford.

Stern, L., Contingency planning: why? how and how much?, **Datamation**, September 1974, pp.83–95. Identify critical applications in terms of money. Ensure these get processed in an emergency.

Steymann, E. H., Justifying process computer control, **Chemical Engineering**, **75**, 12 February 1968, pp.124–9.

Strassman, P. A., Managing the costs of information, **Harvard Business Review**, September/October 1976, pp.133–42. Identify costs, keep score on unit costs, establish standard costing, set up accountability centres, apply competitive pricing, plan for the long term, let the users control, de-emphasise technology, use job enlargement.

Streeter, D.N., Cost–benefit evaluation of scientific computing services, **IBM Systems Journal**, **11**, 3, 219–33, 1972.

Suding, A. D., Hobbits, dwarfs and software, **Datamation**, June 1977, p.92. 8% of hours budgetted did not materialise. 47% of 1314 hours incurred were unanticipated. 87% of group leader (group of four) time spent on overhead, miscellaneous, scheduling. 33% of others' time similarly. 50% over budget overall, but 15% **under** budget on the items that were included in the budget. Suggests relationship between number of items defined and likelihood of omitting an item, e.g. 24–28 items, too many; 10–11 items, too few.

Sutherland, J. W., Tackle system selection systematically, **Computer Decisions**, April 1971. Reprinted in Li. Seminar approach to configurating through consideration of alternatives.

Swanson, C. V., Evaluating the quality of management information, Working Paper No. 538.71, MIT, June 1971.

Taylor, J. W., and Dean, N. J., Managing to manage the computer, **Harvard Business Review**, September/October 1966, pp.98–110. Survey of computer applications of 33 outstandingly successful organisations. Financial and administration (reporting and analysis, accounting, payroll, invoicing, billing). Management planning and control (capital investment analysis, resource allocation). Marketing operations (sales forecasting, sales analysis and control, market research, sales order processing). Distribution operations (warehouse operations, shipment order processing, traffic, inventory control). Factory operations (materials control, production scheduling, quality control). Research and development/engineering (product test, engineering, research, product design and evaluation). Dollars spent versus cost reduction obtained is ineffective yardstick – production efficiency, inventory balance, customer service are benefits which provide competitive edge.

Turton, R., On the relevance of professionalism. In Parkin, 1977.

Verhelst, M., On possible approaches and techniques for determining financial benefits of organisational information. In Frielink, 1975, pp.387-98.

Verhelst, M., **Contribution to the analysis of organisational information systems and their financial benefits**, Ph.D. Thesis, Katholieke Universiteit Leuven, 1974.

Vroom, V. H., and Deci, E. L. (Eds), **Management and motivation**, Penguin, 1970.

Wallace, J. B., An experimental evaluation of simulation techniques for analyzing costs and benefits of information systems. In Frielink, 1975, pp.399-411. Three levels of problem: macro (project mix); intermediate (individual project estimates); micro (optimal design of MIS). Risk analysis economically feasible but not well understood by analysts/managers; ease of use important.

Walsh, H. G., and Williams, A., **Current issues in cost-benefit analysis**, HMSO, 1969, 21pp.

Webster, L. A., The development of an information system for a manufacturing company, 1. The feasibility study, **Australian Computer Journal**, May 1970. Reprinted in Li.

Weinberg, G. M., **The psychology of computer programming**, Van Nostrand, 1971.

Weinberg, G. M., **An introduction to general systems thinking**, Academic Press, 1975.

Weindling, Matthews and Bridgeman, **Management guide to computer feasibility**, American Data Processing Inc., Detroit, 1962. Failure to act can be more expensive (lost opportunity) than abortive feasibility study. Basic rules of thumb for getting computer: 1 over 1000 employees; 2 (a) clerical costs at one location exceed $4000/month (b) so many different items that individual records not kept (c) stockholding costs could be reduced by $25,000 p.a. (d) delayed or late deliveries a serious problem (e) lost items in the production process, need for many expediters, recurrent crises, unused capacity (f) need for centralised control over decentralised operations; 3 Banks, Insurance etc. need clerical costs over £5000/month. Organisation of study: appoint one man to have responsibility; provide terms of reference; provide training/orientation for him; develop a definite schedule with intermediate deadlines; select a study team; appoint and orient a steering committee, management representing each division or department.

Weir, M., Managing the introduction of computers - a comparison of approaches. In Parkin, 1975, pp.7-12.

Weir, M., The effectiveness of computer systems in creating satisfying jobs for users; a method of assessment. In Frielink, 1975, pp.421-26. Two-part questions to determine satisfactions through attitude survey.

Weiss, H. M., Using risk analysis methods, **Data Management**, 15, 1, 42-3 and 66, January 1977. Length of payback: short/long; length of development time: short/long; estimate ranges: narrow/wide; degree of user acceptance: high/low; severity of policy and organisational changes: low/high; severity of procedural changes: low/high; clarity of problem definition: clear/foggy; state of hardware and software: proven/unproven; complexity of system design: simple/complex. Weights and scores method.

Welke, R. J., **Bibliography on information system effectiveness evaluation**, R. J. Welke, McMaster U, Hamilton, Ontario, Canada.

Whelan, W. J., Are your EDP costs reasonable? **Price Waterhouse Review**, Summer 1975, p.28.

Whisler, T., **Information technology and organisational change**, Wadsworth, Belmont, California, 1971. Blurring of line/staff distinction; centralisation issue open; consolidation of operating functions; reduction of clerical workforce; more functional organisation; manager's job more research content; upgrading of skills at all levels; inflexible decision making; fewer decision-making executives, more specialists. Based on US life offices research.

Williams, L., How automation affects the white collar clerical employees. In **Computer technology – concepts for management,** Industrial Relations Counselers, NY, 1965, pp.22-3. Reduced control over timing and patterning of their activities.

Willoughby, T. C., Staffing the MIS function, **Computing Surveys, 4,** 4, 241, December 1972.

Willoughby, T. C., Origins of systems projects, **Journal of Systems Management, 26,** 10, 19-27, October 1975. Factors influencing origination of ideas (descriptive), sources of ideas. Initial study: preparations (user/analyst); initial meeting with responsible executive; data gathering; analysis; design; presentation of informal report; revised formal report.

Yearsley, R., and Graham, R. (Eds), **Handbook of computer management,** Gower Press, 1971.

Zangemeister, C., Measurement of effectiveness of computerised information systems from a management point of view through utility analysis. In Frielink, 1975, pp.440-51.

Index